Intelligence without Fix Up

The UK Intelligence Failure to Fix, French Intelligence Reforms and the Tablighi Jamaat Intelligence Networks in Europe

Intelligence without Fix Up

The UK Intelligence Failure to Fix, French
Intelligence Reforms and the Tablighi Jamaat
Intelligence Networks in Europe

Musa Khan Jalalzai

Vij Books

New Delhi (India)

Published by

Vij Books
(An imprint of Vij Books India Pvt Ltd)

(Publishers, Distributors & Importers)
4836/24, Ansari Road
Delhi – 110 002
Phone: 91-11-43596460
Mobile: 98110 94883
e-mail: contact@vijpublishing.com
www.vijbooks.in

Copyright © 2024, *Musa Khan Jalalzai*

ISBN: 978-81-19438-47-1 (Hardback)
ISBN: 978-81-19438-77-8 (Paperback)
ISBN: 978-81-19438-22-8 (ebook)

Contents

Introduction

The threat of terrorism has been evolving in different shapes since 2001, while the UK police and intelligence infrastructures are facing domestic lone-wolves, extremism and foreign espionage networks. Notwithstanding the collaboration of Counter Terrorism Police with the intelligence community, a professional and technical approach to counter networks of hostile states is a constant need. On 19 January 2024, Reuter reported the establishment of a Counter Espionage Unit by the UK government to further barricade operational mechanisms against extremism and terrorism and foreign espionage. Having commented on the threat of Hostile States networks, head of counter-terrorism policing, Matt Jukes remarked that the challenge posed by Hostile States was "greater now than since the days of the Cold War". The UK Counter Terrorism Coordination Committee (CTCC) is coordinating policing forces in counter-terrorism operations, but intelligence agencies are still complaining of the exponentially growing threat of domestic lone wolves. However, the SERVATOR agency is also tackling terrorism and national security threats, helping the police and secret units, but the performance of the agency has been underwhelming since its inception. The MI5 and other agencies are screaming of growing domestic turmoil, while the government's changing security measures and strategies generated misunderstanding between law enforcement and communities. Black Cloud and climate of fear and consternation ballooned out across the UK, where peace and stability facing the threat of violent extremism and sarcastic behaviour of Hostile States.

States in the EU are accusing each other of political and economic interference in their internal affairs and jeopardising each other's environment of peace and stability. The hostile States are strong and resourceful-using their wealth and resources to destabilize weak states. They are maintaining professional and strongest intelligence infrastructures-targeting weak and crumbling states with their cyber and spying swords and interfering in their internal affairs without fear. One of the fundamental principles of every state is to make its intelligence strong and fit it to the fight against foreign espionage of Hostile States. The fact

1

of the matter is, they want intelligence to be perceived as necessary and indispensable, efficient and effective. It is crystal clear that all states want a strong and reformed intelligence infrastructure despite their different scopes and capabilities. Now, the question is, what kind of secret service is better for a state and how to control it. The democratic control of intelligence services is binding in new democracies. Science and Business in its news report (UK announces new unit to deal with risk of foreign espionage and theft of IP from universities-26 May 2021) noted that "The unit will be based in Manchester and will be responding to requests from UK academics who identify potential risks within projects or proposals. Advisers will also proactively approach research labs and support them to implement advice and guidance already on offer". Science/Business noted. The EU major cities are centres of foreign espionage activities from Hostile States. China has been using different states to advance its own interests and has exploited Taliban and Pakistani ISI's influence in Afghanistan.

The post cold war security and economic confrontations between China and the UK prompted an environment of fear by their changing strategies of intelligence war. China's top spy agency revealed that it exposed the British espionage network in China by arresting the MI6 spy. On 08 January 2024, Reuter reported from Beijing the arrest of a UK spy in China is due to their ongoing heated exchanges and accusations of perceived spying that threatened their respective national securities. China's Ministry of State Security revealed on its WeChat social media account that a foreigner, only identified by surname Huang, was in charge of an overseas consulting agency, and in 2015, MI6 established an "intelligence cooperative relationship" with the person. Reuter reported. "The M16 instructed Huang to enter China several times and instructed him to use his public identity as a cover to collect China-related intelligence."After careful investigation, the state security organs promptly discovered evidence of Huang's involvement in espionage activities, and took criminal coercive measures against him". The Reuter reported. However, Russian police also detained western journalists. Politico in its report on 03 February 2024 (Eva Hartog), noted the arrest of journalists by Russian law enforcement at a protest rally in Moscow. "In comments to the Dutch news agency ANP, Dutch Foreign Minister Hanke Bruins Slot described the detention of two Dutch journalists as "very concerning," and said there would be a reaction. She gave no further details. "You should be able to do your job as a journalist without the risk of landing in jail," she was quoted as saying".

The Guardian newspaper in its news story noted (1,100 scientists and students barred from the UK amid China crackdown. Foreign Office rejected a record number of academics in 2022 on national security grounds, Hannah Devlin, Science correspondent. Guardian, 15 Mar 2023) interception of more than 1,000 educated and professional Chinese from working in the country. "Figures obtained by the Guardian newspaper noted that a record 1,104 scientists and postgraduate students were rejected by Foreign Office in 2022. These reports and commentaries are indicative of a powerful intelligence war between the Bricks member states and the European Union member states. My perceptions of foreign espionage networks and their interference in the internal affairs of Britain became a reality when the British government announced the formation of a counter-espionage unit in 2024. In my book, (Spying with Little Eye: Complexity of Intelligence Challenges in Europe, and the UK, Interference of Russian, Chinese and Iranian Intelligence, Oversight of Intelligence Infrastructure and Post Snowden Reform) I noted that foreign intelligence networks were making things worse due to the unprofessional response of the British intelligence agencies (MI5 and MI6). The MI5 constituted so many spy scandals which are indicative of its sarcastic behaviour, and failure to operate professionally.

Snowden's revelations highlighted MI5's countless breaches of human rights by imposing a heavy blanket of surveillance systems on British citizens. This affected all people whose data was transferred by surveillance communications, digital cables or cloud computing technologies. The irony is that no one dares to complain because irregular and controversial surveillance is legal in the UK. Having analysed the operational mechanism of the British intelligence agencies, I need to focus on the controversial policy of spy agencies. However, on 30 October 2018, journalist Nazia Parveen in her news analysis (MI5 didn't trust black people with secrets in the 1960s, files show. The Guardian, 30 October, 2018) reported that senior MI5 officials admitted they didn't trust black people to hold high-level spying roles in the 1960s because they could be a security risk, according to declassified files uncovered by an academic at Salford University. Mail-online, (06 November 2019) reported the MI5's authorization of its agents to commit serious crimes, potentially including murder, kidnap and torture. Human rights organizations initiated legal action against the agency's illegal assassination campaign. They argued that this illegal assassination policy was kept secret for decades. On 28 January 2023, Daily Mail noted Big Brother Watch concerns regarding the army Brigade-77 controversial role. Secret units operating in the British Cabinet Office and in the Department of Digital, Culture, Media and Sport are spying on politicians. Mail on Sunday journalist Peter Hitchens noted Conservative MP David Davis, and members of staff of Big Brother Watch were all targeted by these secret military intelligence units. Foreign intelligence and espionage networks became stronger and violent while roots of social and political stratification have emaciated.

Intelligence agencies of China, Pakistan, Iran, and Bangladesh are operating illegally in UK cities and towns, recruiting educated men and women and making their networks strong. Connectivity and togetherness ended, and citizens are looking at each other with scorn and sneering. In this age of uncertainty, the state continually faced new and unforeseen threats of economic and geographic collapse. The provinces threatened to part their ways if the centralization of power campaigns remained in place. In yesteryears, MI6 was issuing only statements in newspapers about the presence of Russian intelligence, but practically remained inactive. Foreign and Commonwealth Office and Home Office are dancing in the dark and sleepwalking to hell. The UK intelligence surveillance faced several challenges by breaching human rights. Privacy concerns began to collide with national security interests, and policy makers needed to prepare for a new intelligence war. Edward Snowden exposed communication surveillance that triggered political debate. On 25 July 2022, Human Rights organization Liberty told the investigatory power tribunal that MI5 had breached surveillance laws since 2020, and provided false information to unlawfully obtain bulk surveillance warrants against the public. The troubled and challenging European Union's intelligence cooperation with the United Kingdom has been discussed in books and journals by different perspectives since 2001. Notwithstanding the UK intelligence leadership's determination to establish an advanced and professional intelligence-sharing mechanism with the EU intelligence agencies on law enforcement and counter-terrorism levels, the EU intelligence infrastructure's confusion about the sincerity of MI6, MI5 and GCHQ remained in place.

Intelligence sharing on an emergency level was already in operation but not wholeheartedly as both sides wanted to engage in all sectors of security and counter radicalization. The UK intelligence agencies are now facing numerous challenges due to the recent financial crisis, and the underwhelming role of intelligence in fighting terrorism and foreign espionage. In a modern state, policing and intelligence mechanism is a diverse job, which requires a disciplined approach to counterterrorism and counterintelligence. Many intelligence agencies adopted different approaches like conduct of policy, and disciplinary procedure. Now, we live in an age of risk mixed insecurities, anxieties and Snooper Charter Surveillance. We hoped that the EU and UK policing and intelligence forces would respond to all these tormenting pains and threats with a professional security approach in maintaining security and law and order, but they failed and our hopes vanished. The Snowden revelation regarding mass surveillance in European Union states and the UK generated an unending debate, while media in 2013 began publishing his documents to inculcate the civilian population about their illegal and shameless intelligence surveillance mechanism and the use of Facial Recognition Technologies.

The state body has been tortured by wrongly designed strategies and policies of politicians, governments and asymmetrical religious and sectarian cultures, and now it has become sick and tired of tolerating the burden of a weak economy, social and political inequalities. Brexit, COVID-19, racism, and Islamophobia have further weakened its roots and ties in Northern Ireland, Scotland, Wales and England. Former Prime Minister Gordon Brown (Al Jazeera-25 January 2021) warned that the UK was becoming a failing state: "I believe the choice is now between a reformed state and a failed state," Brown wrote in the Daily Telegraph newspaper. "It is indeed Scotland where dissatisfaction is so deep that it threatens the end of the United Kingdom." 'Whoever in London thought of that?' is a common refrain, reflecting the frustration of people in outlying communities who feel they are the forgotten men and women, virtually invisible to Whitehall," Brown noted. The issues of Islamophobia, reforms, and racism within the state institutions of the country have been widely discussed by experts and commentators in order to divert the attention of the government in power to the looming danger.

These challenges have debilitated the voice of Britain on international forums and incapacitated its enforcement capabilities to energetically respond to the waves of terrorism, foreign espionage, and extremism. External interference damages the state's fundamental institutions. Politicians and parliamentarians help expand foreign espionage networks. There have been several types of interference in the UK that complicated the security of the citizens. Cyberterrorism, foreign espionage and intelligence operations, and targeted killings have badly damaged domestic governance. British intelligence's involvement in rendition and torture cases has been a subject of controversy and legal inquiry. The most notable cases involve allegations that British intelligence agencies, such as MI5 and MI6, were complicit in the illegal rendition and torture of terrorism suspects, particularly in the aftermath of the 9/11 attacks and during the War on Terror. The UK was accused of being complicit in the US's rendition program, where suspects were abducted and transported to secret locations or countries where they faced torture during interrogation. On 02 March 2023, BBC reported shameless failure of MI5 in public inquiry and found it missed a significant chance to take action that might have stopped the 2017 bombing. "Chairman Sir John Saunders said the intelligence could have led to suicide bomber Salman Abedi being followed to a car where he stored his explosives. MI5 director-general Ken McCallum said he regretted that such intelligence was not obtained".

The main functions of French intelligence agencies are to identify and analyse internal and external threats to national security; providing information and advising the management about the nature and causes of these threats. The DGSE safeguards French national security through intelligence gathering and conducting paramilitary and counterintelligence operations abroad. The abrupt outburst in towns and cities of France was a great lesson for all European states that managing a better law and order can be laborious without introducing security sector reforms. As we have seen in yesteryears, terrorist and extremist groups made access to nuclear sites and recruited a good number of European citizens in order to use them for jihad in Europe. These elements later on in Paris inflicted huge fatalities on the civilian population. From the Yellow Vest movement to the recent terrorism (riots) incidents, extremist forces had designed to take control of government installations, cities and towns in order to further and strengthen their agenda. In 2015, France, like many other countries, faced a growing number of security challenges, including the rise of radicalised and extremist groups. The professional approach of the country's intelligence agencies was seen as a good understanding to effectively counter these threats.

The report, Intelligence in a constitutional Democracy: Ministerial Review Commission on the Intelligence in the Republic of South Africa (10 September 2008) argued that "existence of security services in democratic countries gives rise to a political paradox. The establishment of the fusion of intelligence agencies in France in 2015 was indeed a strategic move in response to the evolving security landscape. This decision was taken in the context of a rapidly changing global environment, characterized by the rise of new security threats, particularly terrorism. France, in particular, faced several high-profile terrorist incidents but its intelligence agencies demonstrated professionally to dismantle businesses of evil forces. A more unified intelligence structure was seen as crucial for more effective counter-terrorism efforts in the country. The existence of multiple intelligence agencies with overlapping responsibilities led to coordination and information sharing on the law enforcement level. In France, the threat of jihadism and extremism has been a point of concern, especially the terrorist and extremist elements protested in 2023, which caused destruction, looting and social disobedience. France has multiple professional and well-trained intelligence agencies with different areas of focus, jurisdictions, and methods. Coordinating effectively between these agencies and ensuring timely sharing of information has been a persistent challenge. Effective intelligence work requires significant resources, not just in terms of funding, but also in terms of having a skilled workforce. France has undertaken several initiatives to reform its law enforcement systems in recent years. This excellent book discusses recent security developments in the UK and the European Union.

Musa Khan Jalalzai

March 2024, London

Chapter 1

The Post-Cold War Intelligence Mechanism and Dynamic of Britain's National Security Threats: Foreign Espionage, Extremism and Hostile States

Technology has empowered antagonism with the ability to form near-enough factions that eroded power of state. It has enabled the theft of secrets and the proliferation of dangerous knowledge over vast distances. Governments no longer have a monopoly over information. Secrets are harder to keep than ever before. At the same time, technology has made the dream of near real-time fusion of intelligence come true. It has revolutionized tradecraft and continued to hold out the promise of being able to detect dangerous corporeality. Information technology has ravaged the monopoly that government agencies once enjoyed over intelligence. Public access to internet, database and search engine technology means that government analysts now have to compete with the media, and academics. Of course, satellite and internet technologies from their earliest days have been exploiting it for commercial gain. Experts understand that war makes the state and the state is making the war with the changing relationship of the state. This concept of war made the state navigate technological development in all fields of human society. The cold war did not end at any time. There is a new cold war between China and the United States. Expert Warren Chin (Technology, war and the state: past, present and future: International Affairs, Volume 95, Issue 4, 01 July 2019) in his research paper has highlighted the cold war, defence expenditures and rise of technologies, and argued that the US government funded Internet, virtual reality, jet travel, CCTV, global positioning and computer:

"Once the technology had been created, the civil, commercial sector proved adept at adapting and changing the new capabilities. The critical difference between innovation in the defence market and its civilian counterpart was that, in the latter, high rates of consumption led to product and process innovation by companies. As a result, civil technology providers increasingly took the lead in the information revolution. Given this new dynamism, military power relied increasingly on the existing pool of technological knowledge within the broader economy. The increasing emphasis on quality in war also generated greater complexity during operations. This trend facilitated the rise of private military companies in the post-Cold War era and resulted in western states increasingly subcontracting the provision of internal and external security to the private sector."[1]Lack of concordance and agreement between the United States and Russian Federation over the European order has further complicated the war in Ukraine and re-emergence of al Qaeda and Islamic State in Afghanistan that pose a precarious threat to the integration of both the states. Ukraine, Russia, Syria and Afghanistan are bleeding, while Eastern European states are living in fear of Russian attacks in near future. Estonia and Latvia have reformed and strengthened their intelligence infrastructure and changed its command from military to civilian control.

The Russian Federation vision of EU security and integrity has been made crystal clear by documents that indicated restoration of Russian influence and retreat of NATO forces to the pre-1997 borders. Proposals of former President Medvedev still need to be implemented. The Cold War confrontational standpoints of rival powers left many issues unresolved between the Russian Federation and the collective west, which put security and territorial integrity of EU, Ukraine and Central Asia in danger. Russia invaded Ukraine, the NATO member states and the United States deployed nuclear forces and weapons in Europe, thus, the EU soil became militarised and nuclearized. Experts, Dr. Kristi Raik (Deputy Director and Head of the Foreign Policy Programme of the International Centre for Defence and Security) and Eero Kristjan Sild in their research paper (Europe's broken order and the prospect of a new Cold War Authors. International Centre for Defence and Security. October 2023) have argued that the Russian Federation established the fact that NATO presence near the Russian border was a threat to Russia, while NATO adamantly denied any non-expansion agreements with Russia. The authors maintained that these claims have also been disputed by different commentators and analysts: "Russia has maintained the view of NATO as an existential threat; hence, enlargement has been seen as a direct challenge to Moscow. To the Kremlin, the continued existence of NATO after the end of the Cold War, coupled with Russia's exclusion from the alliance, highlighted that the Alliance was targeted against Russia. For its part, NATO adamantly denied any non-expansion agreements with Russia, stating in a 2014 factsheet that: "No such pledge was made, and no evidence to back up Russia's claims has ever been produced." These claims have also been disputed by many decision-makers and analysts, including former US administration officials who were at the reunification talks with the USSR, as well as by Mikhail Gorbachev himself. NATO's continued enlargement has rejected the Russian claims and affirmed the sovereign right of countries to join. However, NATO countries made a costly strategic mistake by adopting an ambiguous position on the potential membership of Ukraine and Georgia in 2008. Before that, Russia–and Putin–had, on multiple occasions, stressed their good relations with the Alliance, and did not–at least in words–directly oppose the inclusion of the Baltic States. From that moment, according to Putin, NATO's open-door policy towards Ukraine and Georgia became a "direct threat" to Russia".[2]

After the cold war and collapse of the Soviet Union in the 1990s, intelligence agencies were desperately looking for a different mission to justify their existence. War on extremism, terrorism, invasion of Afghanistan and Iraq were the missions, Western intelligence agencies initiated and took forward to justify their importance. In these missions, some Western intelligence agencies crossed red lines by violating basic human rights. In Afghanistan, CIA, and MI6 established military units and private militias, which committed war crimes. The main functions of intelligence services are to protect and manage national security. Secret agencies must operate within the legal frameworks and keeping in view human right respect, their operation need to be professional and their acts must be legal. In order to complete their vital functions, intelligence services throughout the world are able to operate secretly and have special powers to acquire confidential information through surveillance. But sometimes, by protecting secrecy through surveillance, intelligence starts to dance to different tangos and offensively violates individual privacy. These actions might paint a different picture of agencies of a state.

The mandate of intelligence defines its job and stresses the need to perform it within a legal framework and demonstrate resilience and ambitions. In several European states, during the operation of intelligence agencies, many things are not going in the right direction. These kinds of operations have never been successful. Intelligence refers to the product resulting from the collection, and analysis. Post-cold war intelligence can thus be described as 'organised policy related information. A clearly defined mandate helps a security intelligence service to function within a statutory remit. Through various measures, intelligence agencies collect information about sarcastic elements and foreign networks. To address these issues, elaborated collection management systems exist for each of the disciplines that establish validated requirements and priorities. Intelligence gathering in the EU member states and Britain involves protection of national security and identifying internal and external threats. The intelligence agencies are thereby expected to contribute to preventing serious threats to the country. Given these dangers, democratic societies are confronted by the challenge of constructing rules, controls and other safeguards.

Following the post-cold war intelligence mechanism in Britain and European Union member states, the emerging threat of foreign espionage has become precarious to national security as I have already highlighted these threats in my previos books and research papers. My work on French intelligence underscored my expertise in exposing foreign intelligence networks in the country. I meticulously detailed in my books how foreign espionage networks have infiltrated and operated in France and RU member states. By doing so, I contributed significantly to my readers' understanding of international intelligence dynamics, emphasizing the pervasive nature of espionage across national borders. My books not only highlighted the specific challenges faced by France in countering Hostile States and their espionage networks, but also contributed to the broader discourse on national security, sovereignty, and the complexities of global intelligence warfare. My books, such as The UK Big-3: The French and German Intelligence Reforms, Intelligence Diversity and Foreign Espionage and Spying with Little Eye: Complexity of Intelligence Challenges in Europe, and the UK, Interference of Russian, Chinese and Iranian Intelligence, Oversight of Intelligence Infrastructure and Post Snowden Reform, I have explored the nuances of how foreign intelligence agencies have established espionage, terrorist, and extremist networks to influence policy making, target critics, and promote subversive activities. Cyber terrorism and information theft is a second type of threat to the economy and businesses of the government. However, one type of espionage that has not emaciated but rather expanded after the end of the Cold War is economic espionage.

Threat intelligence provides better insight into the threat landscape and threat actors. Foreign espionage is not the one kind of interference in the affairs of the state but damage national security. The hostile States have been attempting to harm and intimidate businesses and infiltrate government institutions to create an environment of fear. Clandestine attempts of interference, or those carried out deceptively or involving personal threats. In these circumstances, secret agencies need internal control in order to ensure strict compliance by their members to the infrastructure, and legislation. In European democracies, public debates on security issues and research help policy makers to easily look through the window. In 2017, the London and Manchester attacks in which terrorists used knives, vehicles and killed several innocent people was a serious failure of MI5 and policing agencies. More than thirty six innocent people were killed and 200 were injured. Public criticism of MI5 raised several important questions. The Manchester arena detailed inquiry report deeply criticized the MI5 leadership and its inattention policy on national security issues. The Chief of MI5 apologized and accepted the failure of his agency to intercept terrorist Abedi. He was later on killed in the explosion. The London Bridge attack was another failure of MI5 to demonstrate responsibly. A Pakistani Khuram Butt, Rachid Redouane and Youssef Zaghba were not followed and arrested before they attacked London Bridge. However, the third great intelligence failure of MI5 was the Finsbury Park attacks. In order to survive as a state, the domestic branches of MI5 needed to demonstrate professionally. Moreover, the domestic branches take years to evolve in themselves. Intelligence must have an organised system, to protect the interest of a state. Dr. Mazzola Stephanie in her PhD thesis (Intelligence services in Post Conflict State Building a comprehensive study of Iraq and Afghanistan Mazzola, Stephanie. War Studies Department, King's College London, July 2021) has highlighted security and intelligence development in post-communist Europe:

"In most post authoritarian and totalitarian states, like the post-communist States in Eastern Europe, these conditions did not prevail. These countries had to face, simultaneously, a political, an economic, a social and a security transformation, commonly resulting into unstable institutions. The fact that many of these states, unlike Western democracies, also lacked a widespread popular identification with the newly established institutions, caused internal fragility and amplified the external sources of insecurity, thus questioning fundamental Rule of Law traits. The fact that norms were still not internally accepted and "absorbed", contributed to the difficulties. The stronger states appeared to be the ones that engaged in regime-society dialogue long before the actual transition, like for instance Hungary and Poland, while countries that did not enjoy a similar dialogue, such as Bulgaria and Romania, were instead less secure and were unable to fully contain the consequences of the armed conflicts that appeared along their borders)".[3]"Intelligence, on the contrary, is the continuation of the information collection process that results out of its processing, forming the basis for the analytical products produced by the relevant intelligence department. Intelligence is the outcome of an analytical process, which interprets the facts in order to offer the decision-makers with the necessary input to manage and utilize it. (The Importance of Counterintelligence Culture in State Security'. Anastasios-Nikolaos Kanellopoulo-GSIN 05 June 2022. The University of Buckingham).

The basic issues for states in bringing intelligence under democratic control is to ensure civilian control of intelligence. Eastern European states experienced a difficult time, where former Soviet intelligence infrastructure was making things complicated and resisting democratic process. In Eastern European states, the reshaping of intelligence and police services has been part of the consolidation process towards democracy. In Czechoslovakia, Bulgaria, Poland, Romania and Hungary, intelligence agencies are experiencing resistance from the old communist intelligence infrastructures. In all these countries, the process started in different ways and brought different results as well. The protection of national security, and prevention of crime are recognised in Article 8 of the European Convention of Human Rights (ECHR). Expert Dovydas Vitkauskas in his research paper, (The Role of Security Intelligence Services in a Democracy- North Atlantic Treaty Organization: Democratic Institutions Fellowships Programme 1997-1999) noted some security developments in NATO member states and also noted the intelligence agencies are operated separately from the police and law enforcement agencies. He also highlighted scandals and of security agencies:

"Security intelligence services in most of the NATO states function in principle separately from foreign or military intelligence services. In some countries security intelligence services function separately from law enforcement agencies as well...Many acute threats of today require a concerted international action. A security intelligence service should also be able to exploit new opportunities in defending national security, including those provided by the technological progression of the private sector. In addition, as regards the analysis of its tasks, the service needs to follow the erratic and varying evolution of models of "traditional" and "new" threats to national security. Therefore, while it is important for a security intelligence service to have a clearly defined statutory mandate, the relevant legislation should be flexible enough to allow the service itself to define its tasks, accommodate resources and prepare for emerging threats in the nearest future. Over the last years there have been numerous events relating to various scandals in the media and investigations in parliaments and courts of sources and methods that security intelligence services use in conducting intelligence and assisting law enforcement authorities".[4]

Some Eastern European intelligence agencies are undergoing a deep crisis of confidence, and national security management. A contest of strength between domestic and foreign intelligence agencies and a misplaced sense of professional approach, poor organisational management, and influence of bureaucratic stakeholders threatened the security of these states. The uninterrupted politicisation of intelligence and policing agencies, enfeebled the operational mechanism of civilian intelligence in these states that resulted in a popular mind-set where every movement, action and way of thinking of their leadership have become militarised, and accordingly seeking a military solution to the Ukraine conflict. In recent years, with the change of political environment, Eastern European states faced complex security challenges after the collapse of the Soviet Union in the 1990s. Military conflicts adopted a religious sectarian shape. Humanitarian crises, migration and terrorism, nuclear proliferation, and war in Iraq, Afghanistan and Ukraine, further generated the clouds of a long war. In European democratic states, most public debate on the operational mechanism of intelligence have been usually focussed on intelligence failure in and outside the continent. Europe became the centre of radicalization and extremism with the arrival of Asian, African and the Arab extremist individuals, leaders and stakeholders who claimed asylum on fake IDs and documents.

Expert of intelligence and writer, Larry L. Watts in his research paper (Conflicting Paradigms, Dissimilar Contexts. Intelligence Reform in Europe's Emerging Democracies, New Democracies, Studies in Intelligence, Vol. 48, No.1) has documented the process of intelligence reforms in Eastern Europe and challenges face be these states in case of resistance from former Soviet intelligence infrastructure in place and communist intelligence operational mechanism: " In many post-authoritarian states, legislatures must first be created—or recreated—and have time to establish their own legitimacy before they can begin to consider the problem of legacy intelligence services, much less oversee their reform. Once created, the parliaments of transition states frequently are unable to devote attention to this domain. In emerging democracies, intelligence reform often has to wait while fledgling institutions struggle to address the most visible public demands— such as economic development, health care, and education. Poland, and, initially, Czechoslovakia—"grandfathered in" substantial numbers of personnel from the former regimes as part of the negotiation process, which caused considerable apprehension in NATO both before and after their accession".[5]

Intelligence reforms in Finland put intelligence agencies at the cycle of reorganization and reinvention process to effectively counter hostile states and national security threats. Finland is a competent state acting for the interests of its citizens. Finland intelligence is responsible for foreign intelligence as well as domestic counterintelligence operations. In 2021, Finland's army published its first military intelligence review amidst a threatening environment and the war in Ukraine that put the security of NATO states and EU in danger. Russia invaded Ukraine on the 24th of February 2022, from multiple directions on land, sea and air, and at the same time expanded the conflict it started in 2014. The NATO Information Security Treaty was brought into force in Finland on 23 August 2023. Expert and analyst, Mikael Lohse, Chief Specialist and Deputy Intelligence Ombudsman at the Office of the Intelligence Ombudsman in Finland in his paper (Finnish intelligence overseers' right of access supersedes Originator Control. About Intel) has highlighted security environment in Finland:

"The two main watchdogs of intelligence operations in Finland are the Intelligence Oversight Committee of Parliament and the Intelligence Ombudsman. The Committee exercises parliamentary control over intelligence activities whereas the Ombudsman supervises the legality of such activities. In practical terms, ensuring that the disclosure, reception, storage and destruction of information complies with the provisions of the Finnish Intelligence and Data Processing Acts, and the Information Security Treaty falls to the Intelligence Ombudsman given his legal role. The Intelligence Oversight Committee, given its parliamentary viewpoint, is concerned with broader issues, such as the role and policy of the Finnish intelligence authorities in the Alliance and the resourcing needs for NATO information exchange. The Finnish Security and Intelligence Service and the military intelligence authorities do provide, on their own initiative, both the Intelligence Ombudsman and the Intelligence Oversight Committee with the information they require on intelligence activities."[6]

The use of Pegasus Spyware by Poland sparked criticism in international media. In 2021, media reported the most intrusive spyware developed by Israel, was used by several states to target journalists and human right activists. The fact of the matter is that the legal system in Poland has never offered any effective remedy against illegal state surveillance. On 01 June 2019, a military and civilian intelligence act was enacted in Finland identifying the legal powers of Finland's security and intelligence agencies and also explained how to collect intelligence information on domestic and international security threats. Finland's intelligence reform represents the most profound change ever made in the Finnish security sector. Expert, Mikael Lohse (The Intelligence Process in Finland. Scandinavian Journal of Military Studies. 19 June 2020) has documented elements and legal framework of the Finland's intelligence agencies:

"Finland adopted civilian intelligence legislation in early June 2019, with the aim of improving our capabilities to protect against serious threats to national security. Such threats include terrorism, proliferation of weapons of mass destruction, espionage by foreign states or disruption of critical infrastructure. The civilian intelligence legislation entered into force at the same time as the military intelligence legislation that enables the Defence Forces to gather information on targets of military intelligence. Civilian and military intelligence authorities engage in close cooperation. The Ministry of the Interior is responsible for the guidance of civilian intelligence. Each year, the Ministry sets priorities for civilian intelligence that guide the activities of the Finnish Security and Intelligence Service and that define the themes on which the Finnish Security and Intelligence Service gathers information and reports.....The Finnish Security and Intelligence Service has the task of gathering information, in accordance with guidance from the Ministry of the Interior, to protect national security, as well as identifying, detecting and preventing such operations, schemes and criminal offences that could threaten state and social order and internal or external security. It must also maintain and develop general readiness to identify and prevent any actions that could threaten the safety and security of society. After the entry into force of the Civilian Intelligence Act, the range of tasks of the Finnish Security and Intelligence Service has expanded and the focus of information gathering has shifted more towards intelligence".[7]

Hager Ben Jaffel and Sebastian Larsson in their research analysis (Why Do We Need a New Research Agenda for the Study of Intelligence? International Journal of Intelligence and Counterintelligence. 06 July 2023) of intelligence transition, intelligence information gathering, mobilization and threats, have generated an excellent picture of intelligence cycle: "The transition from Cold War concerns, such as geopolitical competition, state secrets, spies, and double agents, to a broadening range of emerging "problems" and new security legislation has given rise to a new "problematization" of intelligence. No longer simply about espionage or secret information gathering to inform military strategy and foreign policymaking, intelligence has diversified and become increasingly connected to, and understood as, surveillance, policing, counterterrorism, population management, border checks, and more. New actors have entered, and challenged, the boundaries of intelligence in this regard. It has spread out to a growing number of unconventional sites that are not immediately seen as spaces of intelligence activity, such as prisons, banks, and hospital environments".[8] In a democratic state, security related institutions play a crucial role in peace and stability. These institutions have wide-ranging powers in order to manage domestic security. They are also responsible to professionally respond to internal and external threats. The reform of an intelligence service is not only a legal and constitutional issue, it is at the basis of the process. It is widely known that the intelligence services of contemporary democratic countries collect openly available information. This type of information could be collected and analysed by those institutions. Causes for intelligence failure are usually complex. Reasons for the failure to provide intelligence about threats or in providing only belated intelligence, may be due to mistakes in the organization of intelligence activity.

As intelligence has become an important tool of the state, all states now use it for stabilization and security, and also use it as a weapon against non-state actors, anti-state elements and terrorism. In Europe and Asia, intelligence agencies now became militarised and thinking on a military level, the fact is their measures and strategies are deeply militarised due to their involvement in war zones. They are acting as a militarized unit and operating like militants. This culture of militarization and militancy of the British intelligence agencies have weakened their professional approach to security and law enforcement. In Iraq, Afghanistan, Syria and Ukraine, though the role of intelligence was important but their activities, torture of civilians and training of terrorist and extremist elements raised important question on their way of demonstration in the battlefield. In Afghanistan, intelligence committed war crimes by establishing private criminal militias and used that against the civilian population. The state intelligence (NDS) was kept weak and corrupt and never allowed to operate independently. Experts and writers, David Anstiss, Dr. Cemal Dikmen, and Kevin McTiernan, (Global Lawful and Location Intelligence Outlook: 18 January 2024) in their paper highlighted operation of intelligence the war fatalities in Gaza, Ukraine and Syria:

"Seemingly intractable conflicts continue to arise all over the world, including Syria's ongoing civil war and refugee crisis, the war in Ukraine, and the conflict in Gaza, among many others. As civilians flee military, economic, and other adversity, authorized and unauthorized immigration grows. Border insecurity is already a major source of political instability in many countries, including the US. Desperate people may increasingly turn to human smugglers to help them across borders, exposing them to the dangers of human trafficking and other exploitation. Such widespread human movement also creates changes in the digital landscape, introducing new apps that immigrants bring with them that may spread in their new communities. Such apps may be unfamiliar to local law enforcement, and the encrypted traffic from them can dramatically interfere with traditional lawful intelligence measures. Even known platforms and browsers like WhatsApp and Chrome are introducing "IP Protection" measures that route traffic through proxy servers to conceal the user's IP address."[9]

The role of intelligence in Eastern European states remains the contraption of Cold War espionage studies. Experts and analysts, Daniela Richterova and Natalia Telepneva in their paper, (An Introduction: The Secret Struggle for the Global South–Espionage, Military Assistance and State Security in the Cold War-18 Jun 2020) have documented the global reach of the United Kingdom and benefits of the cold war intelligence mechanism: "Due to its status as an imperial power, Britain ran an extensive network of intelligence and security officers who reported on local developments and managed the often-turbulent transitions to independence. The MI5 also built up new security and intelligence apparatuses in states nearing independence in an effort to develop a 'Commonwealth intelligence culture'. The British also possessed a tremendous SIGINT capacity, with a network of listening stations stretching across the Empire. In 1947-48, London's capability was fostered by the 'Five Eyes' intelligence sharing agreement with the US, Canada, New Zealand and Australia. In the following years, the GCHQ, Britain's signals intelligence agency, established a close 'special relationship' with their American counterpart - the National Security Agency. According to Louis and Robinson, following decolonisation, a close alliance between London and Washington enabled the Americans to pursue their own 'informal empire' to fight the Cold War".[10]

Home Office in its policy paper, (Policy paper. New espionage offences: factsheet. Updated 13 July 2023) has explained the official secret act 1911 that criminalizes espionage by prohibiting certain conduct that is carried out with a purpose prejudicial to the safety of interests of the UK, including obtaining or disclosing information which would be 'useful to an enemy'. Foreign espionage and intelligence infiltration into state institutions is a great misadventure of the post-cold war era, as it became a dangerous virus cruising across Europe and the United Kingdom. During World War II, Britain, Germany, the Soviet Union and the USA put intelligence at the heart of their military operations and had spies operating across Europe,

North Africa and even South East Asia. Unlike European intelligence agencies, Britain had entered the 20th century without intelligence. In 1883, the Special Branch was formed by the British police to fight Irish terrorism. Notwithstanding its lack of manpower, the Special Branch continues spying foreign nationals. Keeping in mind the expanding military power of Germany and Russia, on 01 October 1909, MI5 and MI6 were established in order to protect Britain's secrets. The MI6 was entrusted with the responsibility to protect national secrets. Al Jazeera reported the statement of the Chinese government that it had uncovered a British spy whom it accused of passing on state secrets. "The Ministry of State Security stated that it had discovered that the head of a foreign consultancy was spying for the United Kingdom's MI6 intelligence service. It is the latest in a series of recent accusations traded between Beijing and London. The Chinese spy agency announced the detection of the espionage on its WeChat social media account. It stated that MI6 had recruited Huang Moumou to collect Chinese secrets and information". Al Jazeera noted. The Intelligence and Security Committee of the British Parliament in its report warned: "It appears that China has a high level of intent to interfere with the UK government, targeting officials and bodies at a range of levels to influence UK political thinking and decision-making relevant to China."

Intelligence and Security Committee in its report also noted that Chinese interference activity in the UK was difficult to detect, but even more concerning was the fact that the government may not previously have been looking for it," However, Chief of MI5 on 18 October 2022, warned that all but 20,000 British were approached covertly online by Chinese covert intelligence. "We have seen a sustained campaign on a pretty epic scale," the MI5 Chief told the BBC. "If you're working today at the cutting edge of technology then geopolitics is interested in you, even if you're not interested in geopolitics". Mr McCallum noted. Modern espionage technology put Europe and Britain in danger by using mobile phones, surveillance and other devices to retrieve intelligence information from different government and private institutions. These technologies also generated opportunities to attack the European financial system. In France, for example, implementing regulations of the 2015 intelligence law established two intelligence 'circles'. The 'first circle' is composed of six so-called specialised intelligence services, such as the Direction (DGSI) and the Direction (DGSE). Since 2017, the 'second circle' was later on expanded to include two offices placed under the authority of the director of prison administration, under the Ministry of justice.

Chapter 2

The British Intelligence Remained Imbalanced in National Security Strategy Contents: Lack of Coordination among British Intelligence Agencies and the Police is a Challenging Quiz

Notwithstanding significant efforts made by the British intelligence agencies to prevent radicalization and respond to the threat of terrorism with new strategies and effective weapons, extremism and foreign espionage networks have spread across the country with changing narratives. The MI5 failed, and challenges remained in the imbalanced national security strategy. Lack of coordination among British intelligence agencies and the police has been identified as an issue in some instances, particularly in the context of counter-terrorism efforts. In the past, intelligence agencies like MI5 and MI6 and police forces operated quite separately. Each had its own protocols, culture, and operational methods. The establishment of bodies like the Joint Terrorism Analysis Centre (JTAC) and the Office for Security and Counter-Terrorism (OSCT) by MI5 was aimed at ensuring better coordination and information sharing between various entities involved in national security, but everything was not going in the right direction, there were some broken windows that needed to be fixed. Lack of public confidence and manpower have not only been painful issues, lack of expertise, funds and professional intelligence information causing pain in the neck.

While no significant progress was made in enhancing the coordination between British intelligence and the police, it remains an area of ongoing focus and improvement, given the evolving nature of threats and the complexities of modern intelligence and law enforcement operations. The London Bridge attacks referred to two separate but similarly named incidents: the first on March 22, 2017, involving a vehicle-ramming and stabbing near Westminster, and the second on 03 June, 2017, involving a vehicle-ramming and stabbing spree in the London Bridge and Borough Market area. The attacker Khuram Shazad Butt was known to MI5 but never investigated. However, MI5 never prioritized watching these kinds of suspected individuals. Newspapers reported that MI5 held information and never shared it with police. Perpetrators used encrypted communication channels and sophisticated tactics to avoid detection, while MI5 failed to detect their secret communication system, or pass information to policing secret agencies. The London Bridge and Manchester terrorist attacks led to a period of introspection and review for the UK's intelligence and security services (MI5), with the goal of learning from the incident and preventing future attacks.

My perceptions of foreign espionage networks and their interference in the internal affairs of EU and Britain became a reality when the British government announced the formation of a counter espionage unit in 2024. In my book, *Spying with Little Eye: Complexity of Intelligence Challenges in Europe, and the UK, Interference of Russian, Chinese and Iranian Intelligence, Oversight of Intelligence Infrastructure and Post Snowden Reform,* I noted that foreign intelligence networks making things worse due to the weak response of British and EU intelligence agencies. The MI5 constituted so many spy scandals that are indicative of its sarcastic behaviour and failure to operate professionally. The MI5 was later on tied to a Minister and after the 1994 secret act while its outreach was curtailed in order to dance in a confined legal corridor. The real-life espionage drama, the Guardian news report highlighted with different aspects (Vanessa Thorpe, Arts and Media correspondent, 31 Dec 2023-Guardian):

"In 1983, with a mysterious Moscow death and was followed by the arrest in Britain of a would-be MI5 mole, led to a full-scale internal investigation into the security service and fuelled an escalating diplomatic feud with the Kremlin. The fallout, it is now made clear in papers released by the National Archives, added to worsening relations with the Soviet bloc, which pulled out of the 1984 Olympics later that summer in Los Angeles. It also led to the British expulsion of a top Soviet diplomat, Arkady Guk, who was already known by the UK government to be running foreign agents in London. Lord Owen, Labour foreign secretary from 1977-79 under James Callaghan, was publicly and privately scolded by Thatcher for revealing the identity of the new head of MI5, who had been brought in from outside the intelligence services to shake up procedures and improve accountability after a string of high-profile embarrassments. Owen, who co-founded the SDP, was speaking in the House of Commons on 9 May 1985, just after

Thatcher presented the critical findings of a security commission report into the handling of errant MI5 officer Michael Bettaney, who had been imprisoned for handling sensitive documents over to the Soviet Union. The then leader of the opposition, Neil Kinnock, responded to the prime minister first, with a scathing criticism of poor management inside the security service. Guardian reported."[1]

The MI5 surveillance is watching families in toilets, kitchen and bedrooms. Experts and analysts, Karen Lund Petersen and Kira Vrist Rønn in their research paper (Introducing the special issue: bringing in the public. Intelligence on the frontier between state and civil society- Intelligence and National Security 2019, vol. 34, no.3. Routledge, 12 February 2019) have highlighted complex and threatening environment such as terrorism, radicalization, foreign espionage and global financial crisis: "Complex and uncertain threat environments, with terrorism, cybersecurity and global financial crisis, have made many traditional management tools unfit and profoundly transformed the ways in which intelligence services deal with threats to the nation and its citizens. In this special issue, we argue that intelligence agencies today stand before a defining gap between an increasing demand from society and politicians to provide security and the organization's ability to fulfil those demands and needs. In order to manage this gap between expectations and possibilities for management, new methods, coalitions and partnerships are considered pertinent. These practices include the use of new technologies for collection and analysis as well as arrangements to increase cooperation and partnerships between national and foreign intelligence and security services, between intelligence and police services, between intelligence and security services and the public, and between intelligence and private companies and 'other potentially uneasy bedfellows".[2]

Experts, George Kassimeris and Oliver Price in their paper (How the rise of Militant Tendency transformed MI5's perception of Trotskyism's ability to pose a threat to the British state. LSE British Politics and Policy, a multidisciplinary academic blog run by the London School of Economics and Political Science. 15 November 2021) have also reviewed newly released files available at the UK National Archives that highlight the revolving strategy of MI5 viz-a-viz a Trotskyist group militant in the 1970s and 1980s. In yesteryears, MI5 considered subversive activities that threatened security of the state and making efforts to overthrow parliamentary democracy in Britain:

"The major targets of MI5's counter-subversive operations until the 1970s were Communists and the Communist Party of Great Britain (CPGB), which was subjected to sustained and extensive surveillance following its formation in 1920. The Trotskyist movement, which emerged in Britain during the early 1930s, was regarded by MI5 as being 'too small and chaotic' to be capable of posing any significant subversive threat to the British state. The activities of Militant Tendency (MT), a Trotskyist organisation which came to prominence as a result of its infiltration of the Labour Party in the 1970s and 1980s, transformed intelligence officers' perception of Trotskyists. By the early 1980s, Militant was believed to be capable of posing an equal, if not greater, subversive threat than the CPGB. By 1984, one Whitehall official declared in a memorandum sent to MI5 that 'Militant seems to have replaced the Communist Party as the established focus for subversion within the country'. Militant was considered to pose such a threat because a significant number of its members had managed to infiltrate the Labour Party; they aimed to transform it, from within, into a 'revolutionary party.' At the conference in 1977, Peter Taaffe, deputy leader of Militant, was recorded, by intelligence operatives, stating that the movement would be 'an indispensable weapon of the Revolution in Britain.' MI5 investigations into Militant were eventually highly successful. By the late 1970s, MI5 had identified about 75% of the Tendency's membership through a combination of telephone checks, agent penetration, informants, and".[4]

However, journalist Lara Keay (MI5 'really does have a licence to kill': Spy agency has secretly allowed informants to murder, kidnap and torture for decades, tribunal hears: Four human rights organisations are taking legal action against UK Government. Claim policy allows MI5 agents to commit crimes and get immunity from justice. Mail-online, (06 November 2019) reported the MI5's illegally authorization to its agents to commit serious crimes, potentially including murder, kidnap and torture, for decades. Human rights organizations initiated legal action against the agency's illegal assassination campaign. They argued that this illegal assassination policy was kept secret for decades. Privacy International, Reprieve, the Committee on the Administration of Justice and the Pat Finucane Centre were asking the Investigatory Powers Tribunal to declare the policy unlawful and grant an injunction 'restraining further unlawful conduct'. Four human rights organisations have claimed that MI5 informants employed by the spy agency have been illegally committing crimes for the intelligence services for decades. Ben Jaffey said 'the Security Service (MI5) were permitted under the policy to 'authorise' criminal conduct for a variety of purposes including any national security purpose, or maintaining the economic well-being of the United Kingdom'. He added that 'the agents in question are not officers of the Security Service, but they are 'recruited and given directions by MI5".[5]

The MI5 also missed crucial chances to shut down a Russian spy ring stealing British naval secrets. Journalist Claire Ellicot in his Daily Mail article discovered the ex-wife of agent Harry Houghton had informed his employers that he was 'divulging secret information to people who ought not to get it. The MI5 spy leader, (Security Minister Ben Wallace) in an interview with Daily Mail newspaper painted a disturbing picture of Russian aggression, and Islamic extremism. The inability of MI5 to protect its secret files led to the risk of 600 police experts (2024) working with surveillance agencies and MI5 in Northern Ireland. Expert and writer, Rebecca Camber on 09 August 2023, noted the document was mistakenly released by the Police Service of Northern Ireland (PSNI), identified officers working in the most sensitive roles, including those in 'secret areas' of the force, close protection officers guarding politicians and other VIPs, and others working undercover to thwart terrorists. The list of 10,000 PSNI employees includes more than 560 officers working in intelligence and counter-terrorism, and over 100 in surveillance units. It also identifies almost 40 staff working at MI5's headquarters in Northern Ireland. Rebecca Camber noted.[6]

The 2021 Integrated Review of Security, Defence, Development and Foreign Policy anticipated some but not all of the global turbulence of the last three years. It recognised that the intensification of competition between states was sowing seeds of instability. The review has some weaknesses to address national security threats professionally and its adopted measures and strategies are controversial. Having clarified its approach to national security challenges, Government has been struggling to authenticate its efforts illustrated in integrated review: "The 2023 refresh, therefore builds on the approach set out in the Integrated Review, setting out the next evolutionary step in delivering on its aims, against the backdrop of a more volatile and contested world. Its main conclusion is that unless democracies like our own do more to build our resilience and out-cooperate and out-compete those that are driving instability, the global security situation will deteriorate further, to the detriment of all states and peoples. As in 2021, it paves the way to greater integration across government in pursuit of the four campaign priorities that will guide our national security strategy in this changing context. And it does so with further investment in our national security".[7](Integrated Review Refresh 2023: "Responding to a more contested and volatile world-16 May 2023).

But readers are more experts to identify weaknesses of a government that wants to establish trade cooperation with China on one hand and portray it as a security threat to the existence of the British state on the other. For example, the review noted: "China poses an epoch-defining challenge to the type of international order we want to see, both in terms of security and values–and so our approach must evolve. We will work with our partners to engage with Beijing on issues such as climate change. But where there are attempts by the Chinese Communist Party to coerce or create dependencies, we will work closely with others to push back against them. And we are taking new action to protect ourselves, our democracy and our economy at home". This is a completely controversial approach to engage with China and other nations to make the British economy strong by inviting states to invest in different sectors of the country. British authorities admitted that 'working more closely with others will be vital to these efforts. In 2022, together with the G7 and other partners, the country developed new economic tools, deploying an unprecedented package of sanctions against Russia'. However, in another controversial and hypocritical approach of the British authorities that 'strengthening the UK's domestic resilience and international partnerships, partly in response to the epoch-defining and systemic challenge posed by China under the Chinese Communist Party (CCP) across almost every aspect of national life and government policy.[8]

However, British government again demonstrated and exhibited a hypocritical approach towards China by its screech (Intelligence and Security Committee of Parliament on page 31 and 36 of its China report (1918) stated that 'Ministry of State Security (MSS) lead on China's human intelligence collection through both covert and overt operations, run both overseas and in China. Then says China was sending spies to the UK to collect intelligence information. 'Intelligence is then fed back to a controlling officer based in China via visits, social media or other electronic communications. In terms of espionage, China's human intelligence collection is prolific, using a vast network of individuals embedded in local society to access individuals of interest –often identified through social media. With this controversial approach, no country will wish to engage with Britain.[9] Intelligence failure occurred on many occasions during the agency's fight against radicalization, extremism and national security challenges. History of the failure of British intelligence (MI5, MI6) is of considerable length while their process of reorganization is deeply underwhelming. MI5 is an expert at targeting critics and political opponents.

The COVID-19 was used against critics while from Italy to Australia, critics have accused a "complacent" British government of "massively underestimating" the gravity of the coronavirus crisis. The parliamentary panel rebuked the government for what it termed a "lack of boldness" with the country's virus testing regime and for a failure to boost testing capacity fast enough. Intelligence agencies and the military information brigade-77 were tasked to identify critics and tackle them accordingly. The Brigade-77 is a British Army formation agency, created in January 2015 by renaming the Security Assistance Group which was created under the Army 2020 concept. On 22 April 2020, during the UK coronavirus briefing, General Nick Carter confirmed that the 77th Brigade was working with the Home Office Rapid Response Unit "helping to quash rumours from misinformation, but also to counter disinformation". The Defence Cultural Specialist Unit was used to monitor the internet for content on COVID-19 and to look for evidence of disinformation related to COVID-19 vaccines.[10]

Big Brother Watch claimed that soldiers from the Army's 77th Brigade that a whistle-blower had noted that troops were used to "spy" on the British public. On 31 January 2023, Forces-Net in its analysis of the Brigade-77 role as an intelligence agency during the COVID-19 years (Army 'monitoring of UK citizens' social media posts' to be investigated) quoted Ben Wallace on the Bridge-77 war against misinformation: "Mr Wallace said the unit's counter-disinformation capabilities have been used to assess UK disinformation trends, but added that the Brigade-77 was intended to act against hostile actors overseas. Conservative former Cabinet Minister David Davis, who, according to Big Brother Watch, was monitored as part of a cross-Government group, called for the issue to be reviewed, and Mr Wallace issued an assurance that he had already instructed for it to be looked into.[11] The Defence Secretary told the Commons: "Colleagues may have read reports this weekend about activity conducted by the Army's counter-disinformation unit in 77th Brigade. "Online disinformation from foreign state actors is a serious threat to the United Kingdom, which is why during the pandemic we brought together expertise from... across the Government to monitor disinformation about Covid-19. "The 77-Brigade is a hybrid unit of regular and reserve personnel that was established in 2015." Mr. Wallace said.[12]

Expert and writer, Paul Knaggs in his article (77 Brigade: The British Army spied on its citizens during lockdown-January 30, 2023, Labour Heartland) noted the controversial role of Brigade-77 during the COVID-19 period. He also argued that the Brigade-77 spied on politicians like Keir Starmer, Conservative MPs David Davis and Chris Green: "An investigation by the civil liberties campaign group said a whistle-blower had claimed that troops were used to "spy" on the British public. Military operatives in the UK's 'information warfare' belonging to the 77 brigade were part of a sinister operation that targeted politicians including Labour leader Sir Keir Starmer, Conservative MPs David Davis and Chris Green along with high-profile journalists who had raised doubts about the official pandemic response. They compiled dossiers on public figures such as ex-Minister David Davis, who questioned the modelling behind alarming death toll predictions, as well as journalists such as Peter Hitchens. Their dissenting views were then reported back to No 10."[13] Director for Big Brother Watch, Silkie Carlo, said: "This is an alarming case of mission creep, where public money and military power have been misused to monitor academics, journalists, campaigners and MPs who criticised the Government, particularly during the pandemic". Daily Mail reported.[14]

The 07 July, 2005, attacks on London's public transport system led to questions about the MI5 failure. The attackers were on the periphery of other surveillance operations, leading to inquiries about the prioritization and resource allocation of the security services. As previously noted, the failure of MI5 to identify and stop Salman Abedi raised many questions. The incident led to a public inquiry examining how MI5 handled the incident and shared information. In the lead-up to the Iraq War, the UK government published a dossier on Iraq's Weapons of Mass Destruction (WMDs). The failure of MI5 to find substantial WMDs after the invasion led to criticism of the intelligence used to justify the war and the processes used to gather and present it[15] These incidents raised questions about the MI5 ability to protect individuals on its soil and the need for robust intelligence to counter foreign threats. Reasons for these failures can be varied and complex. Intelligence agencies have finite resources and must make decisions about where to allocate their attention. Failures can occur when different agencies do not effectively share or act upon relevant information. Assessing intelligence involves interpreting often incomplete or ambiguous information. Mistakes can occur in the analysis or the assessment of the credibility of sources. Intelligence can be misused or misrepresented for political ends, or intelligence agencies can be pressured to produce assessments that support certain policy objectives. In response to these failures, the UK has often conducted public inquiries and internal reviews to understand what went wrong and to improve future intelligence work.

The 7/7 attacks refer to a series of coordinated suicide bombings that occurred in London on July 7, 2005. The attacks targeted London's public transport system during the morning rush hour. The attacks were carried out by four suicide bombers: Mohammad Sidique Khan, Shehzad Tanweer, Germaine Lindsay, and Hasib Hussain. The attacks caused widespread chaos and disruption in London, with emergency services stretched to respond. The transport network was heavily affected, with parts of the Underground closed for weeks. Since the 7/7 attacks in London in 2005, extremism and radicalization remained significant concerns for the UK law enforcement agencies. The country has faced various forms of extremism, including Islamist extremism, far-right extremism, and, to a lesser extent, far-left and other forms of ideological extremism. The threat from groups like Al-Qaeda and ISIS has persisted, with these groups encouraging attacks in the West and attempting to radicalize individuals. The UK has seen attacks and plots inspired or directed by these groups, such as the Manchester Arena bombing in 2017 and the London Bridge attack in 2017.[16]

The MI5, also known as the Security Service, operates under the remit of the UK Home Office for several historical and functional reasons. The MI5 is primarily responsible for domestic security and counter-intelligence within the UK. Its focus aligns with the Home Office's responsibilities, which include ensuring public safety and security within the country. The Home Office oversees policing, immigration, and border control, among other duties, making it a logical oversight body for a domestic intelligence agency, but newspapers and journals have been publishing different authors and journalists focussing on the controversial role of MI5 agency. Basically, the structure of the UK's intelligence and security apparatus has evolved over time. The MI5 was officially established in 1909, primarily focusing on counter-espionage. Over time, its role expanded, especially with the growing need for domestic counter-terrorism efforts. The organizational structure reflects this historical evolution. If we read stories in newspapers and journals, we can better understand to what extent MI5 is effective and how it follows legal instruction from the government and how it purveys intelligence information to the accountability bodies. The legal framework that governs MI5's activities, including the Security Service Act 1989, places MI5 under the authority of the Home Secretary.

The MI5's primary roles include protecting national security against threats such as terrorism, espionage, and sabotage, primarily within the UK, but sometimes dancing to political tangos. The London and Manchester terrorist attacks exposed incompetency and failed strategies of MI5 as the agency failed to intercept terror elements before they carried out attacks. MI5 does not have the same powers as the police. For instance, MI5 officers do not have the authority to arrest individuals. The MI5's work is primarily focused on intelligence gathering, while Policing agencies, on the other hand, have a broader remit, including visible community-based policing, responding to emergencies, enforcing laws, and conducting criminal investigations. Another policing intelligence agency is National Intelligence Model (NIM), used primarily by police forces in the United Kingdom to structure their intelligence-gathering and operational activities. It was introduced to standardize the way police handle and use intelligence to make decisions and allocate resources. The oldest and a primitive secret organization is Freemasons, one of the world's oldest and largest non-religious, non-political organizations. Its roots can be traced back to the local fraternities of stonemasons in the late medieval period, which regulated the qualifications of stonemasons and their interaction with clients. Freemasonry is organized into a series of degrees, with the three basic degrees being Entered Apprentice, Fellow-craft, and Master Mason.

On 12 July 2022, while commenting on the security bill, former Home Secretary, Patel said: "The Bill will bring together a suite of new measures to further protect our national security, the safety of the British public, and our vital interests from those who would seek to do us harm. In May 2021, the Home Office published a consultation on legislative proposals to counter state threats. In that document, I discussed the growing, diversifying, and evolving threat from hostile activity by states. State threats are persistent and take many forms, including espionage, foreign interference in our political system, sabotage, disinformation, cyber operations, and even assassinations". The Security Service Interference Alert to Parliament in January was a reminder of the very real and serious threat from those who seek to undermine and destabilize open and democratic societies, as well as the international rules-based system that underpins our stability, security and prosperity. Former Prime Minister Boris Johnson received millions from abroad, and his Ministers also filled and loaded their purses up with that money, and all were dancing to the President Trump tango shamelessly. The Russian intelligence report was delayed for six months, then amended and trimmed with removing all signs of Russian intelligence interference in the UK. The MI5 shamelessly and repeatedly refused to investigate evidence that an alleged Russian spy was attempting to cultivate influence with senior Conservative politicians and channelled illegal Russian funds into the party, a Tory member alleged in a new complaint lodged with the investigatory powers tribunal (IPT). The Guardian noted.

Foreign intelligence and espionage networks became stronger and violent while roots of social and political stratification were emaciated. Intelligence agencies of China, Pakistan, India and Bangladesh are operating illegally in UK cities. On 04 January 2022, National Security and Investment (NSI) Act was enforced as the biggest shake-up of the UK's national security regime. The National Security Bill 2022-23 was introduced in the House of Commons on 11 May 2022. The Bill replaced existing counter-espionage laws with a comprehensive framework for countering hostile state activity analogous to the counterterrorism framework established since 2000. It also limited the availability of civil legal aid and damages to those connected with terrorist activity. Parts 1 and 2 of the Bill and associated schedules created an extensive framework for countering state threats modelled on the counterterrorism framework established under the Terrorism Act 2000 and numerous subsequent pieces of counter-terrorism legislation. The measures of the Bill are included new offences relating to espionage, sabotage and entering prohibited places; foreign interference offences; preparatory conduct relating to state threat activity; powers to take state threat activity into account as an aggravating factor in sentencing; powers to arrest and detain without a warrant; powers to impose civil prevention and investigation measures on individuals suspected of involvement in such activity where prosecution is not possible; and the creation of an independent reviewer to report on the use of the powers.

The MI5 agency has been weak and controversial throughout 21st century-demonstrating intransigence and irresponsibly managing controversial security measures. Never demonstrated as a professional agency according to its historical roots. The agency killed innocent opponents and critics and kidnapped people of its choice. Tortured writers and journalists. Foreign intelligence agencies from South Asia, China and the Arab and African nations were following different strategies and operational mechanisms to strengthen their networks, train more people and generate resources in order to dance professionally for their cause. They recruited cyber fighters, cod-breakers, Mullahs, preachers and religious clerics to reach every corner of the country where they operated. In the EU, the same strategy was adopted to generate financial resources and support. As we have seen in 2022, Chinese intelligence agencies abruptly emerged in Britain with different strategies to approach educational institutions, parliamentarians and civil society. They succeeded in their mission and established police stations in big cities.

Their networks are now strong and they can better invest in people of their choice. South Asian intelligence agencies are more powerful as there are Pakistani, Bengali and Indian communities in Britain who have family members in their own countries working for these agencies. I have come to know and personally interacted with Pakistanis working for British intelligence agencies on many occasions, they are leaking British secrets to their friends, colleagues and governments. In my book, (Spying with Little Eye: Complexity of Intelligence Challenges in Europe, and the UK, Interference of Russian, Chinese and Iranian Intelligence, Oversight of Intelligence Infrastructure and Post Snowden Reform) I suggested that the British government needed to introduce intelligence and policing reforms to make sure and authenticate security of the country. On 20 January 2024, Iran International Television reported the establishment of a counter-espionage unit in the British police to deal with threats posed by Iran, Russia and China ahead of the UK's general election. Assistant Commissioner Matt Jukes, the UK's head of counter-terrorism policing, said that the new unit will be dedicated to specialist investigations regarding the increasing security challenges presented by the three countries. What is the contribution of the MI5 in all these security measures?

The London based Iran International network revealed that the Iranian military intelligence was plotting to assassinate two Iran International television anchors in the UK amid Iranian anti-government protests. Subsequently, Iran International stopped its broadcast operations in London and temporarily moved its studios to Washington DC. In mid-2023, the network relocated to a more secure facility in London. Police vehicles were protecting Iran International's headquarters in London in November 2022. "British Foreign Secretary David Cameron summoned Iran's chargé d'affaires after assuming office and warned that Iran must be sent "an incredibly clear message that this escalation will not be tolerated." In February 2023, an Austrian national named Mohammad-Hussein Dovtaev was detained while filming outside the network's premises. The Central Criminal Court of England sentenced Dovtaev to three years behind bars for attempting to collect information. A Tory member said; "I don't want to be coy. We are talking about parts of the state apparatus of Iran, China and Russia," said Jukes, further adding that the threats of hostile states are considered to be "greater now than since the days of the Cold War."

The new police unit will exercise the powers set forth in a national security act passed last year. The act was introduced to counter attempts made by certain foreign states to interfere with the UK's political affairs, steal confidential trade information, and spy on people. Guardian noted. After the establishment of a group of friends of Russia (Friends of Russia in 2012), Russian Ambassador, Alexander Yakovenko, hosted a lavish launch party for the group in the gardens of his residence in Kensington with guests who included the former Minister of culture, media and sport, John Whittingdale, and Boris Johnson's wife, Carrie Symonds. The Russian government also funded an all-expenses-paid trip to Moscow for a handpicked group of members including the future CEO of Vote Leave, Matthew Elliott." The Guardian reported. These foreign agencies succeeded in killing their critics brutally. In 2020, the government of Boris Johnson published a weak Russian intelligence report. However, in 2022, British intelligence agencies yelled about the interference of Russian and Chinese intelligence agencies. The UK never addressed lapses and flaws in counter-espionage strategies. The Teresa May government failed to introduce counterintelligence and counter-terrorism reforms. Thus the UK espionage strategy also failed shamelessly.

Chinese intelligence interference in the internal affairs of Britain raised many questions that notwithstanding expanding business and investment between the two states, how they became antagonistic on political levels. Expert Dan Sabbagh Luke Harding and Andrew (Guardian-21 Jul 2020) reported from Moscow that the British government and intelligence agencies failed to conduct any proper assessment of Kremlin attempts to interfere with the 2016 Brexit referendum. "It said the government had not seen or sought evidence of successful interference in UK democratic processes" at the time, and it made clear that no serious effort was made to do so. "The UK Government has actively avoided looking for evidence that Russia interfered. We were told that they hadn't seen any evidence, but that is meaningless if they hadn't looked for it." The committee, which scrutinizes the work of Britain's spy agencies, said: "We have not been provided with any post-referendum assessment of Russian attempts at interference".[17]

The Russian interference report revealed too many overlapping agencies with not enough Ministerial accountability and poor decision-making. Nigel Gould-Davies (The Russia report: key points and implications. IISS, 21st July 2020) noted; "the UK government stance on the report and argued that Russia was able to spread its influence for so long because the UK 'took its eye off the ball'. Its responses were limited, reactive, fragmented and unevenly resourced. The ISC is particularly critical of UK domestic weakness that enabled Russia to pose this threat, notably the welcoming 'light touch regulation', golden visas. It points to the role of 'enablers' in the legal, financial, property and PR sectors that profitably laundered money and reputations'. Writer and analyst, Dan Lomas in his article (The Russia Report: Intelligence Expert Explains How U.K. Ignored Growing Threat. Conversation, 21 July 2020) has criticized the report that it is not a page-turner, and nor does it provide all the answers some had expected:

"The long-awaited report follows an eight-month inquiry by the cross party committee of MPs, collecting evidence from the UK's intelligence agencies, senior civil servants and experts. It was published on July 21 after a considerable delay. The Russian foreign ministry called the report Russo-phobia, while the U.K. government rejected the committee's calls for a public inquiry into whether or not Russia had interfered in the 2016 EU referendum......Surprisingly, despite claims of Russian meddling in the Brexit referendum, the ISC's report says little about it. This is only because the committee was unable to get further information, as claims of Russian meddling were seen as a "hot potato" around the government that few wanted to be left with. Despite "credible open source commentary" of Russian involvement in the 2014 Scottish referendum, the ISC concluded that no organization held "primary responsibility" for protecting the U.K. democratic process from "hostile foreign interference". In a stance branded "illogical" by MPs on the committee, U.K. security agencies expressed "extreme caution" two years later over intervening to protect U.K. democratic processes ahead of the Brexit referendum, fearing being drawn into political issues".[18]

Moreover the BBC Reality Check (Russia report: The unanswered questions-21 July 2020) noted that the long awaited Russia report was published with a call for "immediate action" by the government and intelligence services to tackle the threat from the country. The report, by the Intelligence and Security Committee (ISC), covers a number of areas, from allegations of Russian interference in the EU referendum to Russia's "malicious" cyber-activities. Its authors said the 42-page "summary" was "supplemented with a substantial annexure" that gave greater detail but was not being published at that time "in view of the current Russian threat".[19] Home Office in its recent Policy paper on Espionage and National Security Bill factsheet-08 September 2022, elucidated criminalization of espionage by prohibiting certain conduct that is carried out with a purpose prejudicial to the safety of interests of the UK, including obtaining or disclosing information which would be 'useful to an enemy'. The Home Office report also noted: "Espionage is now addressed by three offences in the Bill: obtaining or disclosing protected information; obtaining or disclosing trade secrets; and assisting a foreign intelligence service. The Bill repeals the Official Secrets Acts 1911, 1920 and 1939, which contain the existing provisions. The modern espionage threat endangers the safety and security of the UK and its citizens and, at its worst, can cause loss of life or serious damage to our economic wellbeing".[20]

Another unit called "Project Servator" is a policing tactic that aims to disrupt a range of criminal activity, including terrorism, while providing a reassuring presence for the public. The Project Servator has been successful in gathering intelligence that has assisted Counter Terrorism Units across the UK in investigating and preventing acts of terror. It has resulted in arrests for a multitude of offences and is responsible for removing firearms, knives and drugs from the streets. Project Servator involves police carrying out highly visible and unpredictable deployments that can happen anywhere at any time. The British Intelligence Corps are also responsible for information gathering and intelligence analysis. Modern military operations are dependent on the provision of highly accurate and timely intelligence. The Brigade-77 of the British army played an important role in gathering various types of information during the COVID-19 lockdown from 2019-2022. The Chinese Global Times (21 January, 2024) reported the British government adoption of new National Security Bill, which opposed China's national security legislation for Hong Kong. In response to the establishment of new espionage unit to "counter threats posed by China, Russia and Iran," Chinese experts noted that the UK intends to shift the blame for its domestic underdevelopment issues onto foreign countries while blindly following the US' diplomatic policies.[21]

"The ruling Conservative Party has been unable to address these problems and has instead blamed external factors, such as countries like China and Russia," Zhang said. Some extreme right-wing members of the Conservative Party are constantly seeking out the so-called threats and enemies after Brexit in order to divert public attention, he noted. "Especially with the upcoming general election in the UK, the issues of the Conservative Party's ineffective governance are becoming more prominent, prompting them to work harder to blame their problems on foreign countries." Global Times reported.[22] The British government also enacted a National Security Act in December 2023, which ensures that the UK remains the hardest operating environment for malign activity undertaken by foreign actors." Before the act was enacted, the UK repeatedly accused China of stealing its information or operating unofficial agencies in the country, which China has firmly opposed. The claim that the Chinese side was suspected of "stealing British intelligence" was completely baseless and malicious slander, warned a spokesperson of the Chinese Embassy in the UK in September 2023.[23]

Earlier, in April 2023, the Chinese Embassy in the UK also made it clear that there were no so-called Chinese overseas police stations. "It is important that some from the UK side respect the facts rather than spread false accusations," said an Embassy spokesperson. In June 2023, a police investigation into "secret Chinese police stations" in London concluded that "no criminal activity" was taken place, BBC reported. On 21 January 2024, the Press United noted that the UK in 2023 passed the National Security Act, designed to provide its intelligence agencies with additional measures to tackle state-backed sabotage. The legislation reformed London's existing espionage laws, originally introduced when Britain faced threats from German spies during World War I. The new counter-espionage unit will use the powers afforded by the act to ensure that it "will be the most overt part of the UK security community stepping up its response to those hostile state actions," Jukes added. The Press United noted. However, on 21 January 2024, Agency France Persse reported the statement of Britain's Defence Secretary Grant Shapps that the UK was taking threats of foreign interference in elections 'very seriously'. "Obviously, that's something that we take very seriously," Shapps told the Sky News channel.[24]

Chapter 3

The CONTEST, PREVENT and the Troubled and Challenging European Union's Intelligence Cooperation with the United Kingdom

Since 2018, when CONTEST was last updated, nine terrorist attacks have been reported in the UK. Since March 2017, British intelligence agencies and law enforcement have disrupted more than thirty nine terrorist plots in the country. In July 2023, the UK amended and reshaped the CONTEST strategy due to the country's terrorist threat being unrelenting and evolving. The CONTEST has now become matured but still acting like a weak tool-failing to deliver professionally, and failing to address national security challenges. British Home Secretary Suella Braverman said that the aim of CONTEST was to reduce the risk from terrorism to the UK, its citizens and interests overseas, so that people can go about their lives freely and with confidence, but all of its commitments failed. "The terrorist threat in the UK today is dominated by individuals or small groups acting outside of organised terrorist networks. It is a trend which makes terrorists less predictable and harder to identify, investigate and disrupt. The primary domestic terrorist threat comes from Islamist terrorism, since 2018. "Islamist terrorism is the threat or use of violence as a means to establish a strict interpretation of an Islamic society. For some, this is a political ideology that envisions, for example, the creation of a global Islamic caliphate based on strict implementation of shariah law, drawing on political and religious ideas developed in the 20th century. In the UK the Islamist terrorist threat comes overwhelmingly from those inspired by, but not necessarily affiliated with, Daesh, or al-Qaeda, but they operate within a wider landscape of radicalising influences as set out in the government's response to the Independent Review of Prevent. The New CONTEST-2023 warned.[1]

Home Secretary Suella Braverman suggested that 'an updated version of CONTEST was published on 18 July 2023 that outlined the Government's response to a terrorist threat which was now more diverse, dynamic and complex and sets out the transformational improvements we were making to our counter-terrorism response to meet the key challenges of the current and future terrorist threat and national security context. To counter terrorism and other national security threats, it is crucial that we have the necessary powers and that they are used appropriately and proportionately. The issue of foreign espionage once more appeared in newspapers when the British domestic intelligence agency (MI5) abruptly announced that Chinese intelligence agents were making things worse when they were introduced to parliamentarians. The MI5 said; "a female Chinese national was engaged in political interference activities on behalf of Beijing". But didn't explain why the agency didn't arrest her if she was a foreign agent. On 13 January 2022, Al Jazeera reported MI5's yell against the Chinese woman, and alleged: "she was working on behalf of the Chinese Communist party. MI5's own interference alert, which was circulated to parliamentarians, said anyone contacted by the woman should be "mindful of her affiliation" and its "remit to advance the CCP's agenda".[2]

Many intelligence agencies adopted different approaches, such as the conduct of policy and disciplinary procedures. We live in an age of risk mixed insecurities, anxieties about civilities and anti-social behaviour[3]The Snowden revelation regarding mass surveillance in European Union states and the UK generated an unending debate, while media in 2013 began publishing his documents to inculcate the civilian population about their illegal and shameless intelligence surveillance mechanism and the use of Facial Recognition Technologies. His revelations exposed several states spying on their own citizens. The NSA, BND, MI5 and GCHQ came under severe criticism by mainstream society across EU and the US. Most of the current intelligence challenges of the UK and European Union, whether they relate to predicting surprise attacks, the politicization of intelligence, or questions of ethics and privacy, are old conundrums. However, it is hard to escape the feeling that closer attention to obvious lessons from the past would have assisted intelligence sharing of these states in avoiding the Taliban, ISIS and other ethnic and sectarian group's attacks on civilian and military installations. Bureaucratic control of unreformed intelligence operations, government and private stakeholders, and ethnic and sectarian factors are the most important aspects of any intelligence infrastructure in a state, where these conflicting developments paralyze an intelligence agency. Xinhua News Agency (British security tactics proved ineffective, outdated. March 1, 2015) reported former shadow Home Secretary David Davis that Britain's intelligence services had long utilized tactics that had proved "ineffective, "with a series of security failures showing a "worrying pattern". "One of the results of this policy was that it left known terrorists both to carry out evil deeds and to recruit more conspirators. As a result, the problem on the street grown progressively larger," Davis wrote in the Guardian newspaper.[4]

On 16 December 2020, the Investigatory Powers Tribunal revealed that UK intelligence unilaterally assumed the power to authorise agents to commit crimes in the UK–potentially without any legal basis or limits on the crimes they can commit. The enactment of the Covert Human Intelligence Sources (Criminal Conduct) Act 2021 pre-empted the outcome of the appeal against the decision of the Investigatory Powers Tribunal in the so-called 'third direction' case. In the 'third direction' case the Investigatory Powers Tribunal and the Court of Appeal upheld the lawfulness of an MI5 policy by which its officers were able to 'run' agents who participated in criminality. Each did so on the basis that MI5 had enjoyed the power to implement such a policy before the enactment of the Security Service Act 1989 and that that statute, properly interpreted, continued that power. The Investigatory Powers Commissioner severely criticised MI6 for "several weaknesses" in its agent-running within the UK, leading to "several errors". It found that MI6 needed to "better recognise" and "authorise activity in compliance with" the law in the UK. The Johnson Government sought to put these practices into legislation with the Covert Human Intelligence Sources (Criminal Conduct) Bill, which at present contains no expressed limits on the crimes covert agents may be permitted to commit, even against torture, murder, or sexual violence.

In his Intercept analysis, expert Ryan Gallagher (Inside Menwith Hill: The NSA's British Base at the Heart of U.S. Targeted Killing. 06 September 2016) quoted a British Human Rights Lawyer, Jamima Stratford conversation with Intercept about the questions raised regarding the function of Menwith Hill: "Jemima Stratford, a leading British human rights lawyer, told The Intercept that there were "serious questions to be asked and serious arguments to be made" about the legality of the lethal operations aided from Menwith Hill. The operations, Stratford said, could have violated the European Convention on Human Rights, an international treaty that the U.K. still remains bound to despite its recent vote to leave the European Union. Article 2 of the Convention protects the "right to life" and states that "no one shall be deprived of his life intentionally" except when it is ordered by a court as a punishment for a crime. The UK intelligence surveillance faces several challenges. After the COVID-19 and African Omicron virus's well-built attacks, and Britain's disaffiliation with the EU, the state is going to become fragile. The Labour government had failed in yesteryears, to address mistrust between government and communities.

Correspondingly, and for that reason, the Conservative government continued to affix its footprints to goof up and bounderism. In their recent research paper, Sean Healy and Brigid Reynolds have warned, "If the welfare state cannot be funded in the future, then it will not survive. In fact, the political acceptability of any development in the welfare state is closely linked to economic sustainability." The welfare state in the UK is under pressure from all sides. State institutions are not delivering properly, and literacy rate is going down by the day. A state with an incapacitated and fractured body of national critical infrastructure, unhealthy political and social stratification, and failed foreign and domestic policies, normally, demonstrates the other way around, or unable to speak for all social colours. Fragile urban infrastructure, unemployment, racism, poverty and social disobedience also contribute to the weakness of the state. There has been no attempt in yesteryears to mix unmatched and peerless social colours in European states. Hatred, abomination, abhorrence and racism deeply disturbed their social stratification, and now, in the UK government circles, there has been a substantial debate about the revocation and termination of passports and nationality of criminals and terrorists. The clefts have expanded and social life has been disturbed by statements of government Ministers about the integration of social colours. We have two kinds of states; weak states and strong states. Weak states are of weak capacity to deliver, and strong states are competent, resourceful and reformed. These kinds of states and their institutions deliver services properly.

As a matter of fact, every nation-state fails due to its internal breakdown, social and economic collapse. The United Kingdom is in a deep crisis. Corruption, racism and Islamophobia have fractured the body of the state that is now experiencing a backbreaking burden of challenges. These challenges have debilitated its voice on international forums, and incapacitated its enforcement capabilities to energetically respond to the waves of terrorism, foreign espionage, and extremism. External interference damages the state's fundamental institutions. There have been several types of interference in the UK that complicated the security of citizens. Foreign espionage, cyberterrorism, intelligence operations, and targeted killings have badly damaged domestic governance and public administration. Lack of a coherent society also prompted instability, financial disorganisation and an insecure political and economic environment. Domestic debt and dilapidated relationship with the EU member states, and weak international engagement on different fronts, prompted many challenges. Moreover, Chief Minister of Wales, Mark Drakeford expressed concern over the attitude of Whitehall towards provinces and the future of the Union. In his commentary in the foreword of the report of his administration (Reforming our Union: Shared Governance in the UK-2021), he warned that 'in some important ways the Union failed to keep pace with the full and real implications of the creation of legislatures in Wales, Scotland and Northern Ireland'. He also regretted aggressive action in a unilateral way on behalf of the whole UK without perceiving the status of provinces and their democratic mandates. He also warned that if Whitehall didn't change its attitude towards provinces, the country will be overtaken by competing loyalties and the lure of separatism:

"Beyond slogans, buildings and flag flying, the current UK Government has contributed little to thinking about an energised and viable future for the Union. The Welsh Government has actively tried to stimulate wider debate about UK reform. This document, containing our proposals to protect and reform the Union, was first published in October 2019. We have by no means all the answers. However, it is a contribution to a debate that needs to happen on a range of issues as seen from a Welsh Government perspective. Things move quickly and much has happened since the first publication, and we have updated the document accordingly. Following our election the people of Wales have given a broad endorsement to the Welsh Government's vision and the need to revitalise our Union. In the period ahead we will be engaging directly with civil society and citizens to think through the issues we need to progress in greater detail. I hope that the UK Government in particular, will accept the role it needs to play in cooperating with us and others to mould a forward-looking Union that is fit for purpose and capable of earning the goodwill and respect of all its people. In the election of May this year the choice could not have been clearer. I shared a platform with leaders of parties which argued to abolish devolution on the one hand, and to take Wales out of the UK on the other".[5]

Having shared his concern on government in the UK, on 25 January 2021, former Prime Minister Gordon Brown warned that the public's trust in the way the UK was run was breaking down. He said Covid-19 had exposed "tensions" between Whitehall and the nations and regions, who were often treated by the centre as if they were "invisible". He urged Boris Johnson to set up a commission to review how the country was governed and how powers were shared. "Mr. Brown's intervention comes amid a looming clash between Mr Johnson and Scottish First Minister Nicola Sturgeon, who demanded the UK agree to another Scottish independence referendum if the SNP wins a majority in elections". BBC reported.[6] "Whoever in London thought of that?' is a common refrain, reflecting the frustration of people in outlying communities who feel they are the forgotten men and women, virtually invisible to Whitehall?" Brown said British Prime Minister Boris Johnson should reform the way the UK is governed, warning the country must "urgently rediscover what holds it together, or risk fracturing. He called on Johnson, head of the ruling right-wing Conservative Party, to set up a commission and review how the country is run. Al Jazeera reported.[7]

"I believe the choice is now between a reformed state and a failed state," Brown wrote in Daily Telegraph newspaper. "It is indeed Scotland where dissatisfaction is so deep that it threatens the end of the United Kingdom." 'Whoever in London thought of that?' is a common refrain, reflecting the frustration of people in outlying communities who feel they are the forgotten men and women, virtually invisible to Whitehall," Brown noted.[7] Intelligence and Security Committee (Diversity and Inclusion in the UK Intelligence Community Presented to Parliament pursuant to section-3 of the Justice and Security Act 2013, 18 July 2018) in its report noted comments of intelligence leaders and experts on diversity strategy: Alex Younger, Chief of the Secret Intelligence Service remarked: "Diversity, equality and inclusion are strategic enablers for SIS to succeed in fulfilling our increasingly challenging and complex mission. However, Jeremy Fleming, Director, Government Communications Headquarters said: "Diversity and inclusion (D&I) is at the heart of GCHQ's mission and the organisation we aspire to build. We know if we get this right, we will be better at keeping the country safe – there is no more powerful motivation. Air Marshal Philip Osborn, Chief of Defence Intelligence stated: "I believe it would be professionally negligent not to realise the clear benefits gained from promoting diversity and inclusion in all we do. National Security Adviser in the National Security Secretariat, Mark Sedwill declared: "We are committed to ensuring that the most talented people join the National Security Secretariat and that we support them to develop the most robust policy advice for the National Security Council. Our ways of working must embed creativity and challenge, which is why we have changed the way we develop policy advice for the NSC.[8]

Expert and analyst Daniel W. B. Lomas in his research paper on diversity in the UK intelligence agencies (ForgetJamesBond: diversity, inclusion and the UK's intelligence agencies, Intelligence and National Security), has highlighted diversity and professional reforms within the UK intelligence infrastructure: "In February 2021, The Times reported that Britain's foreign intelligence agency, the Secret Intelligence Service (SIS or MI6), was relaxing rules to allow applicants with dual UK nationality, or with one parent being a UK national or having 'substantial ties to the UK', to apply. Sources told the paper it was just the latest move to access a 'larger talent pool', adding: 'We want a diversification of thought, a diverse workforce, not people who all think in similar ways'. Later, marking LGBT History Month 2021, SIS's Chief ('C') Richard Moore followed other agency heads in apologising for the historical treatment of LGBT (Lesbian, Gay, Bisexual and Transgender) officials and the bar to gay men and women serving in SIS. In a video shared on his Twitter feed, Moore said the ban deprived SIS of 'some of the best talent Britain could offer' and was 'wrong, unjust and discriminatory'.[9]

PinkNews also interviewed two LGBT SIS officers. 'I think the legacy of the ban has been . . . helping people understand that LGBT+ people aren't inherently untrustworthy', said 'Leia', a member of SIS's LGBT Affinity Group. 'It's drawn a line in the sand', she added. The statements and media coverage mark just the latest in a series of announcements on the agency's commitment to diversity and change. In January 2021, tabloid newspapers reported on an SIS recruitment drive, specifically an advert, headlined 'Tell me a secret', calling for 'individuals with diverse skill sets and life experiences' to apply for part-time and consulting roles. Responding, Moore tweeted his service's commitment to 'flexible working' and 'diversity'. 'ForgetJamesBond', he added, acknowledging that Bond often shaped perceptions of the ideal intelligence officer. Sir Colin McColl, 'C' from 1989 to 1994, once described the fictional intelligence officer as, in his view, 'the best recruiting sergeant in the world', yet successive Chiefs, like Moore, have tried to distance themselves, seeing Bond's legacy as both a blessing and a curse. 'For too long–often because of the fictional stereotypes I have mentioned – people have felt that there is a single quality that defines an MI6 officer', Younger told journalists in his first public speech in SIS's Vauxhall Cross headquarters. In July 2018, the Intelligence and Security Domestic Governance, Intelligence Diversity, and Surveillance Committee reported on Diversity and Inclusion in the UK intelligence Community".[10]

Expert Daniel W. B. Lomas, in his research paper on diversity in the UK intelligence agencies, (ForgetJamesBond: diversity, inclusion and the UK's intelligence agencies, Intelligence and National Security) spotlighted professional approach to reforms within the UK intelligence infrastructure:

"There have been significant efforts to change internal culture and promote change, all three agencies having well established networks for women–SIS (DEUCE) and MI5 (GENIE)–and BAME groups- SIS (EMBRACE), MI5 (My5), GCHQ (REACH). LGBT and disability networks have also been formed. For GCHQ, the REACH network has 'led to increased engagement across the organisation, a change in approach to recruitment and traction with BAME communities across the country'. Thanks to internal work the Security Service was named best employer of the year by Stonewall in 2016, remaining in the organisation's top 100 LGBT list of employers. Both SIS and MI5 were also listed in The Times top fifty employers for women in 2018.[11]

Cross border mobility of people, interoperability, interactivity and interface of different policing and intelligence agencies couldn't restore confidence of military establishments, intelligence leaders and law enforcement stakeholders. That clefts and misconstruction still exist. Scientific collaboration, joint ventures and interoperability of police and intelligence infrastructures, and mismanagement of border altercations, further caused miscalculation and mistrust. The process of intelligence sharing among the EU member states has been extremely underwhelming after Brexit. The UK security became vulnerable after its political and judicial separation from the EU project. Thus, Sweden, Finland, Estonia, Lithuania and Latvia jointly managed the flow of strategic and technical intelligence information and helped each other in fighting radicalization and extremism. Collaboration of Intelligence units, and operational police forces in the Baltic Sea and ground, as well as transnational collaboration associated with the rhetorical construction of fighters to defend their territorial integrity and national security helped them in managing a better security infrastructure.

The EU and UK intelligence agencies have been fighting extremism, terrorism and radicalization, war in Iraq, Afghanistan and Libya, but never succeeded to address domestic security challenges since 2001. The UK intelligence agencies suffered deeply due to the bereavement of advanced intelligence information, collaboration and interoperability with the European intelligence agencies. Intelligence sharing among EU member states poses a dilemma. National security threat perception and countering foreign espionage strategies in every member state is diversified while their response to international terrorism underwhelming. Intelligence agencies in all EU member states are not sure of the reciprocation of their partners. Some states understand their security is not under threat. Some intelligence agencies fear that their big partners may not share their national data on terrorism and radicalization. Notwithstanding the importance of data sharing, we know little about the underlying conditions shaping trust among services and intelligence personnel.

There are different public perceptions about the UK intelligence agencies that portray and picture them in different frames. Some support their way of operation and some take them critically and suggest that wide ranging intelligence reforms are needed to make all intelligence agencies competent. After the Anna Chapman spy ring and poisoning of Russian military officer and his daughter, shortfall of public trust increased, while rendition and torture stories further exhibited MI5 and MI6 in controversial pictures. Trust is a key measure in terms of British intelligence infrastructure's confidence and ability to develop public trust and restore a good working relationship with communities. We know the Iraq, and Afghan war and revelations of Edward Snowden about the intelligence led surveillance of our agencies in the UK, generated negative public perception about their operational mechanism and foreign collaboration. At present, MI5-acknowledged under the 1989 intelligence act and MI6 and GCHQ under the intelligence act 1994 have to face the British public. In yesteryears, their dimness and their life in seclusion generated wide ranging controversies that why they remained incommunicado for decades and why this cut-short and absurd relationship with communities. The question is what they were doing in secretion and seclusion.

Anyhow, it was their serious mistake living out of their communities. Intelligence war in Britain generated fear and consternation while some Russians were arrested in Europe, UK and the US. As mentioned earlier, why Russian intelligence selected Britain for its operations, and what is the aim of these operations. Since the 1980s the UK intelligence and armed forces have fought Russia in Afghanistan, and forced its army to withdraw from the country. In 2010, a Russian spy lady Anna Vasilyevna Chapman was arrested in the United States on 27 June 2010 as part of the illegal Program spy ring. At the time of her arrest, she was accused of espionage on behalf of the Russian Federation's external intelligence agency. In 2009, Lady Chapman arrived in New York and started appearing on social media and entered marriage to Michel Bittan, a divorced Israeli-Moroccan restaurant owner. After Anna was arrested in New York on charges of spying, Alex hired media publicist Max Clifford, and sold her story to The Daily Telegraph.

The UK government has been secretly stretching out a controversial surveillance technology that could be capable of logging and storing the web histories of millions of people. Reports noted that in 2022, police deemed the testing of a system that can collect people's "internet connection records". On 14 March 2021, the Mail newspaper reported condemnation of secret 'Snooper's Charter' surveillance trial by Privacy campaigners as the UK Home Office teamed up with two internet firms to test how to track the browsing history of every person in the country. The Edward Snowden revelations in 2013 elucidated and exposed the UK government's surveillance that has gone far beyond what many people are comfortable with. Technology companies and ISPs are all threatening to take away the Internet user's privacy. 'Most recently, the recent Online Safety Bill proposed that providers of secure messaging apps implement a way for Ofcom to access unencrypted messages'. Mark Gill noted. However, the ISP Review in its recent report noted that 'Home Office and the National Crime Agency were making progress on the development of a new internet snooping system and database in 2022, which could soon require broadband ISPs and mobile operators to provide various agencies with access to view a log of your online activity' while Deputy Digital Editor of Wired, Matt Burgess in his article (The UK is secretly testing a controversial web snooping tool- 11.03.2021) has reviewed the UK controversial web snooping strategy:

"The tests, which are being run by two unnamed internet service providers, the Home Office and the National Crime Agency, are being conducted under controversial surveillance laws introduced at the end of 2016. If successful, data collection systems could be rolled out nationally, creating one of the most powerful and controversial surveillance tools used by any democratic nation. Despite the National Crime Agency saying "significant work" has been put into the trial it remains clouded in secrecy. Elements of the legislation are also being challenged in court. There has been no public announcement of the trial, with industry insiders saying they are unable to talk about the technology due to security concerns. The trial is being conducted under the Investigatory Powers Act 2016, dubbed the Snooper's Charter, and involves the creation of Internet Connection Records, or ICRs. These are records of what you do online and have a broad definition. In short, they contain the metadata about your online life: who, what, where, why and when of your digital life. The surveillance law can require web and phone companies to store browsing histories for 12 months – although for this to happen they must be served with an order, approved by a senior judge, telling them to keep the data".[12]

On 30 January 2023, Liberty and Privacy International won a landmark case against MI5's unlawful handling of millions of people's data. Despite knowing of "very serious failings", MI5 continued to handle data unlawfully. Successive Home Secretaries ignored signs of MI5 behaving unlawfully. The MI5 breached its duty of candour to the Investigatory Powers Tribunal in a previous claim by Privacy International. In a landmark judgment, handed down (Monday 30 January 2023), the Investigatory Powers Tribunal has found that there were "very serious failings" at the highest levels of MI5 to comply with privacy safeguards from as early as 2014, and that successive Home Secretaries did not enquire into or resolve this long-standing rule-breaking despite obvious red flags….The Tribunal made declarations that MI5 and the Home Secretary had acted unlawfully under the Investigatory Powers Act, the ECHR and retained EU law. It refused to grant further relief including the quashing of warrants issued during the period of unlawful handling and the Home Office's failed oversight, destruction of data and damages. Although information on whose data has been mishandled is unavailable, it is likely to include many people who are not suspected of any wrongdoing due to the nature of the broad surveillance powers given to MI5. Liberty noted.[13]

On 13 February 2020, Liberty Human Rights organization lawyer, Megan Goulding in her analysis of Intel pointed to the failure of MI5 for more than 10 years: "For nearly a decade MI5 knowingly mishandled data collected through surveillance in violation of statutory safeguards. The service also failed to inform the UK government watchdog IPCO of these unlawful errors. Among other errors, MI5 has neglected the implementation of both serious mechanisms for the review, retention, and destruction of retained data and of effective safeguards relating to lawyer-client communications. MI5's longstanding and serious failings emerged during Liberty's legal challenge to the IPA heard last year. Liberty is a UK human rights campaigning organisation with a long history of holding the UK State to account over surveillance. A document disclosed was an attachment to MI5's Handbook for Judicial Commissioners (JCs) (those at IPCO who review the authorisation of warrants) issued on 1 April 2019."[14] Moreover, on 11 April 2022, Arab News reported the serious failure of MI5 over the Manchester terrorist attacks. "In an interview for "When Worlds Collide," a two-part ITV documentary on the bombing, Lord Anderson of Ipswich QC said "mistakes were made" by the MI5 when it was assessing information before the attack, which killed 22 people as they left an Ariana Grande concert. However, MI5 shamelessly refused to release the secret intelligence report, but Anderson said it was important and linked the bomber Salman Abedi to terrorism months before the attack.[15]

Moreover, expert and writer, Gavin Mortimer (How much longer will MI5 cloak its incompetence in secrecy? The Spectator, 03 March 2023) in his the Spectator analysis of MI5 failure noted that incompetence of MI5 in failing to prevent Salman Abedi detonating his bomb at the Manchester Arena in 2017 beggars belief: "In publishing his 226-page report, Sir John did not spare the intelligence service for missing several opportunities to thwart Abedi, who made little attempt to conceal his extremist ideology. MI5's most calamitous mistake was to sit on a piece of intelligence that they received, information which has not been disclosed for national security reasons. The first MI5 officer to assess the intelligence failed to discuss it with colleagues and did not write a report on the same day as was standard procedure. When the MI5 officer did eventually write the report, noted Sir John, it 'did not contain sufficient context'. Had the officer acted with more diligence, it is likely that Abedi's return to the UK from Libya on May 18, 2017 'would have been treated extremely seriously by the Security Service'. Four days later Abedi blew himself up at the Manchester Arena".[16]On 31 January 2023, Joshua Rozenberg (MI5 and Home Office acted unlawfully: But tribunal rules that a public finding of 'serious failings' is punishment enough) noted the Tribunal statement about the conduct of MI5 leadership as entailing "serious failings in compliance with [its] statutory obligations". Having commented of the Zubaydah-v-Foreign, Commonwealth and Development Office case, expert Dominic Bright (Does English law apply to alleged torts by MI5 and MI6 ("the Security and Intelligence Services") following allegations of torture by the CIA in overseas black sites? [17]

On 20 December, 2023, the Guardian newspaper's Legal affairs correspondent, Haroon Siddique reported some legal aspects of a Palestinian national, Abu Zubaydah's pain inflicted by MI5 and the CIA agents. "Abu Zubaydah, a Palestinian national whose full name is Zayn al-Abidin Muhammad Husayn, said that between 2002 and 2006 he was unlawfully rendered by US agents to Thailand, Lithuania, Poland, Guantánamo Bay in Cuba, Afghanistan, Morocco and finally to Guantánamo Bay again, where he has been held without trial ever since. In 2022, the court of appeal unanimously overturned the decision of the high court that the relevant law was that of the countries where Abu Zubaydah was held rather than the law of England and Wales...There was no suggestion that the UK intelligence services were aware or ever took steps to find out where Abu Zubaydah was. He was rendered to and held in each of the six countries by the CIA without any reference – or access – to the laws of those countries. The MI5 and MI6 were "acting in their official capacity in the purported exercise of powers conferred under the law of England and Wales. Abu Zubaydah claims that the UK intelligence services committed the civil wrongs of misfeasance in public office, conspiracy to injure, trespass to the person, false imprisonment and negligence in a case that threatens to put UK complicity with the CIA's kidnap and torture programme during the "war on terror" back into the spotlight. Haroon Siddique noted".[18]

As the Covert Human Intelligence Sources (Criminal Conduct) Bill 2019-2021 generated debates in domestic and international forums, analyst and expert Joanna Dawson noted that the Covert Human Intelligence Sources (Criminal Conduct) Bill 2019-2021 would 'introduce a power in the Regulation of Investigatory Powers Act 2000 to authorize conduct by officials and agents of the security and intelligence services, law enforcement, and certain other public authorities, which would otherwise constitute criminality'.[19] Former Prime Minister Boris Johnson argued that the coronavirus crisis should serve as a springboard to tackle social and economic inequality in the country so that his government would build more affordable homes, improve education, crack down on crime and invest heavily in 'green' energy, but all his weak and controversial strategies failed. His next step was the introduction of Covert Human Intelligence Sources (CHIS) bill expressly greenlights not merely MI5 but 10 other agencies–including HM Revenue and Customs, the Food Standards Agency, police, and the Gambling Commission–to engage in criminal conduct, as long as they're committing the lesser evil in order to prevent a greater one.[20]

Chapter 4

Failure of British Intelligence to Counter Foreign Espionage, Inexplicable Murder by Viruses and Firearms

As I have already documented the prospect of an intelligence war in Europe in my books and research papers, recent attacks authenticated my perception of espionage networks in the continent. In 1978, writer Georgi Markov was poisoned and killed on Waterloo Bridge. Years later in 2006, Russian writer Alexander Livinenko and MI6 agent Colonel Skripal were poisoned in the UK. These incidents proved my concern of how the British intelligence infrastructure was weak and incompetent to protect citizens of the country. MI5 failed to counter Chinese and South Asian espionage networks in the UK. The most detailed existing accounts of these murders and attempted murder are considered the cases in isolation, while others have focused on UK-based assassinations more broadly. Before his emigration, Mr. Georgi Markov was a novelist and playwright. Expert, Daniel Salisbury and Karl Dewey in their Paper, (Murder on Waterloo Bridge: placing the assassination of Georgi Markov in the past and present context, 1970–2018, Contemporary British History, Volume 37, 2023-issue 1.18 Jan 2023) noted the way Markov and the RFE journalist, Vladimir Kostov were killed:

"On 7 September 1978, as he queued for the bus on Waterloo Bridge, Markov had a strange encounter with a passer-by on his way to work. He later began to feel sick and was unable to broadcast that night. The following day, the family doctor was called and Markov was admitted to St. James Hospital. The following day Markov continued to deteriorate, suffering from acute septicaemia and renal failure, and on 11 September at 10:50am, he died. Nine days before the Waterloo Bridge incident, on 28 August 1978, another Bulgarian defector and RFE journalist, Vladimir Kostov, was attacked on the Paris Metro. Prior to his 1977 defection, Kostov was a Bulgarian intelligence officer working undercover as a journalist in Paris.

According to Kostov, he was exiting the Metro at the Arc de Triomphe stop when he heard a 'muffled crack', like an airgun, and felt a sharp sting in his lower back on the right side just above the kidneys."[1]

Newspapers and journals published stories on the failure of Scotland Yard and MI5 that they knew the killer. The fantastic story about the poisoned umbrella that killed Markov was infected with bacteria. The new bacteriological weapon developed and produced by Bulgaria. In both cases, the British police and intelligence were able to present a clear and detailed narrative encompassing the killers' identities, but they failed to highlight the cases with different perspectives. Expert and writer, Joshua Stewart in his research paper (Responding to Security Threats, the Grey Orchestra: Elastic Communications and the UK's Response to Salisbury, the RUSI Journal. Volume 167, 2022 - Issue 231 May 2022) has documented a detailed story of the Salisbury attacks, British response and Russian reaction:

"The UK response to the Salisbury poisoning attacks of 2018 was a triumph and provides valuable lessons in information advantage and grey-zone competition for the national security establishment. From the poisoning of the Skripals in March to the unravelling of the GRU's operations in October, the UK conducted a phased, managed confrontation, reaching a defined end state. Characterised by the need to establish clarity, authority and authenticity, the UK used an 'elastic communications strategy', which blunted Kremlin disinformation and leveraged the full spectrum of government powers into a potent 'second strike' communications response. The case demonstrates that successful and innovative grey-zone competition can be achieved without sacrificing moral authority. On 4 March 2018, former SIS agent Sergei Skripal and his daughter, Yulia, were found unconscious on a park bench in Salisbury. Overnight, the languid cathedral town became a sprawling crime scene and the epicentre of an onslaught of Kremlin disinformation. A dizzying array of questions confronted the UK government. Who conducted the attack? What was the motivation? How should it respond? Despite an unprecedented information assault and a governmental machinery choked by the Brexit process, the UK was able to cut through the communications space with clarity, authority and authenticity. Through a staggered, methodical approach, the UK leveraged a spectrum of state and non-state powers and blunted the Kremlin's strategy".[2]

Intelligence agencies were left in pain by failing to counter Chinese intelligence in the UK. In 03 December 2018, Chief of MI6, Sir Alex Younger described the key to the UK response as being the operationalisation of values, legal systems and alliances. "We are one of the few truly global intelligence agencies, capable of going to the source of problems anywhere in the world to recruit and run secret agents, penetrate terrorist organisations, provide our government with the intelligence it needs to safeguard the national interest, give UK authorities information they need to disrupt terrorist attacks at home and against our allies, and detect and counter efforts by state and non-state actors to traffic drugs or proliferate nuclear and chemical weapons".(Alex Younger: 'You can tell a lot about the soul of a country from its intelligence services' speech from "C", Head of MI6-St. Andrews, Scotland, UK-Speakola).[3] There was a series of credible criticism on the underwhelming performance of the UK intelligence agencies. The issue of whether MI5 should be investigated for its failure to prevent the Salisbury attack is complex and involves several considerations. Some say intelligence work, especially in the context of state-sponsored attacks, is inherently difficult. The attackers in the Salisbury incident were believed to be part of GRU, a sophisticated Russian intelligence agency, but failure of the MI5 and MI6 to prevent the GRU operation is shameful. Investigations into intelligence services like MI5 often involve highly classified information. The decision to investigate an intelligence agency can be influenced by broader political considerations. The government might have weighed the potential benefits of an investigation against the risk of revealing sensitive methods or straining diplomatic relations.

Expert Kevin P. Riehle in his research paper (Ignorance, indifference, or incompetence: why are Russian covert actions so easily unmasked? Intelligence and National Security, 30 Jan 2024), identified lack of Russian tradecraft and intelligence incompetency: "Investigations by counterintelligence organizations and by journalists have identified multiple instances when Russian tradecraft was lacking. Less than six months after the Skripal assassination attempt, the British government identified the operatives through surveillance camera footage and GRU-linked communications. Two of the GRU operatives went on Russian television a week later and claimed to be simple tourists in the UK. The implausible nature of their claim may be an indicator of Russian indifference. However, the fact that the British investigation forced them to make a public appearance to deny the allegations is an indicator of incompetence in the operation. Russian disinformation is not always well conceived or executed and the tradecraft involved in Russian disinformation is not hard to penetrate. As noted above, the European Union East Strategic

Communications Task Force identified 4,500 messages as Russian disinformation in just a three-year period."[4]

Intelligence agencies in Britain danced with a specific style which doesn't reflect a professional approach to the cause, some of their operations and power abuse caused misunderstanding about their legitimate aspects. As we have seen in the past, MI5 demonstrated irrelevantly and irregularly by adopting a controversial counterterrorism measures, involved in racial politics, as one of its Director General screeched that Muslim communities were a threat to Britain. In the UK, every year, the fluctuation of security threat level becomes questionable when new jihadist networks are introduced to communities. These security threat levels remain irksome as we have been unable to tackle the threat of radicalisation and extremism. Former Prime Minister David Cameron introduced a new strategy called the Tackling Extremism and Radicalisation Task Force (TERFOR) but failed to deliver positively. Extremist and radicalised elements continue to participate in overseas jihadist operations. Moreover, the PPPP strategy has also failed to intercept UK jihadists from joining ISIS and Taliban networks. The scale of danger posed by extremists in and outside the country was underlined when jihadists threatened to kill non-Muslims in the streets of the UK.

The recent reports and official warnings by the UK government about the intensifying threat of cyber terrorism in the print and electronic media prompted torment and cheerlessness in investment and business firms across the country. Cyber security organisations are desperately seeking ways to counter it effectively while private business firms are looking towards the most trusted intelligence agency, the Government Communication Headquarters (GCHQ) for a precursor action against the clandestine networks of hackers and cyber jihadists. As we are being told about the sensitivity of this violent security threat, our intelligence agencies are also restive and anxious about the day-to-day changing mechanism of cyber terrorist groups. The recent violent attacks on the Home Office, Foreign Office, private industry and market economy forced the GCHQ to request cyber technology experts for help in preventing these exacerbating attacks. During the last two decades, cyber terrorists have attacked thousands of websites including the websites of the UK government, causing millions of pounds in damage. Now this war has reached a breaking point. To combat the forces of financial jihad, Britain's Cyber Security Strategy was published in November 2011, which underlined the technicality of the threat faced by the country's institutions from economic jihadists and state-sponsored cyber forces.

The basic objectives of the UK Cyber Security Strategy are to introduce the traditions of partnership and transparency both across business and within the international community in an effort to meet the growing cyber threat. The Whitehall administration has badly failed to confront extremist groups and their networks across the UK. The most interesting thing is that British police, counter terror infrastructure and the government are all complaining against the prevailing extremist culture in the country on the one hand, but avoid any violent action against them due to fear of a backlash from African and Asian communities on the other. Political commentators believe that Britain is losing the battle against extremists and the sectarian mafia groups. Former Home Secretary Theresa May was extremely disturbed by the re-emergence of extremism and sectarianism in Britain. Former Prime Minister David Cameron once said that his country would not tolerate Islamic extremism but, notwithstanding his harsh stand, the PM shared a lot with them at the same table. Experts viewed this apologetically adapted policy of the Cameron government as a major cause of the ineffectiveness of CONTEST.

Secret agencies are facing particular threats from hostile states and terrorist groups from Africa, South Asia and Middle East, because of the nature of their role, and their distinctive characteristic of secrecy. "The intelligence services are thereby expected to contribute to preventing, containing and overcoming serious threats to the country and its people. In order to fulfil their vital functions, intelligence services throughout the world are given special powers. They have the power to acquire confidential information through surveillance, infiltration of organisations, interception of communication and other methods that infringe the right to privacy; to undertake covert operations aimed at countering threats to national security; and to operate with a high level of secrecy".(Intelligence in a constitutional Democracy: (Ministerial Review Commission on Intelligence, Republic of South Africa, 10 September 2008).[5]

Activities of secret agencies in a democratic states demonstrate carefully because there is a watch and monitoring system in operation that control their movement. During the COVID-19 lockdown in the UK, intelligence and surveillance measures were primarily focused on monitoring and controlling society. The Digital Tracking and Tracing system in NHS hospitals developed a contact tracing app, which was a significant part of the surveillance strategy. This app used Bluetooth technology to notify users if they had been in close contact with someone who tested positive for COVID-19. The CCTV and Drone Surveillance was in full operation illegally. Local police forces used drones and CCTV to monitor public spaces. The government of Boris Johnson and his health authorities were acting like vandal against the civilian population by closing their shops and religious places. Social Media monitoring responsibilities were entrusted to the army Brigade-77-information brigade. These measures destroyed the economy and social stratification in Britain. Brigade-77 of the British Army is known for its focus on information warfare, psychological operations, and unconventional methods of modern warfare, ensuring the security of communications and data within Downing Street, protecting against cyber threats and information leaks.

The Brigade-77 by utilizing social media and other platforms to manage public perception and counter misinformation or propaganda that could affect national security or the government's agenda. Providing detailed analysis of open-source information and social media trends to inform government decisions and strategies. The Brigade was advising on and possibly implementing strategies for effective communication from the government to the public, especially in situations that may involve national security concerns. Artificial Intelligence (AI) also played a significant role in combating national security challenges in various ways such as detection, and responding to cyber threats faster and more effectively than traditional methods. The AI helped in processing and analysing large volumes of intelligence data, including images, videos, texts, and signals. It can quickly sort through this data to find relevant information, patterns, or anomalies, aiding in decision-making and strategy development. AI enhanced surveillance capabilities, such as facial recognition or anomaly detection in surveillance footage. On 23 January 2024, writer and analyst, Paul Medina in his article (To Ten Scandal with British Intelligence-23 January, 2024) spotlighted Director of Human Rights organization-Reprieve's Maya Foa campaign that successfully forced the British government to acknowledge their sanctioning of criminal activity by MI5 agents in 2018. The saga, Paul Medina noted, continued into multiple exposés and prolonged trials, and what had emerged from all of it is that MI5 agents were allowed to commit criminal acts, the full extent of which is unknown. The London Bridge attack in 2017 inflicted fatalities was in fact the failure of MI5 operational mechanisms. Between 1974 and 1975, members of British Intelligence allegedly conspired to conduct a smear campaign against Prime Minister Harold Wilson. Paul Medina also noted that book of MI5 officer Peter

Wright that appeared in 1987 titled spycatcher revealed failure of MI5 on many occasions:

"In 1987, a former high-ranking MI5 officer named Peter Wright released a memoir titled Spycatcher: The Candid Autobiography of a Senior Intelligence Officer. In the book, Wright detailed numerous questionable and ethically dubious practices by MI5 members that he had either researched or personally witnessed. The book was immediately banned in England, and any papers who dared to report on its contents found themselves hit with government-issued gag orders. The Cambridge five was another failure of MI5 agency that outsmarted the entire country. Writer Paul Medina also highlighted in brief the MI5 scandal that combing through list after list of British Intelligence failures, the Cambridge Five were likely to be the top in most, and the individual five members on their own were most often the following five entries. At least five undercover Soviet spies successfully infiltrated British Intelligence and relayed state secrets to the Soviet Union for two to three decades. Moreover, they were only discovered when two of them fled to Moscow, and none of the five were ever prosecuted for their role as Soviet moles".[6]

British intelligence was alleged to have provided information or assistance in some of these cases. There have been specific allegations and cases where British intelligence was accused of being directly involved in, or complicit with, the mistreatment of detainees. For instance, the case of Abdel Hakim Belhaj, a Libyan dissident who was rendered along with his pregnant wife to Libya in 2004, allegedly with the help of British intelligence, gained significant attention. Belhaj claimed that he was subsequently tortured by Libyan authorities. The British government faced significant pressure to address these allegations. Various inquiries and reports were conducted, including the Gibson Inquiry and the Intelligence and Security Committee's (ISC) reports. However, critics argued that these inquiries were hampered by a lack of transparency and state secrecy. Some cases led to legal actions and settlements. For instance, in the case of Abdel Hakim Belhaj, the UK government issued an apology and reached a settlement with him and his wife in 2018, though they did not admit liability. It's important to note that these matters involve highly classified information, and many details are not publicly disclosed. The involvement of British intelligence in rendition and torture has been a complex and controversial topic, reflecting broader global concerns about the balance between national security and human rights.

On 29 October 2023, the Guardian reported (Second investigation to open into role of British spies in torture of Guantánamo detainee. Lawyers for Abd al-Rahim al-Nashiri claim UK intelligence was 'complicit in his ill-treatment' by the US, Guardian Sunday 29 Oct 2023) judicial investigation into the allegations that MI5 was complicit in the CIA's post-9/11 secret torture and rendition programme. "The investigatory powers tribunal (IPT), the Guardian noted, said it will open a second investigation into allegations that the intelligence services were involved in the mistreatment of a prisoner detained by the US. In a ruling released the secretive court said it would examine a complaint filed on behalf of Abd al-Rahim al-Nashiri, a Saudi Arabian citizen held at the US military prison at Guantánamo Bay in Cuba. Nashiri, who was alleged by the US to have plotted al-Qaida's bombing of an American naval ship in Yemen, was captured by the CIA in 2002 and transferred to Guantánamo in 2006. He was held in indefinite detention ever since. Lawyers for Nashiri argued that there was an "irresistible inference" that the UK's intelligence agencies, including MI5, MI6 and GCHQ, participated in intelligence sharing relating to al-Nashiri and "were complicit in his torture and ill-treatment. The IPT's decision to investigate the claims comes after it agreed in May to examine a similar complaint by another man held at Guantánamo, Mustafa al-Hawsawi". Guardian noted.[7]

After consecutive failures of MI5, now all the UK intelligence agencies were lobbying the government to weaken surveillance laws, they argued to place a "burdensome" limit on their ability to train artificial intelligence models with large amounts of personal data. The Guardian newspaper on 01 August 2023 reported (UK spy agencies want to relax 'burdensome' laws on AI data use: GCHQ, MI6 and MI5 propose weakening safeguards that limit training of AI models with bulk personal datasets- Harry Davies, The Guardia Tue 1 Aug 2023) lobbying of the UK intelligence agencies for weakening surveillance laws to ease their burden. "Privacy experts and civil liberties groups expressed alarm at the move, which could unwind some of the legal protection introduced in 2016 after disclosures by Edward Snowden about intrusive state surveillance. The UK's spy agencies are increasingly using AI-based systems to help analyse the vast and growing quantities of data they hold. Privacy campaigners argue rapidly advancing AI capabilities require stronger rather than weaker regulation. MI5, MI6 and GCHQ frequently use BPDs that are drawn from a wide range of closed and open sources and can also be acquired through covert means. The agencies, who argue these datasets help them identify potential terrorists and future informants, want to relax rules about how they use BPDs in which they believe people have a "low or no expectation of privacy". The Guardian reported.[8]

MI5 lost control of its data storage operations and has been obtaining surveillance warrants on the basis of information it knows to be false, the high court heard. The security agency was accused of "extraordinary and persistent illegality" in a legal challenge brought by the human rights organisation Liberty failures were identified by the official watchdog, the investigatory powers commissioner, Lord Justice Fulford, and admitted in outline by the former home secretary, Sajid Javid. Moreover, the secret policy of MI5 allows its agents to commit crimes. Journalist Dan Sabbagh in his recent article (MI5 policy allowing agents to commit crimes was legal, say judges: Human rights groups indicate they will seek to take the case to the Supreme Court after appeal court judgment.[9] The Guardian, 09 March 2021) noted that MI5's partially designed secret policy of allowing agents to participate in serious crimes in pursuit of intelligence was legal. The three judges held that MI5 was "not above the law" because the long-established power did not equate to an immunity from prosecution, in the latest step in a long-running legal case brought by four human rights groups. At a hearing in the case in January government lawyers told a court that MI5 officers could in theory authorise an informer to carry out a murder if they were "an extremely hostile individual". Human rights groups indicated they would seek to appeal to the Supreme Court. Maya Foa, the director of Reprieve, said: "The idea that the government can authorise undercover agents to commit the most serious crimes, including torture and murder, is deeply troubling and must be challenged." Critics say agents operating in Northern Ireland have repeatedly been accused of colluding in murder. The Guardian noted.[10]

In 2019, Greater Manchester Police (GMP) estimated that there were 940 victims of the attack who survived. Of those 940 victims, 337 people were in the city room at the time of the explosion and a further 92 people were in the immediate vicinity. Of the victims, 237 people were physically injured. A total of 111 people required hospitalisation. A total of 91 people were categorised as being seriously or very seriously injured.[11](Manchester Arena Inquiry: Volume 2: Emergency Response. Volume 2-II. Report of the Public Inquiry into the Attack on Manchester Arena on 22nd May 2017. Chairman: The Hon Sir John Saunders. Presented to Parliament pursuant to section 26 of the Inquiries Act 2005, Ordered by the House of Commons to be printed 3 November 2022).The Manchester Arena bombing on May 22, 2017, carried out by Salman Abedi, was a tragic event that led to intense scrutiny of the UK's security services, including MI5. Following the attack, reports emerged that MI5 had been aware of Abedi and his potential risk. Salman Abedi was known to MI5, but he was not considered a high-risk subject at the time of the Manchester attack.

Inquiries into the attack revealed that there were potential opportunities to detect Abedi's plot or to place him under closer scrutiny. Retrospective analysis by MI5 and counter-terrorism police suggested that the available intelligence could have been interpreted differently, potentially altering the handling of Abedi's case. While recognizing the complexities of counter-terrorism work and the volume of potential threats, these reviews pointed out areas for improvement in information sharing, risk assessment, and investigative procedures. The MI5 and UK counter-terrorism policing failed to react on time. While MI5 faced significant challenges in identifying and thwarting every potential threat, the Manchester Arena bombing led to introspection and changes aimed at preventing such tragic events in the future. The MI5 chief apologized shamelessly for the failure of his agency to prevent the Manchester Arena attack. The head of MI5 expressed the apology as a gesture of taking responsibility and being accountable for the agency's actions. The MI5 is always a failed agency not in this case, in many cases MI5 never demonstrated professionally.[12]The MI5 lost public confidence and trust which is crucial for its management. The apology was also a way to address public concerns, demonstrate transparency, and show that the agency is committed to learning from its mistakes and improving its practices. The apology was a confession that his agency needed reform and a monitoring system but MI5 never took responsibility and shamelessly responded to the incident with a false statement and never realized that the agency had committed crime. The MI5 Chief aimed to convey empathy and commitment to doing everything possible to prevent such tragedies in the future. Experts and analysts, Karen Lund Petersen and Kira Vrist Rønn in their research paper (Introducing the special issue: bringing in the public. Intelligence on the frontier between state and civil society- Intelligence and National Security 2019, vol. 34, NO. 3. Routledge, 12 Feb 2019) have highlighted complex and threatening environment such as terrorism, radicalization, foreign espionage and global financial crisis:

"Complex and uncertain threat environments, with terrorism, cybersecurity and global financial crisis, have made many traditional management tools unfit and profoundly transformed the ways in which intelligence services deal with threats to the nation and its citizens. In this special issue, we argue that intelligence agencies today stand before a defining gap between an increasing demand from society and politicians to provide security and the organization's ability to fulfil those demands and needs. In order to manage this gap between expectations and possibilities for management, new methods, coalitions and partnerships are considered pertinent. These practices include the use of new technologies for collection and analysis as well as arrangements to increase cooperation and partnerships between national and foreign intelligence and security services, between intelligence and police services, between intelligence and security services and the public, and between intelligence and private companies and 'other potentially uneasy bedfellows".[13]Experts, George Kassimeris and Oliver Price in their paper (How the rise of Militant Tendency transformed MI5's perception of Trotskyism's ability to pose a threat to the British state. LSE British Politics and Policy, a multidisciplinary academic blog run by the London School of Economics and Political Science. 15 November 2021) have also reviewed newly released files available at The UK National Archives that highlighted the revolving strategy of MI5 viz-a-viz a Trotskyist group militant in the 1970s and 1980s. In yesteryears, MI5 considered subversive activities that threatened security of the state and making efforts to overthrow parliamentary democracy in Britain:

"The major targets of MI5's counter-subversive operations until the 1970s were Communists and the Communist Party of Great Britain (CPGB), which was subjected to sustained and extensive surveillance following its formation in 1920. The Trotskyist movement, which emerged in Britain during the early 1930s, was regarded by MI5 as being 'too small and chaotic' to be capable of posing any significant subversive threat to the British state. The activities of Militant Tendency (MT), a Trotskyist organisation which came to prominence as a result of its infiltration of the Labour Party in the 1970s and 1980s, transformed intelligence officers' perception of Trotskyists. By the early 1980s, Militant was believed to be capable of posing an equal, if not greater, subversive threat than the CPGB. By 1984, one Whitehall official declared in a memorandum sent to MI5 that 'Militant seems to have replaced the Communist Party as the established focus for subversion within the country'. Militant was considered to pose such a threat because a significant number of its members had managed to infiltrate the Labour Party; they aimed to transform it, from within, into a 'revolutionary party'. At the conference in 1977, Peter Taaffe, deputy leader of Militant, was recorded, by intelligence operatives, stating that the movement would be 'an indispensable weapon of the Revolution in Britain.' MI5 investigations into Militant were eventually highly successful. By the late 1970s, MI5 had identified about 75% of the Tendency's membership through a combination of telephone checks, agent penetration, informants, and".[14]

The UK Intelligence Failure to Transform and Reorganize its infrastructure: The Role of Army Brigade-77 in COVID-19-Spying Program, the Manchester and London Attacks and the Landscape of Extremism and Radicalization

History of the failure of British intelligence (MI5, MI6) is of considerable length while their process of reorganization is deeply underwhelming as there are no absolute and out-and-out reform to make MI5 fit to the fight against hostile forces.[15]MI5 never demonstrated on the right direction just waited terrorist attacks one-by-one and closed eyes to human fatalities in every terrorist attack.[16]The agency is expert of targeting critics and political opponents. Boris Johnson committed war crimes by using COVID-19 as a weapon against the British citizens."[17]Director for Big Brother Watch, Silkie[18]Carlo, said, "This is an alarming case of mission creep, where public money and military power have been misused to monitor academics, journalists, campaigners and MPs who criticised the Government, particularly during the pandemic". Daily Mail reported.[19]Intelligence failures in Britain, as in other countries, have occurred over the years, and they often lead to significant introspection, policy changes, and sometimes public inquiries. Addressing these root causes is a long-term challenge that goes beyond the scope of any single strategy. Critics argue that some aspects of the CONTEST strategy, such as surveillance and control orders, may infringe on individual rights. Measuring the success of a counter-terrorism strategy is inherently challenging. Preventing attacks and radicalization is crucial, but it's often hard to quantify what doesn't happen due to successful interventions.[20]

While the CONTEST strategy has faced challenges and criticisms, it's also important to recognize its successes and the continuous efforts to adapt and improve the approach in response to an ever-changing threat landscape. It's an ongoing process that requires vigilance, adaptation, and a balanced approach. During the Prime Minister Boris Johnson reign, state institutions, government circles and communities were facing the wrath of Chinese, Russian and Iranian espionage and intelligence nests while they began using their hackers and spy agents to retrieve strategic information and metadata. While Boris Johnson was clandestinely a supporter of Russian intelligence networks in the UK by furthering the political and economic agenda of the Russian government and the Trump administration. France

24 reported Junior Health Minister Maria Caulfield's revelations that her party acted promptly to drop the two potential candidates for parliament after MI5's intervention. (UK government spy scandals fuel calls for tougher stance on China. 13 September 2023) Caulfield was speaking after a report in The Daily Times said MI5 raised concerns that the pair had linked to the Chinese Communist Party's United Front Work Department, a body charged with influencing global policy and opinion.

Details of the advice, given in 2021 and 2022, comes days after it emerged a parliamentary researcher was arrested in March on suspicion of spying for Beijing. The suspect, said to be in his 20s, was arrested at his home in Edinburgh, along with another man in his 30s. Both were detained on suspicion of offences under the Official Secrets Act and have been released on bail until October, pending further investigations. France 24 reported.[21] On 20 December 2023, the Home Office determined to implement the core measures put in place by the National Security Act passed in July 2023. The Home Secretary, James Cleverly hoped that law enforcement agencies can now be able to use the new tools and modernised powers to deter, detect and disrupt threats from those acting on behalf of foreign states against the UK and its interests. He also views recent evolved security threats while Russia, China and Iran have all posed acute threats to the UK, through interference, poisonings and attempted kidnappings. Home Secretary, James Cleverly, noted:

"There are foreign powers who have shown their willingness to make threats to the UK and our freedoms. The National Security Act will prove critical in helping police and intelligence partners to make it even more difficult for them to do so, and as the core measures come into force today, the UK becomes a safer country. We will always do everything possible to protect the United Kingdom. Further activities which can now be put before the UK courts includes updated espionage offences, including the theft of trade secrets, foreign interference, including in the UK's political system, sabotage, and modern ways of attempting to access the UK's most sensitive sites".[21] However, Deputy Prime Minister, Oliver Dowden, said: "The National Security Act is the most significant reform of espionage law in a century and demonstrates that the Government will always act to protect the UK from threats to our security, prosperity and interests. State threats are an evolving challenge and the new offences and powers in the National Security Act will ensure that our intelligence services and law enforcement have the tools they need to counter them. The act has brought into effect modern laws to tackle such threats, replacing previous espionage legislation that was primarily designed to counter the threat from German spies before and after the First World War". (New national security laws come into force: Policing and intelligence partners now have more powers to foil covert foreign influence, with espionage laws updated to tackle 21st century threats. 20 December 2023).[22]

The Security Minister in his comment categorically remarked: "The UK has been facing a rise in foreign state-directed threats with various attempts to harm our citizens–we have not stood back but have created a new set of powers to confront it. Our new national security laws can now be applied, and those who would seek to undermine our democracy can be held to account. These new tools will protect us and hold all malign foreign actors responsible for any threatening activity. The new tools available to operational partners will also provide the means to stop those seeking by illegitimate means to influence public figures. It will also improve the process for the use of existing powers within the Counter Terrorism and Border Security Act 2019, which grant police officers the ability to stop individuals at ports and retain items that could ascertain their involvement in hostile activity by foreign states". (New national security laws come into force: Policing and intelligence partners now have more powers to foil covert foreign influence, with espionage laws updated to tackle 21st century threats. 20 December 2023).[23]

Britain's internal security challenges are indeed multifaceted and complex. I have heard from some intelligence Heads in UK about their personal commitment to include LGBT in the ranks of MI5, MI6 and GCHQ infrastructures, but things are evolving differently and we still have not heard how they accommodate these people and what role they need to play. For diversification and the work they need to do to create more inclusive workplaces it still needs to be specified. In 2015, Intelligence and Security Committee in its report noted: "This is not just an ethical issue: it is vitally important from an intelligence perspective …Logically, if all intelligence professionals are cut from the same cloth, then they are likely to share 'unacknowledged biases' that circumscribe both the definition of problems and the search for solutions. Diversity should therefore be pursued not just on legal or ethical grounds – which are important in themselves–but because it will result in a better response to the range of threats that we face to our national security."[24](Intelligence and Security Committee, Women in the UK Intelligence Community, 2015).

Security threats to national security have been common in all EU member states, but in the UK these threats evolved differently due to its military involvement on different fronts. The UK faces a substantial threat from terrorism. Higher levels of effective and visible protective security at national infrastructure sites are likely to act as a deterrent to terrorists, who increasingly favour 'soft' targets. Nevertheless, with the continual diversification of the threat, the ambition and capability of terrorist groups to target UK infrastructure is likely to continue to evolve. In June 2022, the NATO heads of states gathered in Madrid and declared that the organization facing the specific threat from China: "We face systemic competition from those, including the People's Republic of China, who challenge our interests, security, and values and seek to undermine the rules-based international order"[25]According to the House of Lords Library report (China: Security challenges to the UK in Focus, 08 July, 2022); 'On 6 July 2022, the heads of the UK Security Service (MI5) and the US Federal Bureau of Investigation (FBI) held an "unprecedented joint address" to warn of the "immense" threat from China.[26]

The government's position on China was deeply criticised by the report of the House of Lords International Relations and Defence Committee in September 2021. A Daily Times article from 01 November 2021 reported that Elizabeth Truss, the Secretary of State for Foreign, Commonwealth and Development Affairs, had previously accused China of committing genocide against the Uyghur population in Xinjiang. This accusation was alleged to have taken place during a private meeting in October 2020 when Ms Truss was the Secretary of State for International Trade.1 Currently, the MI5 does not collect intelligence information about extremism but leaves this to its sister organization, the counter-terrorist police and the police force more generally. Yet the 1989 Security Service Act places on MI5 the statutory duty of 'protecting national security...from actions intended to overthrow or undermine parliamentary democracy by political... or violent means' (Legislation, government, 1989), but MI5 doesn't care about it intransigently and does not wish to exercise this role. But this is not something that MI5 should, by itself, be entitled to determine.[27]

Chapter 5

Collective Expulsion of Russian Diplomats from the US and EU Member States, Hostile States and the Chinese and Iranian Intelligence Networks in Britain

As I have already documented the UK national security challenges in my books and research papers, the country faces a range of national security threats from terrorism, foreign espionage and hostile state. Unfortunately, the current data across the intelligence community is not sufficiently robust as MI5 and MI6 need to share their data with the state institutions wholeheartedly. However, MI5 failed to cooperate with the Intelligence and Security Committee and other institutions of the British state. It means that MI5 must cooperate with national security organizations without holding its secret information and data. The security challenges include Britain's threat from both international terrorism and radicalization and foreign espionage. The UK, being a significant global player and a permanent member of the UN Security Council, holds considerable influence. Hostile states might target the UK to weaken its influence or to alter its foreign policy decisions. Targeting the UK's financial institutions, industries, or infrastructure can provide economic leverage or disrupt the UK's economic stability.

The UK's advanced digital infrastructure makes it a target for cyber-attacks aimed at causing disruption, stealing intellectual property, or gaining strategic advantages. Hostile states may also target the UK due to ideological differences, aiming to destabilize or challenge Western democratic ideals and values. By targeting the UK, hostile states might aim to disrupt alliances such as NATO or the "Five Eyes" intelligence-sharing network, thus weakening collective definitions and intelligence cooperation. Responding to the Russian intelligence involvement in the country, the UK expelled dozens of Russian diplomats in 2018. The Guardian reporters Julian Borger and Patrick Wintour and Heather Stewart reported that Western allies expelled scores of Russian diplomats over the Skripal attack: "US ordered expulsion of 60 officials as a succession of EU states announce similar moves. The Russian Foreign Ministry issued a statement denouncing the expulsions as "an unfriendly step" based on alliances rather than evidence. "The provocative gesture of the so-called solidarity of these countries with London, which blindly followed the British authorities in the so-called Skripal case and which never got around to sort out the circumstances of the incident, is a continuation of the confrontational policy to escalate the situation," the statement said". The Guardian noted.[1]

The collective expulsion from the US and EU member states was a remarkable show of solidarity with Britain, even more so because it comes at a time when UK-EU relations were strained due to the Brexit negotiations. Donald Tusk's noted that there could be "additional measures" was a signal to Moscow as it considered how it will respond. This incident led to a significant deterioration in UK-Russian relations and prompted a series of similar actions by other Western countries, showing solidarity with the UK and taking a stand against what was perceived as a pattern of aggressive and harmful actions by the Russian state. Russia expelled 189 diplomats from various countries in retaliation for the wave of ejections of Russian officials. A total of 342 diplomats were expelled and returned to home countries. The UK-China espionage tussle is part of the broader concerns over national security, economic espionage, and geopolitical rivalry. Several factors contribute to these tensions: The UK has raised concerns about cyber-attacks originating from China, targeting government and commercial entities to steal sensitive information and intellectual property.

On 07 December 2023, British authorities warned that Russia's intelligence services targeted high-profile British politicians, civil servants and journalists with cyber espionage as part of years-long attempts to interfere in U.K. politics. The Foreign Office said Russia's FSB agency was responsible for a range of sustained cyberespionage operations in the U.K. The UK's relationship with China also deteriorated after banning Huawei in the UK, a Chinese telecom giant, from its 5G network over security concerns reflecting the apprehension about potential espionage and cyber vulnerabilities. There have been worries about Chinese attempts to infiltrate universities and industries to acquire technological and scientific research. The UK has criticized China over human rights issues, especially concerning Hong Kong. On 08 January 2024, Al Jazeera reported a statement of Chinese intelligence about a British spy whom China accused of passing on state secrets.[2]

The Ministry of State Security stated that it had discovered that the head of a foreign consultancy was spying for the United Kingdom's MI6 intelligence service. It was the latest in a series of recent accusations traded between Beijing and London. Al Jazeera reported. (China accuses UK of sending spy to access state secrets: China and the UK and its Western allies have traded barbs, accusing each other of espionage) [3] The term "crisis of UK domestic security" could refer to a variety of challenges and threats that the United Kingdom has faced or is currently facing due to its unreformed intelligence infrastructure-failing to counter foreign espionage networks and radicalization. British agencies have failed on many occasions, particularly MI5 and the policing agencies failed to intercept terrorist Abidi before the Manchester attacks. These challenges often evolved and can be diverse, including terrorism, cyber security threats, organized crime, and issues related to border control and immigration. The UK has been a target of various terrorist attacks and plots. This includes both international terrorism, often linked to groups like ISIS or Al-Qaeda, and domestic terrorism, including far-right and Northern Ireland-related terrorism. Issues include dealing with illegal immigration, human smuggling, and trafficking, while ensuring the legitimate flow of people and goods, and Policing and Law Enforcement Resources. The UK's establishment of a new espionage unit is a response to the evolving and increasingly complex landscape of international espionage and cyber threats.

The dynamic and covert nature of espionage means that the success of such units might not always be visible to the public but is a crucial part of a country's national defense strategy. The UK is facing significant security challenges from, China, and Iran, according to statements from the heads of Britain's foreign and domestic intelligence agencies, MI6 and MI5 respectively. MI6 Chief Richard Moore identified China, Iran, and international terrorism as the "big four" security threats to the UK. Mr.Moore specifically highlighted China as the agency's top priority, pointing to its large-scale espionage operations, efforts to distort public and political discourse, and the export of technology that can enforce authoritarian control. Journalist Jill Lawless (MI6 spy chief says China, Russia, Iran top UK threat list-November 30, 2021) in his AP article reported remarks of the MI6 Chief on the interference of Russia and China in the internal affairs of Britain:

"Calling China "an authoritarian state with different values than ours," he said Beijing conducts "large-scale espionage operations" against the U.K. and its allies, tries to" distort public discourse and political decision-making" and exports technology that enables a "web of authoritarian control" around the world. "Beijing's growing military strength and the (Chinese Communist) party's desire to resolve the Taiwan issue, by force if necessary, also pose a serious challenge to global stability and peace," Moore said. The self-ruled island of Taiwan split from mainland China in 1949, and Beijing still claims it as part of its territory. "Beijing believes its own propaganda about Western frailties and under-estimates Washington's resolve," Moore added. "The risk of Chinese miscalculation through overconfidence is real." Moore said the U.K. also continues "to face an acute threat from Russia." He said Moscow has sponsored killing attempts, such as the poisoning of former spy Sergei Skripal in England in 2018, mounts cyberattacks and interferes in other countries' democratic processes. "We and our allies and partners must stand up to and deter Russian activity which contravenes the international rules-based system," the MI6 chief said". Jill reported.[4]

Asian Lite International (UK government taking poll interference threats seriously-23 January 2024) in its news report argued that the UK government taking foreign espionage threat seriously: "The UK is taking threats of foreign interference elections expected later this year "very seriously", the defence minister said on Sunday, after a warning from a counter-terrorism official. "Obviously, that's something that we take very seriously," Shapps told the Sky News channel. Counter-terrorism bodies and other institutions would "be looking very carefully at that", he said. UK counter-terrorism chief Matt Jukes said Friday that the espionage threat from foreign states such as China, Russia and Iran — is greater now than it has been "since the days of the Cold War".[5]Similarly, MI5 Director General Ken McCallum warned about China, and Iran, noting their use of coercion, intimidation, and even violence to pursue their interests on foreign soil. He stressed that Iran's intelligence services are ready to take reckless action against opponents, evidenced by at least ten potential threats uncovered by UK authorities this year, involving plans to kidnap or kill British or UK-based individuals viewed as enemies of the Iranian regime. McCallum also highlighted the challenges posed by Russia's espionage and China's strategic efforts to reshape global norms and recruit influential figures in British politics and public life.

On 15 January 2024, British Defence Secretary, Grant Shapps, in his speech at Lancaster House in London, in which he criticised political and intelligence interference of China, Russia and Iran in the UK institutions through their espionage networks. In the past few years we've seen terror attacks on the streets of London, attempted assassinations in Salisbury, theft of intellectual property, attempted interference in political processes, a cost-of-living crisis, that's hurting families here at home. And now, our trade, 90 percent of which comes by sea, is the target of terrorists. Proving that not only do our adversaries have the intent to target us but they have a widening array of weapons with which to wreak havoc. In our online world our adversaries don't need to jump in a tank, board a sub or strap into a fighter jet to hurt us. Cyber warfare simply means hacking into our networks and watching the economic carnage unfold. Defence Secretary, Grant Shapps noted.[6]

Expert and writer, Kyle S. Cunliffe in his research paper (Cyber-enabled tradecraft and contemporary espionage: assessing the implications of the tradecraft paradox on agent recruitment in Russia and China-Intelligence and National Security Volume 38, 2023-Issue 7. 02 Jun 2023) explained espionage and human intelligence: "Espionage, or what is more often known as human intelligence, Merely convincing a foreign official to walk a path that too often ends in execution or imprisonment is a delicate task, while the personal foibles which intelligence officers exploit to recruit spies seem just as likely to sow the seeds of distrust and doubt. As such, at the heart of spying lies the trusting bonds between those who spy and the operatives who enable them. Those bonds, as with all relationships, are best developed face-to-face, but personal meetings are 'almost always the most precarious and dangerous part' of any operation. In the past, the perils of street surveillance, meaning the physical observation of foreign intelligence officers, led to new innovations in 'tradecraft', the methods used to recruit and handle spies. But as the espionage world enters into a changing security landscape, one defined by a new age of street surveillance threats, innovation is rising up the agenda".[7]

During the past 20 years, more than 1,500 Soviet diplomats were expelled from diplomatic and other government representations around the world. Expert and writer, Kevin P. Riehle in his research paper (Soviet and Russian Diplomatic Expulsions: How Many and Why? 06 Dec 2023) noted and explained expulsion of Russian diplomats by 34 states: "In reaction to Soviet intelligence officer defectors and intelligence obtained from penetrations of Soviet intelligence services, and, most frequently, in retaliation for espionage. Recent expulsions are modern adaptations of a method that was common during the Cold War with commonalities of purpose, but some variations, especially in scale and level of international cooperation. Since February 2022, 34 countries, mostly in Europe, expelled over 700 officials from Russian diplomatic establishments. That follows a wave of expulsions in the aftermath of Russia's attempt to assassinate Sergey Skripal in 2018, and the closure of Russian diplomatic establishments in the United States after Russia's manipulation of 2016 elections. These are modern adaptations of a method that was common during the Cold War but had become more sporadic in the post–Cold War era".[8]

These assessments underlined multifaceted and evolving nature of the threats faced by the UK, spanning state actors engaging in espionage and coercion, as well as non-state threats including terrorism and cyber-attacks. The emphasis on the need for vigilance and preparedness reflects the complex security landscape in which the UK operates. The British National Security Act of 2024 is a significant reform of espionage law and aims to counter modern threats, including those posed by countries like China, but some experts view it as a frustrated move of intelligence and political establishment. It introduces new offences, modernizes powers, and enhances the ability to tackle espionage, foreign interference, and sabotage. The Act makes it an offence to be an undeclared foreign spy materially assisting the activities of a foreign intelligence service in the UK. It provides law enforcement agencies with tools to deter, detect, disrupt, and prosecute threats from actors representing foreign states. The Act updates espionage offences, including the theft of trade secrets, and covers foreign interference in the UK's political system and sabotage attempts.

It replaces outdated espionage legislation and gives operational partners new tools to prevent illegitimate influence on public figures and protect sensitive sites and information. This realization highlights the need for a comprehensive approach that encompasses various aspects of national security, including cybersecurity, commercial data protection, and infrastructure safety. In yesteryears, countless acts were passed and numerous laws were promulgated in Britain, but successive governments shamelessly failed to control extremists, terrorists and foreign espionage networks. The country's intelligence agencies have also failed to demonstrate professionally. Harassing critics, intimidating political opponents and targeting writers and journalists now become a culture of intelligence agencies. National security challenges and threats are diverse and persistent. The form they take is varied and includes espionage, foreign interference in the British political system, sabotage, disinformation, cyber operations, and even assassinations and poisonings. These actions often take place in the shadows, but the harm is very real. These words of the British government are clearly indicative of the frustration of the British policing and intelligence infrastructure, which failed to respond to these security threats traditionally. Foreign espionage is now a bigger challenge. An offence of assisting a foreign intelligence service reduces the ability of such agencies to carry out a range of hostile activities, extending beyond traditional espionage activity.

According to the new national security laws; "The principal aim of the foreign interference offences is to create a more challenging operating environment for, and to deter and disrupt the activities of, foreign states who seek to undermine the UK interests, institutions, political system, and rights. But my two books have deeply highlighted all these national security threats and foreign espionage in the country". The British leadership and intelligence agencies now realized that my information, analysis and assessment of national security threats were crystal clear and authenticated facts. An official of British intelligence infrastructure and a member of counter-extremism and foreign espionage centres in 2023 told me that my assessment and analysis of foreign espionage and exponentially growing national security threat helped them in the decision-making process. And told me that I was better competent and well-aware compared to their security management.

The National Security Act-2023 made a number of changes to the TACT 2000 to either strengthen existing or introduce new safeguards, or implement recommendations made by the Independent Reviewer of Terrorism Legislation, but my perception is that these changes and measures need coordination and concordance among the No-10, MI5 and policing agencies, otherwise it will remain on paper. The National Security Act-2023 created by the Prime Minister and the Intelligence and Security Committee to consider if any amendments to the coordination between the PM and the Intelligence Committee, as outlined in section-2 of the Justice and Security Act 2013, are required as a result of the changes arising out of the National Security Act. With this new legislation, the UK is now a harder target for those states who seek to conduct hostile acts against the UK, which include espionage, foreign interference, sabotage, and acts that endanger life, such as assassination. This is the biggest overhaul of security legislation for a generation. The Security Act is providing the security services with greater powers to tackle threats from spies and state-backed sabotage and reform existing espionage laws, like the Official Secrets Act, to better tackle threats faced by hostile states like Russia and China. Overhaul of espionage laws comes into force: The National Security Act became law in July after it was passed by Parliament and got Royal Assent. Express and Star.com on December 20, 2023, noted that as in 2023 the MI5 yelled and told MPs that Ms Lee, a prominent London-based solicitor, was engaged in "political interference activities" on behalf of China's ruling communist regime. Some media outlets in their comments refused to accept this perception, but some published stories of their choice. Home Secretary James Cleverly said the laws will "prove critical" in helping police and intelligence agencies make it even more difficult for foreign powers to pose a threat to the UK.[9]

Notwithstanding all these security measures of the UK government in 2024, China's State Council Information Office released a white paper titled "China's Legal Framework and Measures for Counter-terrorism." This is China's first comprehensive white paper on the subject. In the face of terrorism, the common enemy of human society, the scientific and effective construction of China's counter-terrorism legal system is fully reflected and demonstrated in this 13,000-word document, providing valuable reference for the world's fight against terrorism. Global Times noted. "Those who have criticized China's counter-terrorism actions should read it carefully, as it will surely lead to a different understanding as long as one does not have a preconceived stance". Global Times editorial noted. In April last 2023, French President Emmanuel Macron tweeted about his trip to China on social media, saying that "there is so much for us to do together." What does he mean by saying "so much for us to do?" Which fields are promising in our future cooperation? The Global Times (24 January 2024) in its editorial page noted President Macron's recent announcement that France will not join the US-UK joint strikes on Houthi sites in Yemen.[10]

'Chinese spies are targeting British officials in sensitive positions in politics, defence and business as part of an increasingly sophisticated spying operation to gain access to secrets, the British government warned. The government, responding to a parliamentary report in July that found the government's approach to the threat posed by China was inadequate, highlighted the "prolific" scale of Chinese espionage. (Andrew Macaskill and Kylie Maclellan-Reuter, September 14, 2023).[11]The U.K. government also agreed to establish a National Security Procurement Unit to oversee future procurement decisions through a national security lens. China is engaged in espionage overseas, directed through diverse methods via the

Ministry of State Security (MSS), the Ministry of Public Security (MPS), the United Front Work Department (UFWD), and the People's Liberation Army (PLA) via its Intelligence Bureau of the Joint Staff Department, and numerous front organizations and state-owned enterprises. On 08 January 2024, Al Jazeera reported the Chinese government's remarks about the UK intelligence war against China. The Chinese spy agency announced the detection of the espionage on its WeChat social media account.[12] The state security body did not disclose the nationality or gender of the suspect. Al Jazeera noted.[13]MI5 boss said Chinese espionage in UK on 'epic' scale with 20,000 people approached by spies. On 18 October 2023 the Independent reported Chinese spies' online visits to make contact with over 20,000 people in the United Kingdom. "We have seen a sustained campaign on a pretty epic scale," Ken McCallum told the BBC during an unprecedented public appearance alongside his counterparts from the Five Eyes intelligence-sharing alliance. The British intelligence chief spoke at the event in California, hosted by the FBI, alongside fellow spy chiefs from the US, Canada, Australia and New Zealand. Independent newspaper noted.[15]

BBC Security Correspondent, Gordon Corera in his detailed report (Has the UK woken up to the China spy challenge? 11 September 2023) assessed relationship between the UK and Chinese leadership: "The nature of China's engagement, influence and interference activity in the UK is difficult to detect, but even more concerning is the fact that the government may not previously have been looking for it," the ISC said. The security services have also long complained that they did not have the tools to confront the new reality of what foreign intelligence services get up to. In particular, they argued the Official Secrets Act was not fit for purpose. Under the UK's laws, even being an undercover intelligence officer for China or Russia was not in itself illegal".[16]The Chinese interference activities described above are not solitary cases. They are part of a broader strategy of the United Front work, a system that gathers intelligence about and works to influence private citizens overseas. Under the Chinese counterespionage law, Chinese citizens are obliged to cooperate with the Chinese security apparatus. In December 2022, Richard Moore, head of MI6, warned the rise of China was the "single greatest priority" for his officers. He warned Beijing was increasing its espionage activities and focusing on politicians and government workers. (British Intelligence Shines Light on Chinese Spy 'Hiding in Plain Sight-VoA, January 14, 2022, Jamie Dettmer).[17]

Chapter 6

The UK Security Challenges, Democratic Transition and Security Sector Reform in Eastern Europe

The United Kingdom is facing the threat of terrorism, extremism and foreign espionage networks operating in towns and cities, but the country's intelligence and law enforcement infrastructure lives back in 20th century. Lack of reform, public confidence and modernization, and concordance and lack of manpower and professional approach have caused various political and ethnic diseases. The MI5 and MI6, GCHQ, Home Office and all policing agencies are living under the umbrella of racism and discrimination and established that all educated Asian, African and Central Asian writers, academics and researchers are their slaves. But the situation changed now and educated professionals no longer want to live in Britain for some reasons. According to their culture of spying, while every educated refugee and asylum seeker retrieves British Passport, he/she is bound to work for intelligence agencies. But not all educated people are bound to do so, some highly educated and professional men prefer to leave the country for Europe and the United States. Notwithstanding this untraditional pressure to bring educated people close to their business, people of conscience are not willing to be involved in their espionage business. The Home Office is the most racist institution that mentally tortures applicants of British Passport. There is no law in the country to force passports applicants to wait for six months.

The annual report of the Intelligence and security committee (2023) has noted threats coming from different sources, including Northern Ireland related terrorism and right-wing terrorism, but there is no countering mechanism to protect the lives of vulnerable British citizens. The Intelligence and Security Committee of Parliament annual report for 2022–2023 noted that foreign intelligence agencies in and outside the country making things worse, while the British intelligence agencies have failed to counter foreign espionage: "The threat to the UK from hostile activity by states also includes the efforts of foreign states to exert covert and malign influence on UK policy, democracy and public opinion through attempts to influence social media, journalism and political figures. There is a growing threat of state-sponsored assassination, attacks and abductions of those perceived as dissidents. Since the start of 2022, there have been at least 15 credible threats to kill or kidnap British or UK-based individuals by the Iranian regime. In October 2022, a pro-democracy protester appeared to be the subject of violence outside the Chinese consulate in Manchester. The threat to dissidents in the UK from the Russian state, which we saw manifest in the attempted assassination of Sergey Skripal in 2018, has not abated".[1]

Yes, we know that Chinese intelligence has been targeting its critics and dissidents, while in Britain political and social critics are also punished by a cruel means. The basic issues for countries undergoing a democratic transition in Eastern Europe is fighting the old communist security and intelligence infrastructure and bringing secret agencies and the police. Central and Eastern Europe lack of democratic culture has caused many challenges. Transformation in Eastern Europe has been complex and it will take time to completely reform and reorganize all state institutions. The threat to Eastern European states from overseas continues to diversify. Presence of Al-Qaeda, Taliban, Islamic State, and African and South Asian extremist organizations in these states are making things worse. Iran and China remain aggressive cyber actors with a range of espionage, and destructive cyber capabilities. Cyber actors associated with these States have also been implicated in attacks against victims in many countries. Research scholar and intelligence expert, Mazzola Stephanie in her PhD thesis (Intelligence services in Post Conflict State Building a comprehensive study of Iraq and Afghanistan King's College London- July 2021) has discussed instability factors in Afghanistan and Eastern European states, and also noted reshaping of intelligence services in Europe which is a consolidated process a democratic process:

"In Eastern Europe, the reshaping of the intelligence services has been part of the consolidation process towards democracy. In Bulgaria, Czechoslovakia, Hungary and Poland, all chose to keep the original structure of their intelligence services (including the personnel serving under the communist regime)....Moreover, the ideal reform scenario presumes the existence of stable democratic institutions and a secure environment free of perceived immediate threats which may affect the process. In most post authoritarian and totalitarian states, like the post-communist States in Eastern Europe, these conditions did not prevail. These countries had to face, simultaneously, a political, an economic, a social and a security transformation, commonly resulting into unstable institutions. The fact that many of these states, unlike Western democracies, also lacked a widespread popular identification with the newly established institutions, caused internal fragility and amplified the external sources of insecurity, thus questioning fundamental Rule of Law traits. The fact that norms were still not internally accepted and "absorbed", contributed to the difficulties. Many post-communist countries had problems during their transition because they became procedural democracies which fitted into societies that suffered from a lack of trust in all state institutions".[2]

Different bodies oversee the work of European intelligence operations, including judiciary, parliamentary committees and data protection authorities. Many intelligence services were divided into small units in Eastern European states to effectively counter terrorism and radicalization. However, this is the only aspect that the western model and the post-communist one have in common. According to FRA report, (Surveillance by Intelligence Services: Fundamental Rights Safeguards and Remedies in the EU Volume II: field perspectives and legal update-European Union Agency for Fundamental Rights, 2017), "While all EU Member States have at least one independent body in their oversight framework, some lack such decision-making powers". The lack of expertise in dealing with secrecy and with technical matters is also an issue, both with judicial and non-judicial actors. In the judicial context, Member States have found several ways to address this issue, including by developing alternative adversarial procedures to allow for the use of classified information; creating cooperation mechanisms, including with intelligence services, to tackle the lack of expertise, and establishing quasi-judicial bodies".[3]

The three terrorist attacks of 2017 caused the public's lack of confidence in law enforcement agencies and MI5 for a variety of reasons, including agencies' failure to disrupt terrorist plots, deteriorating law and order situation, and media criticism of the government's lack of a strategic approach to security threats. Secret agencies are not sharing all information with the state institutions. Privacy International in its report noted: "In the UK, we have experienced different types of watchdogs, spy networks and private intelligence and intelligence agencies collecting information and data by illegal means. Privacy and human rights organizations filed numerous cases against the state surveillance swords and courts, and trying to convince stakeholders that this way of privacy interference can alienate citizens from the state, but state, notwithstanding domestic pressure, resorted to blanket surveillance, in which every kind to privacy is being plundered". According to Byline Times recent analysis, "we believe border regimes and immigration systems have their roots in racism and Islamophobia. Now, as Prevent could be forcibly imposed into immigration and asylum processes, migration advocacy organisations and Muslim organisations must wake up to Islamophobia's grip on UK border regimes. Prevent is used as a form of surveillance.

At present, Byline noted the Prevent duty requires public-facing authorities such as education, health, local authorities, police and criminal justice agencies to 'prevent' people from being "drawn into terrorism." It is a fundamentally flawed and discriminatory mechanism that leads to thousands of people (mainly Muslims) being treated with suspicion on the basis they are assumed to be more likely to commit a 'crime' such as terrorism". Byline Times noted. In December 2023, the Home Office published an Independent Review of Prevents report and the Government's response by William Shawcross (Independent Reviewer of Prevent) in which he recommended the Government explore extending Prevent into the immigration and asylum system. The expansion of the Prevent Duty into the UK immigration system would further embed racism and Islamophobia in borders. (The UK's Immigration System is Islamophobic and Racist. Expanding Prevent into it will Re-traumatised Refugees'. Julia Tinsley-Kent. 26 January 2024).[4] The UK's immigration strategy disproportionately targets minority population by deprivation of citizenship powers. "Deprivation of citizenship powers has been used to strip British citizens of citizenship on the grounds of national security, after being accused of suspected terrorist activities. Evidence shows subjects of citizenship deprivation on national security grounds have been almost exclusively Muslim and from a Middle Eastern, South or West Asian or North African background". Julia Tinsley-Kent of Byline Times noted".[5]

However, the Byline Times analysis (Tens of billions in Government and Council pandemic spending unaccounted for as local authority auditing scandal worsens. David Hencke. 26 January 2024) noted that "some £55 billion spent by the Government and local councils during the pandemic year remains unaudited and unaccounted for two years later, a new report by MPs has revealed. The House of Commons' Public Accounts Committee lambasts the Treasury for being "too passive" in chasing up the cash which is resulting in inaccurate figures being published by Whitehall and making it difficult for ministers to plan future spending. The Treasury's report on the latest Whole of Government Accounts for 2020-21–an annual report comprehensively listing all public expenditure for each financial year– was published 27 months late and is incomplete, inaccurate and too long delayed, according to the committee. It also raises the question of whether the Government will ever be able to account for the £372 billion spent by ministers on the pandemic because the Treasury plans to end monitoring of Coronavirus spending next year". David Hencke Noted.

Where these billions of pounds gone and how and where this money was spent, and which group, sector and agency was financed? Nothing known and there is no record of more than $500 billion Dollars in government papers. Analyst and writer, Emma DeSouza in her article (How Long can the UK Government ignore the collapse of Governance in Northern Ireland? Rather than adapting to a new political landscape, leaders are laying roadblocks in place. Byline Times, 19 January 2024) revealed that Northern Ireland has been without a functioning government, and all political and financial decisions were taken since the past two years: "Northern Ireland has been without a functioning government for 735 days. The previous collapse in 2017 went on for 1,097 days. Artificial deadlines have come and gone, the bluff of fresh elections has been called, and rudderless leadership steers Northern Ireland further out to sea. This isn't just a crisis of power-sharing–this is the final gasp. Speaking in the chamber, First Minister designate Michelle O'Neill MLA said the political institutions of the Good Friday Agreement are in "free-fall". "There was a dangerous attempt under way to discard the democratic outcome of the Assembly election, and this threatened our democratic governance, public administration, reconciliation, and the fabric of this society," she told the Assembly. Journalist Emma DeSouza noted.[7]

The Power sharing issue was later on settled in February 2024 in Northern Ireland. The UK has undertaken a small package of intelligence reforms over the years to challenging security threats and technological advancements, but now everything is not going in the right direction as questions raised by different circles about the weak performance of MI5. Law such as the Investigatory Powers Act 2016 have updated the legal framework for surveillance and data collection, but there are numerous complaints that the Investigatory Power Act-2016 doesn't respond to public complaints against the attitude of intelligence agencies and their illegal harassment. This author registered several complaints to the office of Investigatory Power Commissioner in 2023, but received no response. These laws aim to give intelligence agencies the powers they need while incorporating safeguards for privacy and civil liberties. Reforms have sought to strengthen oversight of intelligence agencies, while in reality, no oversight existed. This includes the work of bodies like the Investigatory Powers Commissioner's Office (IPCO) and the Intelligence and Security Committee of Parliament, ensuring that intelligence work is subject to rigorous independent oversight. The MI5 and other British intelligence agencies remained silent about the public complaints against their illegal harassment.

Experts, Jeanine de Roy van Zuijdewijn and Edwin Bakker in their research paper (Twenty years of countering jihadism in Western Europe: from the shock of 9/11 to 'jihadism fatigue', Journal of Policing, Intelligence and Counter Terrorism-26 Apr 2023) have highlighted legal developments in Belgium, Denmark, France, Germany, UK and the Netherlands that can be applied without the interference of a judicial entity: "Belgium, Denmark, France, Germany and the Netherlands focused on new and more extensive administrative measures, which could be applied without the interference of a judicial entity. For instance, in the Netherlands, the law changed in 2017, enabling the authorities to revoke citizenship if a person joined a terrorist organisation. The UK has had such a measure in place since the 1980s and could also apply this to citizens without dual nationality after 2014. Belgium started to regard travelling abroad for terrorist purposes as a criminal offence in 2015. Eventually, across Western Europe, an extensive set of tools and measures was used, ranging from the prevention of radicalisation and travelling abroad to dealing with online propaganda and supporting the reintegration of convicted terrorists returning from prison. Abroad, military instruments again became important counterterrorism tools. Western European countries joined the Global Coalition against Daesh that was formed in September 2014 after IS had proclaimed the caliphate. Many of them executed air strikes against IS targets. Some countries, most notably the UK and France, also executed targeted killings against their own foreign fighters in Syria and Iraq".[8]

Since 2018, British intelligence agencies have never made concerted efforts to improve diversity within their ranks. The primary goal of these initiatives was to ensure that the intelligence community reflects the rich diversity of the society it serves, enhancing its operational effectiveness by bringing in a wide range of perspectives and skills, but unfortunately they are male dominated agencies. The effectiveness of the British counter-extremism strategy, particularly the "Prevent" program, has been a topic of debate and analysis in intellectual forms and newspapers. Some communities, especially Muslims, have felt that Prevent has unfairly targeted them, leading to feelings of alienation and mistrust. This could potentially undermine the very goal of preventing radicalization. The strategy's broad and sometimes vague definitions of extremism and radicalization have been criticized for potentially encompassing a wide range of legal, non-violent opinions and beliefs. There has been a lack of transparent and comprehensive evaluation of the program's effectiveness. It's important to note that these points represent a combination of criticisms and challenges identified by various groups, including academics, community leaders, and human rights organizations.

In 1999, the National Criminal Intelligence Service established National Intelligence Model (NIM) which is based upon the "collective wisdom and best practice", but counter-extremism and counter-intelligence capabilities of the British state have broken to control these illegal activities. The failure in intelligence cooperation between the UK and the EU can be attributed to a combination of political, legal, and operational factors. The UK's decision to leave the EU created significant uncertainties and disruptions in intelligence cooperation with European states. However, the EU has stringent data protection laws (GDPR), and there have been concerns about the UK's adherence to these standards. Intelligence sharing is built on trust, while the EU doesn't trust the UK intelligence infrastructure. Differences in technology and operational methodologies can also hinder seamless intelligence cooperation. The UK was adamant that its intelligence information collection technology was strong, but the EU was also using the strongest intelligence technology. The UK's and EU's relationships with third countries also play a role. The involvement of US intelligence and political leadership in the EU and UK was another obstacle to their cooperation. In comparison, these factors contributed to challenges in intelligence cooperation.

If there's a perception that information sharing is not mutual or beneficial, it can lead to reluctance in sharing sensitive data. The UK conservatively said it had concerns about the control and dissemination of its intelligence within the EU's broader network. If there are doubts about operational security or the handling of classified information, the UK might limit what it shares. The legacy of former communist intelligence infrastructure in Eastern Europe has indeed been an obstacle in intelligence cooperation, particularly in the post-Cold War era. Former communist regimes of Eastern Europe were replaced by democratically elected governments. In Poland, Hungary, East Germany and Czechoslovakia, newly formed centre-right parties took power for the first time since the end of World War II. The Eastern Bloc was the coalition of communist states of Central and Eastern Europe. They were also wary of the reliability and compatibility of the intelligence apparatus in former communist states. Victoria E. Bonnell, Centre for Slavic and East European Studies. University of California at Berkeley).[9]The new successor states and those largely satisfied with the settlements after World War-I (Poland, Czechoslovakia, Yugoslavia, Romania, and Greece), as a rule, allied themselves with France, the most powerful state in Europe, and entered into local alliances with one another, directed against the irredentism and revisionism of Austria, Hungary, and Bulgaria.

The British intelligence services, specifically the Secret Intelligence Service (SIS), MI5, and GCHQ, have been in crisis to increase their openness and public engagement. This crisis of greater transparency is deep-generating controversies and challenges. Traditionally, these agencies maintained a low profile, but recent initiatives have seen agency heads and representatives actively participating in public discussions and media engagements, but they still have no place in society as they have failed to maintain stability and diversity in their ranks. For instance, SIS Chief Richard Moore is occasionally facing but giving political speeches and interviews to persuade communities and government about the work of his agency, but newspapers' record shows his agency's credibility is quite different. In terms of public confidence, there has been a notable decline in the UK, particularly in the context of intelligence and the police. This decline is attributed to several factors, including high-profile cases of spy agencies misconduct, institutional involvement, and failures in handling certain types of security threats. The public's trust has also been impacted by perceptions of institutional racism. These incidents have revealed deep-rooted problems within the intelligence culture, leading to a decrease in public confidence.

While intelligence agencies have never been effective in certain areas, such as counter-terrorism and handling new threats like cryptocurrency-related crimes, and foreign espionage, the overall decline in public trust reflects a need for more profound systemic changes and improvements in day-to-day interactions with the public. At the same time, the MI5 is facing challenges in maintaining public confidence due to various internal and systemic issues, underscoring the need for substantial reforms. The UK intelligence agencies were falsely proud of their intelligence gathering and process and didn't want to share that information with the EU member states. In fact the UK intelligence agencies mostly collect low quality intelligence information through illiterate people. The Chinese Intelligence Services may use bulk data to provide additional intelligence to support their targeting efforts against UK politicians. (Intelligence and Security Committee of Parliament China-2023). There's often a fear of information leakage or manipulation. In the post-communist transitions in central and Eastern Europe, competing priorities also distracted attention from intelligence reform as political, economic, and other security institutions simultaneously underwent changes.[10]

The security challenges faced by Britain, particularly in the context of Northern Ireland, are indeed multifaceted and complex. The absence of a functional government in Northern Ireland since 2021 exacerbates these challenges. The lack of a formal government in Northern Ireland leads to political instability. The power-sharing arrangement, as set out in the Good Friday Agreement (1998), requires cooperation between unionist and nationalist parties. The issue of foreign espionage once more appeared with a different face in newspapers when the British domestic intelligence agency abruptly warned that Chinese intelligence agents were making things worse. Intelligence agencies across Europe and the UK maintain a very poor record of professional approach when they come to countering foreign espionage networks and activities of foreign embassies. The end of the cold war changed the whole intelligence infrastructure, operational mechanism, priorities and intelligence surveillance techniques in Europe. Eastern Europe was liberated by Afghans after the dismemberment of the Union of Soviets in 1990s, Germany united and Central Asia retrieved independence. A decade later, the US war on terrorism and globalization once more divided the world in three blocks. Russia and China challenged the US hegemony in Asia and Africa.

There was another side to the Cold War as Reg Whitake has explained a decade's long campaign in which assaults were made behind enemy lines, casualties sustained, battles won and lost. Intelligence information cooperation between the EU member states is not a new prodigy; it has been appearing in different shapes through intelligence and security sector reforms since 2001. After the Paris, London and Madrid terrorist attacks, the EU member states introduced wide ranging intelligence reforms to make their intelligence gathering process update and reorganize their intelligence organizations. At the same time, cooperation with intelligence and security actors from outside the European Union also changed. Many former communist countries had to undergo significant institutional and legal reforms to align their intelligence services with democratic norms and standards of accountability. Given recurrent intelligence and "political policing" problems in the transition states, it was inevitable that reform in those domains would eventually become a western priority, particularly after NATO opened its doors to new members in 1993. (Intelligence Reform in Europe's Emerging Democracies. Larry L. Watts- Studies in Intelligence, New Democracies, vol. 48, No.1).

The European Union's response to the protests in Paris in 2023, particularly the ones related to pension reform and government actions, is not widely reported in the sources I accessed. The protests in Paris, which escalated with clashes between police and protesters, were mainly in response to President Macron's decision to raise the retirement age and bypass parliament. This decision led to widespread discontent and demonstrations. The protests, drawing parallels with the Yellow Vest movement of 2018, highlighted issues like economic inequality and dissatisfaction with government policies. It's important to note that the EU typically does not intervene in the internal matters of member states unless they pertain to violations of EU laws or fundamental rights. The absence of a vocal EU stance on the Paris protests could be attributed to this policy of non-interference in domestic affairs of member states, especially when it comes to internal political issues and national reforms. The European Union's typically cautious response to internal matters of member states, like the 2023 Paris protests, can be attributed to its policy framework and the nature of its role. His approach is consistent with the EU's foundational principles of respecting national autonomy and avoiding overreach into member state-specific issues.

Romania's security sector reform, particularly since the 1990s, has been a significant process, marked by efforts to modernize and align with Western standards, especially in the context of joining NATO in 2004 and the European Union in 2007. The reform aimed to bring the security sector under democratic control and civilian oversight, a stark contrast to the Communist-era practices. Efforts were made to professionalize the armed forces and other security institutions, including updating equipment, training, and procedures. Romanian intelligence services underwent significant restructuring to operate within a democratic framework and to provide transparent and accountable security operations. The success of these reforms can be gauged by Romania's effective integration into NATO and the EU, increased professionalism and capabilities of its security forces, and enhanced regional stability. These reforms were aimed at making the Belgian intelligence and security apparatus more proactive, efficient, and coordinated in the face of evolving terrorist threats. The effectiveness of these measures continues to be a subject of ongoing assessment and refinement.

European intelligence cooperation is in crisis as majority of member states do not share their national secrets. The EU maintains numerous institutions, networks, and databases for collaboration and intelligence sharing with partner services in Europe and beyond, but they are reluctant to share real intelligence information. This book highlights intelligence and security sector reforms within the European Union, radicalization, espionage and the Lone-Wolves attacks. The Romanian revolution that saw the seeds of self-government in December 1989 was the main starting point of the country's independence from the former Soviet Union. Communist leader Nicolai Ceausescu was executed and the National Salvation Front (FSN) took power to lead the nation towards the establishment of a new and modern democratic state. The new government managed economic reforms but also designed national security measures to end dictatorship and introduce democratic culture of governance. Political and security sector reforms were an irksome state due to the strong networks of former communist administration, internal opposition and bureaucratic stakeholders. There was a political and bureaucratic stakeholder's culture that deeply influenced foreign and domestic policies of the state. These stakeholders did not allow democratization and modernization of state institutions.

At national level, Romania has the National Intelligence Agency (ANI), the High National Security College (HNSC), as well as specialized training units within other intelligence agencies, whose programs rely heavily on NATO/Western curricula and teaching expertise and reflect the new security features. The intelligence and security sector reforms received mixed messages from the international community. The persisting complications in Romanian intelligence are corruption, stakeholders, and the operational mood of former Securitate agents. Democratization of secret services and the policing forces in Romania has been a complicated issue since the dissolution of the Soviet Union when the old communist intelligence infrastructure refused to allow democratic reforms. The agency was also accused in the press of illegally investigating journalists, media agencies, and politicians. Often, the political struggle between parties or within parties to obtain the leadership of ministries that control the spy agencies is acute.

All secret agencies are weapons of the state against enemies and domestic terror and extremist organization that want to destabilize the state. After the collapse of Soviet Union in 1990s, Eastern European states were left in crisis including border management and democratic culture, and they were confused what kind of government would be suitable to run their crumbling states. They were still surrounded by former Soviet security infrastructure and bureaucratic system. Security Sector Reforms and political transition in Romania and Poland was of great importance. Romania's problem with corruption became transparent while the European Commission accepted its membership, but created natural selection, and oversight of Security Sector Reforms. On 18 January 2017, the Intellnews reported the resignation of the deputy head of Romanian intelligence, Florian Coldea when the country government decided to bring all security organs and the policing agencies under democratic control. Dr Florian Coldea had held the position of the Deputy Director of the Romanian Intelligence Service for twelve years. He ran all operations for Romania's most significant domestic intelligence agency. Mr. Florian was forced to resign on 17 January 2017, while the head of anti-corruption came under pressure to explain his position about the revelations of businessman Sebastian Ghita who claimed that the security service was involved in shaping the DNA in partnership with the State Intelligence Agency (SRI).

The EU gradually increased its strength to professionalize domestic security, and intelligence infrastructure, reform law enforcement agencies and digitalize border security. The EU member states have also improved intelligence information sharing on law enforcement level to effectively address the issues of radicalization, extremism, terrorism and illegal immigration. Some Western European states helped Eastern European states in bringing intelligence infrastructure under democratic control. Expert of intelligence and Former Rand consultant and adviser on military reform to the Romanian Defence Ministry, and advisor of the Romanian government on intelligence matters, Larry L. Watts in his research paper (Conflicting Paradigms, Dissimilar Contexts: Intelligence Reform in Europe's Emerging Democracies. Larry L. Watts-Studies in Intelligence, New Democracies, Vol. 48, No. 1) highlighted some aspects of intelligence reforms in Eastern European states and their democratic transition. He also noted reform packages in Czechoslovakia, Hungary, Poland and Romania:

"Czechoslovakia's immediate post-communist foreign-intelligence branch, for example, continued to function "under KGB tutelage and tasking" until the collapse of the Soviet Union. And after Czechoslovakia divided, the

Slovak intelligence service sent its officers to Moscow and welcomed Russian instructors to run programs in Slovakia until at least July 1996. Analysts have continued to air concerns about "Russian penetration and vested interests" in Bulgarian intelligence because of Sofia's traditionally close relationship to Moscow. Hungary, Poland, and, initially, Czechoslovakia-"grandfathered in" substantial numbers of personnel from the former regimes as part of the negotiation process, which caused considerable apprehension in NATO both before and after their accession. Thus, establishing sovereign national control over the domestic security apparatus and the loyalty of its personnel became major objectives of post-communist reform efforts. Romania's situation was somewhat the reverse of its regional confreres, with residual Russian influence stronger among intellectual and dissident groups than within the security services, a circumstance that affected post-communist intelligence missions, personnel, and institutional culture. States that either engaged in more organized transformations (Czechoslovakia, Hungary, Poland) or built their intelligence services from scratch (the Baltic States) received aid sooner than the states of south eastern Europe where greater transformation problems existed across the board."[11]

In some cases, there might have been resistance within these countries to fully reform the intelligence services, either due to political reasons or due to the vested interests of those within the agencies. But, there was a strong resistance from the old security infrastructure and didn't allow the reform campaign to proceed. Despite these obstacles, significant progress was made in introducing security sector reforms. Several former communist states in Eastern Europe successfully integrated into Western defence and intelligence structures. Intelligence and security reform in countries like Poland and Romania had faced different challenges, but succeeded in many ways and it encountered significant hurdles. Both the states inherited intelligence structures from their communist past. Intelligence and security agencies in these two states have sometimes been subject to political interference, intransigence of stakeholders and private partners. Effective reform requires expertise and resources. Developing a professional intelligence cadre, free from past allegiances and equipped with modern skills, is a resource-intensive process. Both Poland and Romania were strategically important countries, and their intelligence reforms were often subject to external influence and pressure. They took significant steps to reform their intelligence and security sector.[12]

Experts and writers, Aidan Wills, Mathias. Hans Born, Martin Scheinin, Micha Wiebusch and Ashley Thornton in their research paper

(Parliamentary Oversight of Security and Intelligence Agencies in the European Union- European Parliament, Brussels, 2011) have argued that due to the illegal practices of intelligence agencies and their involvement in illegal activities after the cold war, democratic intelligence surveillance and oversight were the only tools to monitor their activities and operational mechanism: "Many states created parliamentary and other specialised bodies to oversee intelligence agencies in light of revelations about their involvement in illegal and/or improper activities, e.g., Canada, the Czech Republic, Norway, Poland, South Africa, and the US. Notably, during or immediately after the Cold War, it became clear that in many Western states, governments had used intelligence agencies to disrupt persons involved in legitimate expressions of the rights to freedom of association, assembly and expression. Elsewhere, intelligence agencies were found to have exceeded their legal mandates and powers in tackling domestic terrorism. Against this backdrop, effective oversight (and legal regulation) of intelligence agencies came to be seen as essential for ensuring that they contribute to the security of the populations they serve without undermining democratic processes and human rights. That is, to 'secure democracy against internal and external enemies without destroying democracy in the process'. Needless to say, the development of oversight of the EU's AFSJ bodies is taking place in a vastly different climate from the types of conditions that led to the establishment of oversight bodies on the national level".[13]

Expert and analyst, Larry L. Watts in his research paper (Conflicting Paradigms, Dissimilar Contexts: Intelligence Reform in Europe's Emerging Democracies. Studies in Intelligence, New Democracies, Vol. 48, No.1), has noted that intelligence agencies need to cooperate instead of competition to open the road to reform in Europe. He also noted that there were competition and rivalries between the old and new democratic systems. "The imperative for intelligence services to cooperate rather than compete with each other against the variety and multiplicity of post–Cold War threats also proved a major boon to intelligence reform in central and Eastern Europe. Cooperation has required the creation of mechanisms for judging the effectiveness and control of services in emerging democracies and has provided experience to officers of those services regarding the organization and procedures of more effective and better-controlled Western services. It has even created an informal set of common standards. The demands of procedural interoperability in the new security environment have already contributed to the success of these services in adapting to the new paradigm".[14]

The 9/11 attacks in the United States, the London, Paris and Germany attacks generated so many external and domestic security challenges. Nuclear terrorism became topic of discussion on intellectual forms and in newspaper pages. The risk of a complete nuclear device falling into the hands of terrorists caused consternation in the region. There are three basic groups of biological agents that could likely be used as weapons: bacteria, viruses and toxins. Biological agents can be spread by spraying them into the air, person-to-person contact, infecting animals that carry the disease to humans and by contaminating food and water. The gravest danger arises from the access of extremist and terror groups to the state-owned nuclear, biological and chemical weapons. Some EU member state have no idea of fighting this war. The growing use of chlorine bombs became a matter of concern when a former commander of the Joint Chemical, Biological, Radiological and Nuclear Regiment of UK told The Times that the UK needed to take strong security measures and control the availability of chemical weapons such as chlorine bombs to the terrorists. Improvised explosive devices and chemical and biological weapons are easily available in some Asian and African markets and can be transported to the UK and France through human traffickers.

For more than two decades, the threat of nuclear and biological terrorism has been at the forefront of international security agenda. Nuclear experts have often warned that terrorists and extremist organisations operating in South Asia and Europe must be prevented from gaining access to weapons of mass destruction and from perpetrating atrocious acts of nuclear terrorism. The greatest threat to the national security of Europe stems from nuclear smuggling and terror groups operating in different states. Increasingly sophisticated chemical and biological weapons are accessible to organisations like ISIS, Mujahedeen-e-Hind (MH), the EU extremist groups, and Central Asia terrorist organizations based in Afghanistan and Pakistan. There are more than 31 terrorist groups operating in Afghanistan with the support of Pakistan and the Taliban terrorist regime. Majority of these groups want to retrieve nuclear and biological weapons. In January 2024, a delegation of Taliban nuclear weapons experts arrived in North Korea for talks on nuclear weapon. These groups can use more sophisticated conventional weapons as well as chemical and biological agents against Europe. As international media focused on the looming threat of chemical and biological terrorism in Europe and Central Asia while the Taliban providing training of sophisticated weapons to the Afghanistan based suicide brigades of different terrorist organizations. Intelligence agencies in Europe need a comprehensive internal control in order to ensure strict compliance with the legislation, Ministerial directives and the headquarter policy. This internal control is proper systems of authorisation, decision-making, and supervision of staff; monitoring and audit systems to detect noncompliance; and a disciplinary system for addressing any breaking of the rules.

The security of French nuclear facilities is a critical aspect of France's national security and environmental safety. France is one of the world's largest producers of nuclear power, with a significant portion of its electricity generated from nuclear energy. The French Nuclear Safety Authority (Autorité de Sûreté Nucléaire, ASN) is the primary regulatory body responsible for nuclear safety and radiation protection. France has implemented stringent cybersecurity protocols to protect the digital infrastructure of its nuclear plants. Former British Minister Boris Johnson and his allies intentionally debilitated Britain and destroyed the state institutions, intercepting operation of nuclear submarine and looted huge money from treasury. He allowed foreign espionage networks to operate in Britain. Every foreign agency was controlled by their stakeholders independently in Britain, foreign embassies had established their own spying networks. Staff of some embassies told this author that they were running behind their target in towns and cities. The MI5 failed to dance on right direction and was fighting against its own people by inflicting uncontrollable surveillance and spying blankets.

Chapter 7

France's National Security Challenges, the Fight against Foreign Espionage, Radicalization, and Extremist Organizations

War in Gaza and Ukraine further complicated the task of French intelligence agencies to detect, arrest and prosecute foreign intelligence operatives in the country. The French intelligence agencies have been struggling to manage a better domestic security amidst intelligence war in the continent, but hostile states have managed to establish terror and espionage networks everywhere, finance terrorism and radicalization and penetrate into state institutions. These networks are struggling to manage access to biological and nuclear weapons in the country where networks of extremism are well-established and strong and their members are working in state institutions. Border insecurity in several EU states is a strong source of domestic instability as terrorists and extremist elements easily cross borders with their weapons and firearms. Such widespread human movement across Europe caused major changes in the digital landscape. Expert, Michael Jonsson (Espionage by Europeans: treason and counterintelligence in post-Cold War Europe. Intelligence and National Security Journal. 11 Sep 2023) in his paper argued that due to the lack of comparative studies, spotlighting trends of antagonistic intelligence agencies is a complicated issue:

"The role of intelligence and security services of Central-Eastern European countries in the Global South remains the 'black box' of Cold War espionage studies. Thus far, most literature on intelligence and security activities of 'Moscow's satellites' has focused on the domestic – detailing human rights abuses and reconstructing the organisational structure of these complex security bureaucracies. This has been a mammoth task pioneered by hundreds of archivists, historians and social scientists often employed by specialised national memory institutions set up in the early 2000s to study the security and intelligence apparatus of the state socialist regimes. These detail-oriented and largely descriptive accounts have gradually enabled scholars to move beyond the domestic and discuss issues such as that of the 'agency' of state security and intelligence organisations across the Soviet Bloc. While early observers often considered state socialist regimes in Central-Eastern Europe to be Soviet proxies, new scholarship has highlighted their independent agency, as well as disagreement and rivalry within the Soviet Bloc. Nevertheless, the international legacy and impact of Central-Eastern European security and intelligence organisations has thus far not received enough attention. We continue to be largely unaware of how Prague, Bucharest or Warsaw used their intelligence services to pursue their foreign policies. The Global South is no exception".[1]

In these circumstances, global reach of some European states became emaciated, particularly, the British government and its intelligence infrastructure has been confined to some areas due to its financial crisis and shortage of funds. France has been targeted by a global intelligence alliance to destabilize the country with all aspects. Its neighbouring states are dancing within the country with evolving mechanisms and exhibit that they are friends of France and they want the country aggrandised, but in reality, they clandestinely support terror and extremist forces to create disturbances and war like situations. In 2023, they trained and adorned these sarcastic forces to hijack security and attack public and government installations. They set fire to French cities and towns and harmed its financial market, challenged authority of the state and threatened law enforcement agencies and intelligence with more violent actions. Expert and writer, Tara Varma (Unrest in France challenges Macron's ambitions, Brooking March 31, 2023) has noted one million extremists and protestors took to the streets in France on March 24, 2023. Current security crisis in France is linked to its domestic and international engagement.

Chief of the French domestic intelligence agency, Mr. Nicolas Lerner recently warned that the Islamic State (ISIS) propaganda was attracting the young generation in France and his agency closely monitored radicalized elements. In his interview with Le-Monde newspaper, (07 December, 2023, Soren Seelow) Director Nicolas Lerner elucidated challenges monitoring terror elements and professional criminals. The French are maintaining professional intelligence agencies with their National Intelligence and Counter-Terrorism Coordination (CNRLT) that serves French authorities and the intelligence community.[2]In 2017, establishing the CNRTL marked an important development in France that this organization will better identify the country's national security threats. As National Intelligence Coordinator, Pascal Mailhos hoped "that the intelligence services (DGSE,

DGSI, DRM, DRSD, DNRED, TRACFIN and DRPP, SCRT, SNRP, and SDAO) work together and provide guidance to the President of the Republic". Since its inception, the counter-terrorism governance revolving around CNRLT/CNCT at strategic level and the DGSI at operational level has been an important response to the lessons learned from the 2015 and 2016 attacks. Experts, Michael Jonsson, Deputy Research Director at FOI Swedish Defence Research Agency and analyst Jakob Gustafsson (Threat of spies is increasing in Europe: A series of high-profile cases that have recently led to arrests and convictions shows that the threat posed by spies seems to have increased in Europe over the past decade. Swedish Defence Research Agency, 16 May 2022) in their recent analysis have asserted that the threat of spies is increasing in Europe. Mr. Michael Jonsson has recently conducted a research study "Espionage by Europeans 2010–2021",in which he noted European citizens working for foreign agencies. "The recruitment of a new spy often begins cautiously, with the intelligence officer asking for innocuous information that is already available from open sources".[3]

However, Deputy Research Director at the Swedish Defence Research Agency, Michael Jonsson in his analysis (Europe's decade of the spy: American moles of the 1980s are well-known amongst intelligence scholars—and they may soon be joined by equally infamous European traitors. Politico, 05 February 2023) has also noted the arrest of two Swedish brothers convicted of spying for Russia's military intelligence: "From 2014 and 2018, espionage convictions more than tripled compared to those between 2010 and 2013, reaching almost six per year. And since Russia's war of aggression against Ukraine began, those numbers have been surging: In 2022 alone, at least seven individuals were convicted of spying for Russia, and three for China. Given that a decade ago there were only one to two convictions per year in Europe, this represents a clear step change. Interestingly, these convictions have mainly occurred in northern Europe—particularly in the Baltic States, which represents over seventy percent of convictions despite having less than two percent of Europe's population. Estonia especially has concluded that the best way to counter espionage is to prosecute, calling out the instigator in a bid to deter would-be spies".[4]

Russia has been maintaining the strongest and well-trained professional intelligence network in Europe since the Cold War, and it infiltrates can everywhere. Russia-phobia in Europe and the UK has caused anxiety and frustration, while it has become a schizophrenic disease. Russia wants to protect its interests across Europe and everywhere it understands its interests are in danger, strengthen its presence, because the west once broken the Russian empire and again wants to destabilize Russian federation/or dismember its geographical infrastructure. On 31 January 2024, Politico (As the European Parliament investigates a Latvian lawmaker suspected of being a Russian spy, her co-nationals in the chamber are warning there are others like her. Jakob Hanke and Nicolas Camot. January 31, 2024) in its report raised the question of Russian interests in European Parliament: "European Parliament opened an internal probe into Latvian MEP Tatjana Ždanoka after an independent Russian investigative newspaper, the Insider, reported she had been working as an agent for the Russian secret services for years, Ždanoka has denied those claims. She was one of just 13 MEPs who in March 2022, voted against a resolution condemning Russia's full-scale invasion of Ukraine, which caused her to be expelled from the Greens/EFA group. Zdanoka now sits as a non-attached MEP. "We are convinced that Zdanoka is not an isolated case," the three Latvian MEPs wrote, citing concerns over suspicious "public interventions, voting record[s], organised events, as well as covert activities".[5]

The cold war intelligence was an open hostility started in World War-I and intensified again in cold war military and political confrontations in Europe. Spy networks of US, UK and Russian appeared in different shapes and revolved in various moods, and now every political and military conflict is revolving around intelligence operations. Socialist ideology very soon spread across Europe. To confront Russian military power, the West formed a NATO alliance. Intelligence operatives entered at different times the other side passing important documents and military information to rival powers. The cold war intelligence was an operation with changing strategies and operational mechanisms. On 25 October, 2022, Le Monde newspaper (Russia is rebuilding its spy networks throughout Europe: Following Russia's invasion of Ukraine, French intelligence detected several agents belonging to Russia's military intelligence services in strategic parts of Europe. Jacques Follorou. October 25, 2022) reported war in Ukraine forced Russians to escape Western sanctions imposed on Moscow, the country's "partial" mobilization, or simply to travel.1 Salisbury was a unique case in the UK confronting hostile state actors in the grey zone by leveraging information advantage principles without sacrificing.[6]

Moreover, on 20 February 2023, IntelNews (Russia's spy networks in Europe see greatest post-Cold War setback, experts claim. Joseph Fitsanakis) reported Russian human intelligence operation in Europe suffered damage and this damage was caused western campaign to cripple Russian intelligence network in Europe: "The initial blow against the Kremlin's spy network was delivered last year, when a wave of mass expulsions of Russian diplomats resulted in more than 400 suspected Russian intelligence officers being ordered to leave various European capitals. According to observers, the expelled Russian diplomats were in reality intelligence officers, who were active across Europe under diplomatic cover. Since that time, European counterintelligence agencies have launched a series of "precision strikes" against what remains of Russia's human intelligence network across the continent. The recent wave of expulsions of Russian intelligence personnel was not unprecedented. But it does suggest a degree of collaboration between Europe's counterintelligence agencies that is difficult to match with historical examples. The Finnish Security and Intelligence Service (SUPO), who claims that the Russian capability to conduct human intelligence operations in Europe "was degraded considerably".[7]

'The most prominent post–Cold War expulsion for political manipulation occurred in the United States in two consecutive presidential elections. In January 2016, President Barack Obama expelled 35 Russians officials in retaliation for election interference, and then in April 2021, President Joe Biden announced the expulsion of ten officials. Although there have been numerous additional reports of Russia manipulating elections, for example in France, Montenegro, Spain, and the United Kingdom, the reactions to those events did not elicit public diplomatic expulsions'. (Soviet and Russian Diplomatic Expulsions: How Many and Why? Kevin P. Riehle. International Journal of Intelligence and CounterIntelligence-06 December 2023).[8]Russian intelligence continued to do its job and several European states to protect national interests of Russia. On 04 April 2023, Politico in its news report (Critical infrastructure is a key target for Russia's intelligence gathering, the priority being to monitor 'the production and supply of Western arms to Ukraine.' Jamie Dettmer) noted that Russian wants to reorganize its intelligence networks across Europe: "And there's now growing evidence that Russia's foreign intelligence service (SVR) and its military intelligence agency (GRU) are aggressively trying to rebuild their human espionage networks—particularly with an eye toward military aid going to Ukraine. Finland's Security and Intelligence Service (SUPO) warned expulsions of Russian intelligence officers, and visa refusals for their replacements, have substantially weakened Moscow's intelligence operations in the Nordic region.[9]

In 2021, the French government passed a major reform of the legislative framework for intelligence surveillance. But on several key issues, such as international data sharing, open-source surveillance or the right to information, French law still lags behind international standards in intelligence oversight. This is all the more worrying given that the staff and resources of major French agencies have vastly expanded over the past few years. The legal framework for the French intelligence received less attention from Parliamentarians and successive governments, but surveillance measures are in place to help the police in managing law and order. Adopted by the Parliament in June 2015, the new surveillance law was corroborated by the President on July 24, 2015 and published in an Official Journal in July 2015. On 06 August 2015, Director of the Law and Digital Technology Studies Winston Maxwell wrote in Chronicle of Data Protection that new surveillance law was presented by the French government after the 2015 terrorist attacks to create a single legal framework for intelligence gathering activities. On 08 February 2024, journalists Matt Strudwick and Tash Mosheim reported to Mailonline that a Russian Afghan spy' met Prince Charles and Prince William after 'working for MI6' having been given asylum in the UK by falsely claiming he was fleeing the Taliban in Afghanistan. "The alleged spy–who also claims to have worked for the Foreign Office, the Ministry of Defence and GCHQ–is said to have gained access to 'top secret' documents. He obtained both Russian and British citizenship and worked under Prime ministers Gordon Brown and David Cameron, a court heard. He also met Prince Charles and Prince William when he made visits to Afghanistan while working for the Foreign Office in the late 2000s. After the refugee, identified only as C2, arrived in the UK in 2000 the Home Office granted him the right to remain after he suggested he fled Afghanistan directly from the Taliban. The alleged spy, who also claims to have worked for the Foreign Office, the Ministry of Defence and GCHQ ¿ is said to have gained access to 'top secret' documents. Matt Strudwick and Tash Mosheim reported.[10] However, GB news reported an Afghan Russian agent's life in Russia since 1994. He was working for GCHQ and MI6.

On 26 September 2023, BBC (Five alleged Russian spies appear in London court. Daniel De Simone, BBC news 26 September 2023) reported the arrest of five Bulgarian spies, Orlin Roussev, Bizer Dzhambazov, Katrin Ivanova, Ivan Stoyanov, and Vanya Gaberova. Spies carried out surveillance on people and places targeted by Russia between August 2020 and February 2023. Their surveillance activities, according to the BBC, were alleged to have apparently been for the purpose of assisting Russia to conduct hostile action against the targets, including potential abductions. However, Reuter on 15 August 2023, reported the arrest of three suspected Russian spies arrested in Britain. They were held in February 2023 under the Official

Secrets Act by counter-terrorism detectives at London's Metropolitan Police. The individuals were Bulgarian nationals-alleged to be working for Russian security services. The police named them as Orlin Roussev, Biser Dzambazov, and Katrin Ivanova. Britain has been sharpening its focus on external security threats while the country passed a new national security law, aiming to deter espionage and foreign interference with updated tools and criminal provisions. Police have charged three Russians, agents of Russian military intelligence (GRU).[11]

The real issue of foreign espionage needed to be addressed within Europe, because without security sector reforms countering foreign espionage are impossible. Secondly, in yesteryears, the EU member states spied on each other's institutions, intelligence agencies and politicians that resulted in mistrust and a new intelligence war between Britain and Germany. The three states that countered foreign espionage in a professional way were France, Germany and the Netherlands. These states intercepted foreign intelligence operatives who had planned to retrieve economic and military data and spy on the civilian population. The Netherlands, Norway, Sweden, and Brussels and French intelligence agencies have lived through different phases of experiments, experiences and participation in the US and NATO war on terrorism in Afghanistan, and built professional infrastructures that protected the national security of their states. One thing, I want to elucidate here is the causes of failure of intelligence agencies within the EU project. In fact, the lack of adequate intelligence information, trained manpower, flow of low-quality intelligence information purveyed by untrained, illiterate and ill-educated agents, failure to understand modern technology, and proper intelligence sharing with policy makers. The British, French and German intelligence agencies suffer from lack of check and balance and influence.

In Central and Western Europe, some states introduced major reforms in the field of law enforcement and intelligence, but the way their intelligence agencies are operating is not a professional way of operation due to their consecutive failure to tackle national security threats. These reforms have had mixed results; sometimes states adopted a democratic model, and at times, it looked as though hardly anything had changed. The most important concerns relate to the regime change in Ukraine, the emergence of the Islamic State and a new wave of terrorism in Europe. The crisis continues to have significant repercussions for the member states. While terror elements started infiltrating from one state to another state, the EU member states individually decided to manage their own borders to tackle the crisis of migration and free movement of people. This unexpected infiltration forced them to introduce security sector reforms and apply new means of intelligence surveillance to identify terror suspects. In 2015, after the Paris terrorist attacks, President Hollands declared was against Daesh that killed more than 130 innocent people. Expert, Benjamin Dodman in his analysis (Riots, protests and climate uprisings: The 2023 was a tumultuous year in France. FRANCE 24. December 28, 2023) has argued that the Pension Reforms sparked countrywide protests that caused financial destruction and social disobedience:

"Violence flared in March 2023 when Macron ordered his government to ram the reform through parliament without a vote, using special executive powers. The move sparked several nights of unrest and turned the festering social dispute into a crisis of French democracy. Police crackdowns and controversial rulings by France's constitutional court helped snuff out the movement, handing Macron a pyrrhic victory–though in the weeks that followed he could scarcely take a step outside the Élysée Palace without being greeted by protesters banging pots and pans. Running battles between riot police and pension protesters revived a long-standing debate on police brutality in France – with human rights monitors both at home and abroad raising the alarm over officers' "excessive use of force". The scrutiny only increased in late June when towns and cities across the country erupted in rage at the killing of Nahel M.a 17-year-old of North African origin who was shot dead by police during a routine traffic stop in the Paris suburb of Nanterre. Social media footage of the incident, which contradicted police claims that Nahel had posed a threat to officers, kicked off several nights of rioting in France's deprived and ethnically diverse suburbs, known as banlieues, where non-white youths have long complained of being singled out by police".[12]In 2015, the French government introduced intelligence and security sector reforms to effectively and collectively respond to prevailing radicalization and extremism, and make intelligence agencies fit to the fight of foreign espionage. Experts and analysts, John Wihbey and Leighton Walter Kille in their paper have raised the question of social integration, (France, Islam, terrorism and the challenges of integration: Research roundup: 2015 review of research related to Muslims in France, and the terrorist attacks on the French satirical news outlet Charlie Hebdo and a chemical plant near Lyon. The Journalist's Resources. November 16, 2015) radicalization and the 2015 terrorist attacks in Paris: "The 2015 string of terrorist attacks across Paris that killed 129 people has again raised concerns across French society about jihadist violence and ISIS-inspired domestic terrorism".[13]

Chapter 8

The French Intelligence Reform, the Charlie Hebdo Assassination Attacks, Foreign Espionage, CNCTR and Democratization of Post-Cold War Intelligence in Europe

Intelligence is generated from collection, analysis and information. Modern intelligence can be elucidated as organised policy related information, including secret information. For an intelligence agency focussing on every aspect of national security threat is impossible to establish priorities for all aspects of intelligence operation. On 13 November 2015, terrorist attacks in Paris killed 129 people and threatened authority of the state but never harassed and consternated French citizens. France is a democratic country-maintaining friendly diplomatic relationship with the Muslim world and involved in countering terrorism and radicalization in different fronts. Muslims community in France is highly diverse, and some are secular while others are observant. After the Charlie Hebdo assassination attacks, there were hundreds of spontaneous mass demonstrations across Europe to condemn new wave of terrorism and violence. The Charlie Hebdo work and expertise attracted criticism from Pakistan and African states. Charlie Hebdo reprinted cartoon of prophet Muhammad (PUH) published by Danish newspaper that provoked Muslim groups in France. Years later, technological developments further complicated the work and operation of French security agencies. In the past decade, modern technology launched Brain-Project and one of emerging technology enabled by Brain Project is brain-computer interfaces that allow interactive communication between external tools and the brain waves.

A major characteristic of the information era is the continuous increase in interconnectedness created by a worldwide electronic network. Experts James J Giordano and Bert Gordijn in their research paper (Possibilities, limits, and implications of brain-computer interfacing technologies.

Cambridge University Press:07 May 2010) have noted that the computer usually creates an interface between us and the digital world: "An ultimate connectedness between our minds and the information pool of the Internet can be fantasized within a science fiction scenario as represented in the movie The Matrix. Brain–mind operation could be connected to a computer, which might afford an opportunity to enter a direct interaction with a virtual world. Such brain–machine interfaces would have to fulfil a two-directional task: one is to give the human user the opportunity to communicate with the system by sending signals to the computer; the other is brain stimulation by a device in order to let us experience the virtual world".[1]

Like past scientific and technological breakthroughs, cognitive sciences research is purported to have an impact on future security policies. Mind Control knowledge, or telepathy could allow for instantaneous clear communication between government officials, military personnel, and intelligence agents, leading to improved coordination and faster response times during emergencies or operations. As this author personally developed telepathy of mind control knowledge, telepathic abilities could be used to gather intelligence more effectively, bypassing conventional communication barriers and encryption. My major research has been helped by telepathic approach, and telepathic capabilities could be employed to detect and prevent threats to national security more efficiently. It might also be used to identify and counter espionage activities. In Second World War, intelligence gathering relied on conventional methods like espionage, and code-breaking, but telepathic approach to war and controlling enemy mind was of most importance. However, state intelligence aims to protect the nation's interests, sovereignty, and security. It often involves gathering intelligence about foreign governments, organizations, and sometimes individuals while policing intelligence seeks to prevent, investigate, and solve crimes.

Now we can judge the terrorist attacks carried out by extremist organization in 2015-2016 in France. In these attacks, terrorists were not successful to inflict huge fatalities due to the French intelligence immediate reaction. The failure to prevent jihadist attacks in France are complex issues involving both policing intelligence agencies. Thousands of asylum seekers in France submitted their claim on fake documents, fake IDs and fake information like wrong date of birth and fake names. The French intelligence agencies are competent and professional in their operations, strategies and measures to tackle these people. Successful counter-terrorism efforts often require effective collaboration and information sharing between policing intelligence and state intelligence agencies. There are legal and operational constraints that can limit the effectiveness of both policing and state intelligence. The nature of jihadist terrorism, often characterized by radicalization, decentralized planning, and low-tech, high-impact attacks, can make it particularly challenging to detect and prevent. Involvement of private intelligence in national security mechanism can assist state intelligence and law enforcement agencies in maintaining stability in a state, but this collaboration needs to be managed with care. Private intelligence agencies often employ experts with specialized knowledge in areas like cybersecurity, financial crimes, or international affairs, which can complement the skills of state agencies.

The main functions of French intelligence agencies are identifying and analysing internal and external threats to national security; providing information and advising the management about the nature and causes of these threats. The DGSE protect and enable French citizen to live without fear and consternation. The DGSE can trace its roots back to 27 November 1943, when a central external intelligence agency, known as the DGSS was founded by politician Jacques Soustelle. The services are obliged to respect the political rights enshrined in the Constitution. A French parliamentary inquiry investigating the Paris terrorist attacks in 2015, suggested that the country's many intelligence agencies be merged to create a single agency. In my perception, I am not agree with this proposal. The commission was set up to investigate the police failures that led to two terrorist attacks in France. Intelligence in a constitutional Democracy report, (Ministerial Review Commission on the Intelligence Republic of South Africa, in its final report-10 September 2008) argued that all intelligence agencies need to operate secretly in order to retrieve confidential information through surveillance and its affiliated organizations comtetent interception communication system."Notwithstanding their grave responsibilities and the perils they might have to face, the intelligence agencies and other security services are at all times and in all respects bound by the Constitution".[2]

Al Jazeera (02 Jul 2023) reported the 2023 riots in which extremist and foreign elements clashed with police overnight and targeted a mayor's home with a burning car. 'Police made arrests nationwide in an attempt to quell France's worst social upheaval in years. 'French Prime Minister Elisabeth Borne condemned the attack. "We will let no violence get by" unpunished, she said, urging that the perpetrators be sanctioned with the "utmost severity". Al Jazeera noted.[3] A Police officer fatally killed an African French national in June 2023 during the traffic stop. This incident caused unrest and demonstration of extremist elements who set fire to thousands of businesses across France. Violent demonstrations were reported in nearly 300 cities and towns around the country during this period. French politics is often viewed as complex and sometimes indescribable for several reasons. Unlike two-party systems, France has a multi-party system where several political parties compete for power. This diversity can lead to a wide range of political views and coalitions, making the political landscape more intricate. France combines aspects of both presidential and parliamentary systems.

The President holds significant power, but this is balanced by the powers of the Parliament. The complexity and sometimes indescribable nature of French politics stem from its unique combination of historical, cultural, and structural factors, along with the dynamic nature of its political processes and public discourse. Terrorist groups used modern technology and military-grade weapons to attack governments and private properties. Foreign spies managed rioters and their strategies. Some extremist and terrorist elements have crossed borders from neighbouring states to help their group's members in looting, vandalism and fear marketing. In France, more that 70 percent asylum seekers have submitted fake documents to the immigration departments-with their fake names and group's affiliation. Intelligence challenges in Europe need a professional assessment to address issues of sharing, analysis, and process and information dissemination. By taking this step, policy makers must be purveyed processed intelligence information and they must be led in the right direction. "There is also some work on the typology of the intelligence problem as a whole, (Christiaan Menkveld. Understanding the complexity of intelligence problems-08 Feb 2021).[4] There is also quite some work on the application of complex adaptive systems on the field of international relations. Associate researcher at CNRS and post-doctoral analyst at CERI Sciences in Paris, Felix Treguer in his paper (Major oversight gaps in the French intelligence legal framework. 25. March 2022) has noted surveillance techniques of French intelligence, and also highlighted parliamentary and legal oversight of agencies:

"In 2021, French Government introduced major intelligence and law enforcement reforms to make its intelligence infrastructure, but some issues have not been highlighted in detail, suchlike intelligence dissemination, sharing, open source surveillance and international standard of intelligence oversight. Experts stressed the need for legal and parliamentary oversight and coordination of intelligence agencies with law enforcement agencies. Revelations of Edward Snowden forced the French parliament to pass an intelligence revision act after the 2015 terrorist attacks in Paris. The reform passed in 2016 is certainly much less ambitious than its 2015 predecessor. Yet, strengthening oversight should be a priority, given the role of intelligence in government. Since 2015, French intelligence agencies have seen their workforce increase by 30 percent, in particular to develop their technological capabilities. In this context, the use of various surveillance techniques have increased significantly, in particular in areas that are especially sensitive for civil rights. For instance, following criticisms by civil society organisations during the parliamentary debate in 2015, the CNCTR has warned in several annual reports about an important oversight gap regarding the sharing of data between French intelligence services and foreign agencies".[5]

Legal system of French intelligence surveillance is also of greate importance. The French law also views open surveillance differently, especially twitter and Facebook. In France, transparency is difficult to be judged notwithstanding the CNCTR in its report claimed accuracy of information. Associate researcher at CNRS in Paris, Felix Treguer in his paper (Major oversight gaps in the French intelligence legal framework. 25. March 2022) has noted transparency and accuracy of intelligence information: "In France, such a degree of transparency seems unimaginable for the moment. Even if the CNCTR has made some progress in the accuracy of the information it provides in its reports, it often sticks to mere descriptions of the state of the law and its evolution, or issues general statistics on the types of measures authorised and their purposes. This is still a far cry from the level of detail feeding the public debate and the work of parliamentarians, journalists or NGOs in countries such as the United Kingdom or Germany. French law also makes no mention of so-called open source surveillance, especially on social networks such as Facebook or Twitter – an activity about which little has been leaked to the press but known to have grown in importance over the last ten years."[6]

In the years leading up to 2015, France, like many other countries, faced a growing number of security challenges, including the rise of radicalised and extremist groups, foreign espionage and the wrath of hostile states. The professional approach of the country's intelligence agencies was seen as a good understanding to effectively counter these threats. The report of Intelligence in a constitutional Democracy, Ministerial review commission on the intelligence in the Republic of South Africa (10 September 2008) argued that existence of security services in democratic countries gives rise to a political paradox. On the one hand, the security services are established in order to protect the state, its citizens and the democratic order and they are given special powers and capabilities for this purpose. The intelligence services present a particular challenge because of the nature of their role, their intrusive powers and their distinctive characteristic of secrecy. Their main functions typically include identifying and analysing internal and external threats to national security."[7]

An Associate Researcher at the CNRS Centre for Internet and Society and a Postdoctoral fellow at CERI-Sciences. Professor Félix Tréguer in his recent research paper (Overview of France's Intelligence Legal Framework. December 2021) has reviewed legal developments in the French Parliament after the 2015 terrorist attacks. The French intelligence (DGSE) and security (DGSI) agencies identified the threat of ISIS, al-Qaeda-affiliated entities active in Pakistan, Afghanistan and African states. To make intelligence agencies more competent and professional, an Intelligence Bill was introduced to the Parliament on 19 March 2015 by former Prime Minister Manuel Valls. "Despite widespread mobilisation, the Bill was adopted with 438 votes in favor, 86 against and 42 abstentions at the National Assembly and 252 for, 67 against and 26 abstentions at the Senate. It was made into law on 24 July 2015. Although framed by the government as a response to the Paris attacks of January 2015, the passage of the Intelligence Act has a much longer history. The previous law providing a framework for the surveillance programs of French intelligence agencies was the Wiretapping Act of 1991, aimed at regulating telephone wiretaps. Many surveillance programs developed in the 2000s –especially to monitor Internet communications—were rolled out outside of any legal framework. As early as 2008, the French government's White Paper of Defence and National Security stressed that "intelligence activities do not have the benefit of a clear and sufficient legal framework,".[8](Professor Félix Tréguer- Overview of France's Intelligence Legal Framework. December 2021).

In France, the threat of jihadism and extremism has been a point of concern, especially the terrorist and extremist elements protested in 2023, which caused destruction, looting and social disobedience. Some neighbours interfered in France and supported sarcastic elements, extremists and terrorist groups. French intelligence services have often warned of a likely surge in Islamist terrorist attacks, considering these high-profile events as potential targets and creating what they term a "perfect storm" of threat conditions. Salafi-jihadism, Wahhabism, Tablighi

Jamaat, Taliban, ISIS and extremist organizations of Africa, Middle East and South Asia have been major causes of unrest and terrorism in France. They are most visible, active, and threatening violent extremist movements operating in the heart of Paris. While the global terrorist threat landscape is complex and multifaceted, involving various groups and geopolitical dynamics, the situation in France is particularly sensitive due to its history of dealing with Islamist terrorism and its prominent global and regional role, but its intelligence agencies professionally tackled with these groups. Security sector reform in France after the consecutive terror attacks since 2015 faced several challenges and complexities, but succeeded.[9] (Rise of the Reactionaries: Comparing the Ideologies of Salafi Jihadism and White Supremacist Extremism. (Alexander Meleagrou-Hitchens, Blyth Crawford, Valentin Wutke, the Program on Extremism, George Washington University, December 2021).

France has multiple professional and well-trained intelligence agencies with different areas of focus, jurisdictions, and methods. Coordinating effectively between these agencies and ensuring timely sharing of information has been a persistent challenge. Effective intelligence work requires significant resources, not just in terms of funding, but also in terms of having a skilled workforce. France has undertaken several initiatives to reform its law enforcement systems in recent years. These reforms aim to address various issues, including police conduct, community relations, and the overall effectiveness of law enforcement. Majority of French intelligence agencies are now skilled, professional and dealing with foreign espionage and domestic security threats with their professional security approach. The success of these reforms typically depends on a range of factors, including political will, community engagement, and the adaptability of the law enforcement institutions themselves. Experts and analysts, Laurence Bindner, Hugo Micheron, Aaron Y. Zelin (Policy Analysis, Policy Watch 3400. Terrorism in France: New and Old Trends in Jihadism. The Washington Institute for Near East Policy, 13 November 2020) in their research paper have noted some aspects of the 2015 terrorist attacks in Paris and the role of jihadist groups in these attacks:

"France has experienced escalating tensions in the past few months surrounding two developments: the trial of the suspects who perpetrated the 2015 terrorist attacks in Paris, and the republican this September of the Charlie Hebdo cartoons depicting the Prophet Muhammad. These events have sparked worldwide condemnation, boycotts, and incitement to violence, all exacerbated when President Emmanuel Macron refused to publicly condemn the cartoons. His October address on related matters reiterated France's respect for freedom of speech and spoke of "Islamist separatism"—a stance that some Muslims viewed as a provocative endorsement of the cartoons' content and a critique of Islam as a whole".[10]France has faced multiple social and security challenges in recent years, notably the Yellow Vest movement, contentious pension reforms, and a surge in extremism. Despite these challenges, it's worth noting that France has made significant efforts to reform its intelligence services post-2015.[11](The EU's response to terrorism: Fighting terrorism is a top priority for the EU. Member states work closely together to prevent terrorist attacks and ensure the security of citizens. Council of the European Union). The French intelligence legal framework is designed to govern the activities of the country's intelligence agencies, ensuring that their operations are conducted within the bounds of the law while safeguarding national security and individual freedoms.

France has passed several intelligence acts, including significant ones in 2015 and 2016, which provide a legal basis for intelligence operations. These acts define the missions of intelligence agencies, the scope of their powers, and the conditions under which certain surveillance activities can be carried out. Expert and writer, Jacques Follorou in his article (Intelligence-gathering: French oversight board alarmed by the rise in requests concerning political activism. In its annual report, the secret services watchdog stated that it increased disciplinary warnings and requests for additional information. The commission warned of the weakness of its oversight measures, which are ill-adapted to 21st-century technology. Le Monde, in June 16, 2023 highlighted function of CNCTR Commission oversighting operations of intelligence agencies:

"The proportion of surveillance techniques used in cases of "collective" violence is 12%. For these purposes more than any other, the CNCTR stressed that it has been forced to multiply the number of disciplinary warnings and requests for additional information "to assess the merits" of surveillance "whose motivations are sometimes too abstract, even stereotyped." It said it had often attached "reservations and conditions to its favourable opinions, aimed at limiting the impact of the technique: reducing the authorization period, for example, or preventing possible impacts on family and friends." Finally, the increase in the number of unfavourable opinions, numbering 629 cases in 2022, "mainly concerned requests submitted for the prevention of collective violence." For an alarm to be heard, it has to make noise. It is unlikely that the warning issued by the Commission Nationale de Contrôle des Techniques de Renseignement (CNCTR, the French national regulatory commission on intelligence techniques), in its 2022 annual report, will resonate across the public. And it's a shame. Born in late 2015 from the very first law on intelligence and the only independent watchdog for government surveillance, the CNCTR monitors the activities of the French secret services. As soon as agents employ a technique to gather information–wiretapping, geolocation, computer data, image and sound capture, etc.–they must seek the CNCTR's advisory opinion".[12]

The legal framework includes provisions for oversight to ensure that intelligence agencies operate within the law. This includes parliamentary oversight committees and independent regulatory bodies that review the activities of intelligence services. The European Union Agency for Fundamental Rights in its new surveillance report has reviewed the EU surveillance mechanism and operation and new development taken place, including the new oversight bodies. (Surveillance by intelligence services: Fundamental rights safeguards and remedies in the EU–2023). New developments such as new surveillance bodies and constitutional courts' decisions and the impact of the 2016 European data protection reform were taken place, which brought to light 18 bodies overseeing work of intelligence agencies in EU-27: "In 2023, 18 expert bodies are overseeing the work of intelligence services in the EU-27, compared with 16 in the EU-28 in 2017. These developments are viewed in the light of minimum requirements shaped by the Court of Justice of the European Union (CJEU) and the European Court of Human Rights (ECTHR). In this context, the current report refers to a selection of relevant FRA opinions drawn from the 16 opinions published in the 2017 FRA report, alongside key findings from this earlier report. It also highlights relevant developments over time. Several key legal developments have taken place since the publication of the 2017 FRA report. For example, the CJEU and ECtHR issued seminal judgments on the transatlantic flow of data and surveillance by intelligence services; the General Data Protection Regulation (GDPR)".[13]

The 2017 FRA report noted some aspects of intelligence surveillance in European Union member states. Countering foreign espionage is a critical aspect of France's national security strategy. Given the complex and evolving nature of espionage threats, France employs a multi-pronged approach. French intelligence agencies, such as the DGSE and the DGSI play a crucial role in identifying and monitoring foreign espionage activities. They gather intelligence, analyse threats, and conduct counter-espionage operations. The framework is supported by judicial and law enforcement agencies capable of acting on intelligence information. Recognizing that foreign espionage also targets the private sector and research institutions, the French government works closely with these entities to enhance their security measures.[14] Members of the EU have established different oversight bodies to hear citizens' complaints of their privacy violation and address this issue. While such remedies do not need to be of a judicial nature, they need to be effective. France and Germany maintain professional intelligence infrastructures and implemented notable surveillance reforms, particularly in light of security concerns and technological advancements. In Germany, the Federal Intelligence Service (BND) is authorized to gather and analyse information from telecommunications networks deemed relevant for national security. In France, the government has taken steps to implement extensive surveillance measures, especially in preparation for the 2024 Paris Summer Olympics.

The French National Assembly has approved the use of AI-powered video surveillance cameras. Additionally, the French National Assembly adopted a bill that allows law enforcement to remotely activate devices' cameras, microphones, and location services for investigating serious crimes. The Euronews on 09 July 2023 reported France's intelligence authorities of violent actions by the ultra-right organizations. Director General of France Domestic Intelligence, Nicholas Lerner in his interview with Le Monde newspaper warned that; "we have witnessed very worrying resurgence of violent action".[15] He also warned in his interview that senior civil servants were concerned. He also said, "The fight against global warming is a legitimate battle that deserves to be fought with determination. The French far right in the political sphere has painted several faces. The General Directorate for Internal Security is a French Security Agency. It is charged with counter-espionage, counter-terrorism, countering cybercrime and surveillance of potentially threatening groups, organisations, and social phenomena. The agency was created in 2008 under the name Central Directorate of Interior Intelligence. The French successive governments have introduced intelligence and security sector reforms to make intelligence competent.

Research Scholar and intelligence expert, Mazzola, Stephanie in her research paper (War Studies Department. PhD Thesis: Intelligence services in Post Conflict State Building: a comprehensive study of Iraq and Afghanistan. July 2021, Kings College London. UK) noted the nature of intelligence and evolution of intelligence in most authoritarian and totalitarian states:

"To understand the nature of the intelligence services today, however, one ought to firstly go back to the military doctrine of espionage and "survival of the state" as the winning party of a war, and ought as well to understand the evolution of these organisations from pure "servants" of the regime in power to guarantors of the interests of all State institutions. In most post authoritarian and totalitarian states, like the post-communist States in Eastern Europe, these conditions did not prevail. These countries had to face, simultaneously, a political, an economic, a social and a security transformation, commonly resulting into unstable institutions. The fact that many of these states, unlike Western democracies, also lacked a wide spread popular identification with the newly established institutions, caused internal fragility and amplified the external sources of insecurity , thus questioning fundamental Rule of Law traits. The fact that norms were still not internally accepted and "absorbed", contributed to the difficulties. The inability of the West to dedicate the right attention to the different security realities impeded the quick identification of a correct direction to the reform of the intelligence sector. This is particularly pertinent given that when Western democratic countries undertook intelligence reform none of them was simultaneously engaged in fundamental institutional reform".[16]

According to the French Foreign Minister, Catherine Colonna's remarks that 'Russian actors had been involved in a digital information manipulation campaign, including several in Europe. German Interior Minister Nancy Faeser's report confirmed the involvement of Chinese intelligence that has focused on protecting the country's national interests in Europe. "To maintain control over the Chinese diaspora, overseas police stations are run by "Chinese expatriates loyal to the line–often with German citizenship." Alina Clasen noted. State transformation and security sector reforms in Germany have further professionalized tactics of domestic and foreign intelligence agencies. In 2022, foreign espionage, radicalization and extremism have taken root there, while Chinese, Iranian, Turkish and Russian secret agencies have been operating in all European states. Expert and analyst Alina Clasen in her recent analysis (Intelligence reform and the transformation of the state: the end of a French exception German intelligence services point to increased hybrid security threats. EURACTIV.de-19 July 2023) has quoted the German domestic intelligence services (BfV) and German Minister of the Interior Nancy Faeser reports on the intelligence reforms and interference of foreign agencies in domestic affairs of Germany and other EU member states:

"Espionage, illegitimate influence peddling, disinformation campaigns, and cyber-attacks increased in Germany in 2022, with activities mainly linked to Russia, China, Iran, and Turkey, according to a report by the domestic intelligence services (BfV). The Federal Office for the Protection of the Constitution sees a connection between the increase in hybrid threats and the Russian war of aggression against Ukraine initiated in February 2022 and China's growing confrontational approach with the West. "The Russian war of aggression against Ukraine has changed the security situation across Europe. We have taken strong measures to arm ourselves against espionage, disinformation campaigns, and cyberattacks," explained German Minister of the Interior Nancy Faeser at the presentation of the report. Besides Russia, the main actors are China, Iran, and Turkey, and the impact of activities–like cyberattacks, disinformation, and espionage–varies. The report emphasises that the illegal actions of foreign intelligence services affect national sovereignty and cause considerable operational and economic damage. In particular, the increased use of social media as a means for disinformation was identified with the aim of weakening social cohesion, disrupting the free formation of opinion, and destabilising democracy."[17]

The French intelligence was implicated in a multifaceted crisis, while if we look at its past historical status, French intelligence has been a competent agency during the First and Second World Wars, and extensive Cold War. In his Aljazeera analysis, Bruce Crumley noted that the Paris attacks occurred due to the police failure. He has also documented the US warning about the ISIS attacks in France. He is of the opinion that terrorists were on the radar of French authorities as radicals and potential threats—with at least one charged in a terrorism-related case. (Were the Paris attacks a French intelligence failure? Al Jazeera November 17, 2015).[18]On 23 December 2022, BBC reported a gunman opened fire in central Paris, killing three people and wounding three others. The attacker targeted a Kurdish cultural centre and shot local community members. The police investigated a possible racist motive.[19]On 28 October 2020, Paris based Le Monde newspaper reported the killing of three people in a knife attack at a church in Nice, in what French President Emmanuel Macron said was an "Islamist terrorist attack". He said France would not surrender its core values after visiting the Notre-Dame basilica in the southern city. An extra 4,000 troops are being deployed to protect churches and schools.[20]

Moreover, on 05 July 2016, Associated Press reported multiple failings by French policing agencies including their lack of cooperation with their partner agencies, communities and political leadership. "Our police have failed," Fenech said at a news conference called to present proposals growing out of the nearly six-month investigation....Investigators found that intelligence was not the only failure rivalry and rules stymied various police and military units who arrived at the scene of the November Paris attacks.[21] The French inquiry argued changes to intelligence services in light of failures. An investigative committee of France's Parliament announced that it had found intelligence lapses leading up to the November terror attacks in Paris. Georges Fenech, head of the special parliamentary commission noted the Paris 2015 attacks: "Our intelligence services have failed. On 05 July 2016, New York Times (Aurelien Breeden) reported a parliamentary committee examining two devastating terrorist attacks in France in 2015, "called for the nation's intelligence agencies to be streamlined and merged, finding widespread failures in the collection and analysis of information that could have helped prevent the attacks.[22]

Once again France's intelligence agencies confronted extremist and radicalized elements in streets and towns to intercept them from looting, and destroying shops, historical places and markets in 2023. The French government focussed on intelligence and security sector reforms, while social reforms also needed serious action in order to integrate all extremists, radicalised jihadists and sarcastic so-called Muslims into the French society. More than sixty years after the promulgation of the first intelligence act, French lawmakers once more want some intelligence and security sector reforms. Expert and journalist, Jacques Follorou in his commentary on the French intelligence reforms (France's tepid intelligence reform, 07 June 2021, About Intel) is of the view that by these reforms "government also aims to provide new capabilities to the services. The bill includes a provision dedicated to the surveillance of a new generation of satellites. Small in size, placed by the thousands in low orbit, these satellites provide high-speed Internet access outside of traditional operators, and escape the "big ears" of intelligence. The government wants to fill this gap, just as it wants to legislate a way to bypass the technical hurdles posed by 5G networks. Since 2016, a terrorism-related data storage centre, nicknamed "the warehouse", has been operating outside any legal framework. Article L. 863-2 of the Internal Security Code, also adopted in 2016, provides that intelligence agencies can "share all the information useful for the accomplishment of their missions"[23]

In my articles and research papers published in newspapers and journals in 2015, I have already suggested some intelligence reforms in France to undermine the ring of terrorist and jihadist organizations. The 2015 terrorist attacks in Paris exhibited police failure in France. The French government, later on, constituted a fusion of all intelligence agencies to effectively respond to the threat of radicalization and international terrorism. After intelligence and security sector reforms, terrorist incidents decreased in France. Writers and experts, Griff Witte and Loveday Morris (Failure to stop Paris attacks reveals fatal flaws at heart of European security-Washington Post, 28 November 2015) also noted in their analysis terrorist attacks that left 130 people dead in Paris, the killers relied on a cunning awareness of the weaknesses at the heart of the European security services charged with stopping them: "Poor information-sharing among intelligence agencies, a threadbare system for tracking suspects across open borders and an unmanageably long list of home-grown extremists to monitor all gave the Paris plotters an opening to carry out the deadliest attack on French soil in more than half a century. Two weeks later, European security experts say the flaws in the continent's defenses are as conspicuous as ever, with no clear plan for fixing them. "We lack the most obvious tools to deal with this threat," said Jean-Charles Brisard, chairman of the Paris-based Centre for the Analysis of Terrorism.[24]

France has entered a political, social and economic transformation phase. The Niger crisis and military takeover has deeply disturbed political and military leadership of the country, and the arrival of Wagner militia and other stakeholders created a threatening security environment. In all these and other events, French intelligence exhibited its professional approach and proved that a strong and reformed secret agency can better manage national security crises. In fact, secret agencies were not conceived in France as a functional tool in the hands of the decision-maker, but later on they realized the importance of intelligence infrastructure. Persistent intelligence and security sector reforms were in fact the reorganization and reinvention of French security infrastructure. As France has been a strong colonial power, its agencies have also been struggling to adopt modern intelligence tactics. French reform is based on the action of an attempt to explain or justify behaviour or an attitude of secret agencies with logical reasons, or mechanism in which apparent logical reasons are given to justify behaviour. Government and the state have decided to modernise and centralise secret agencies. Expert and writer, Anne Lise Michelot (Reform of the French Intelligence Oversight System-30 November 2028) has documented some aspects of the French intelligence oversight and reform:

"French intelligence remains a very secretive world from the public view, and the little presence it occupies in the press or public debate is more often than not one of scandal, abuse or failure. In 2008, the government initiated a reform process of the intelligence organisation, and continued in 2015, following the numerous terrorist attacks on the national territory. The result of this long process of reshaping the intelligence community has included attempts at perfecting, and in some cases creating, oversight mechanisms. These reforms have been the subject of public and parliamentary debates for the past decade, as many politicians, scholars and journalists pointed out the lack of supervision and the relative freedom intelligence agencies enjoyed in performing their activities. Today, the French oversight system comprises a specific institution for each type of control. This diversified/ plural system was completed with the creation of a new institution, the Commission Nationale de Contrôle des Techniques de Renseignement, CNCTR (national commission for the control of intelligence techniques) in 2015. The creation of the CNCTR in 2015 to oversee the usage of intelligence techniques has attempted to bring France up to high democratic standards in terms of intelligence oversight. However, the commission's limited means hinder its ability to perform fully its duties."[25]

Chapter 9

The Tablighi Jamaat and its Intelligence Units Constitute a Perilous Security Threat to France and the European Union

The role of Tablighi Jamaat in recruiting of radicalized elements of French, German and Netherlands citizens has caused perilous development. While Tablighi Jamaat's group have been involved in radical activities in EU. However, it's important to note that such instances do not necessarily reflect the organization's ethos or objectives. It's also important to consider the broader context. The process of radicalization is influenced by a variety of factors, including individual experiences, social and economic conditions, political contexts, and exposure to extremist ideologies. Therefore, any connection between Tablighi Jamaat and radicalization would be part of a much larger and more complex picture. Given the sensitivity and complexity of such topics, it's always recommended to consult a range of sources and perspectives, including academic studies, government reports, and analyses from reputable think tanks, to get a comprehensive understanding.

One of the largest Islamic extremist intelligence networks of contemporary times, in terms of both geographical spread and number of activists, the Tablighi Jamaat has received attention of states where it operates with different intelligence shapes, strategies and recruitment plans. Tablighi Jamaat, a South Asian Deobandi-Barelvi organization that played an ambiguous role in India and Pakistan, spying for Britain, Taliban and Pakistan, it trained and recruited Muslims and Christians, and established intelligence networks in more than 100 European, Asian and African countries. Tablighi Jamaat is playing important role in intelligence operations of the Taliban intelligence (GDI). Tablighi Jamaat members are spying on Afghani civilians. With increasing frequency, terrorist plots in the West uncovered Tablighi Jamaat's linkages. A unit of Aadhyaasi Media and Content Services Private Limited, OpIndia in its news commentary

(Tablighi Jamaat and its links to terrorist organizations: History of association to Al Qaeda, Taliban and Kashmiri terrorists: Secret US documents released by WikiLeaks in 2011 revealed that some Al Qaeda operatives used the Jamaat to get visas and fund their travel to Pakistan. They also lived in and around Delhi, the documents said-31 March, 2020) noted the role of Tablighi Jamaat in spreading COVID-19 in India, and its relations with Al Qaeda terrorist group:

"The role of Tablighi Jamaat in the spreading of the Wuhan Coronavirus across numerous states of India has come to light. At least ten people have died thus far after attending an Islamic religious event organized by the Islamic missionary organization in Markaz, Nizamuddin at the national capital. India is not the only country affected by the recklessness of the Tablighi Jamaat. Other South Asian countries are bearing the brunt of it as well. Under such circumstances, the Tablighi Jamaat's links with terrorist organizations such as the Al Qaeda become hugely significant. Secret US documents released by WikiLeaks in 2011 revealed that some Al Qaeda operatives used the Jamaat to get visas and fund their travel to Pakistan. They also lived in and around Delhi, the documents said. Referring to Saudi Arabia national Abdul Bukhary, as "a veteran jihadist", the report prepared by US authorities in-charge of Guantanamo Bay in Cuba, said a Jamaat member, whom he met in 1985-1986 helped to procure his visa for Pakistan. "One of the JT (Jamaat Tablighi) members procured detainee's visa for Pakistan, after which detainee and another Saudi travelled to Lahore," the report prepared on July 25, 2007 said. "While in New Delhi, detainee was introduced to the leader of the JT and asked to make a life commitment to the organisation. Detainee told JT that he needed to think about it because he did not want to commit his life to servitude, pilgrimage, and missionary work. Detainee returned to Lahore for two weeks and then travelled to Saudi Arabia," the document revealed by WikiLeaks said."[1]

The Tablighi Jamaat is also facilitating extremism and terrorism in France, and recruits Muslims and Christians to balloon out its infrastructure to cities and towns. Harkat-ul-Mujahedeen, the Taliban and al Qaeda are being facilitated in Afghanistan and Pakistan by Tablighi Jamaat and its intelligence units-trained by Inter Services Intelligence (ISI). French, German, Italian and Netherlands Muslim groups are being facilitated and trained by Tablighi Jamaat and inviting them to join its intelligence networks in Pakistan and Afghanistan. Once a facilitator identifies such candidates, he often will segregate them from the main congregation in the mosque or community center and put them into small prayer circles or study groups where they can be more easily exposed to jihadist ideology, Stratfor noted. On 07 July 2005, Experts and analysts, Fred Burton and Scott Stewart in their report (Tablighi Jamaat: An Indirect Line to Terrorism-The Stratfor January 23, 2008), highlighted terror links of Tablighi Jamaat in Europe, US and Asia: "Like Khan and Tanweer, many jihadists desire to travel to Pakistan for training, while others want to get to Afghanistan, Kashmir or other places to fight jihad". The mode adopted by Tablighi Jamaat is to facilitate terrorist groups in Europe and Africa. Tablighi Jamaat remained out of the limelight due to its unorganised structure and missionary nature, but after the US invasion of Afghanistan, it became clear that the group was involved in recruitment of EU Muslims and Christians.[2]

Tablighi Jamaat aided Al Qaeda and Taliban members to get visas and funds to travel from Pakistan. Moreover, several other cases from Kenya, Somalia and Pakistan make it amply clear that Tablighi Jamaat is used as an acceptable conduit by Islamic terrorist organisations to facilitate travels of their members. In UK the group has established mosques networks where the collect money for Taliban and the ISI agency. A Deobandi Islamic scholar, Maulana Muhammad Ilyas established Tablighi Jamaat in 1926 in India. National Security Adviser and a former Director General of intelligence Bureau (IB) of India, Mr. Ajit Doval argued: "The movement was never viewed adversely by the government." But the Tablighi Jamaat has been banned in Saudi Arabia and some Central Asian countries such as Uzbekistan, Tajikistan and Kazakhstan, whose governments see its puritanical preaching as extremist". Expert and analyst, Arsalan Khan in his recent research paper (Contested Sovereignty: Islamic Piety, Blasphemy politics and the paradox of Islamization in Pakistan-08 Jun 2022) explained the rise of a range of Islamic forces in Pakistan and the role of Tablighi Jamaat in popularizing Blasphemy:

"Pakistan has witnessed the rise of a range of Islamic forces that claim to be defending Islam from what they imagine to be a deluge of incidents of blasphemy, a veritable moral panic organized around a set of blasphemy laws pertaining to the regulation and protection of Islam. The violence of blasphemy politics, which is disproportionately directed at sectarian and religious minorities, is predicated on the claim that is the duty and mandate of the state to enforce the blasphemy laws, and where the state fails, the onus falls on ordinary Muslims to fulfil the demands of Islam. I focus here on the response to this blasphemy politics by Pakistani Tablighis, practitioners of the transnational Islamic piety movement the Tablighi Jamaat. Like other Islamic groups in Pakistan, Tablighis consider blasphemy to be a grave sin and a deep threat to the Islamic community, but Tablighis believe that the solution to the growing incidence of blasphemy is to spread virtue through their distinct form of face-to-face preaching (dawat).[3]" South Asia Democratic Forum in its research paper (Policy Brief 10–Tablighi Jamaat and its role in the Global Jihad. South Asia Democratic Forum 11 December 2020) has noted some aspects of extremist and intelligence training of the Tablighi Jamaat in Europe and Asia:

"In spite of this, up until this point, the majority of critical evaluations by international intelligence have not reached public discourse or political decision-making processes in the states where TJ holds a significant presence. Especially in Europe and the US, TJ remains largely unknown outside Muslim communities–and when known, actions and motives are misread. This lack of knowledge regarding the dissemination of an Islamic supremacist agenda facilitates TJ's function as a driving force for Islamic extremism and as a major recruiting agency for the cause of Global Jihad- the movement bluntly threatens societies based on liberal and democratic norms. TJ has a relatively clandestine character, but reports point to TJ being extremely effective at spreading Islamic fundamentalism. In sum, TJ is seen as an essential component of a phenomenon which the French political-sociologist Bernard Rougier (2020) calls an 'Islamist Ecosystem'. We believe this concept is most useful to understand the role that TJ plays in the Global Jihad. It appears that there is a growing awareness within Germany's intelligence community regarding potential causal links between TJ's missionary activities, particularly religious training and instruction courses, and the radicalisation of individual followers. The BfV warned already in 2005 that 'trainings by TJ can constitute for individual young Muslims an entry into Islamism and–subsequently–also into Islamist-terrorist groups'. The federal agency emphasizes the significance of study tours abroad [namely those to Pakistan] offered by TJ. It is stated that 'successfully proselytised people are often provided several months of training events in Pakistani Quranic schools [madrasas]. Such intensive training courses can indoctrinate participants and make them receptive to Islamist ideas'. 'In individual cases, trainees then found their way to quote Mujahedeen training camps in Afghanistan (BMI 2006, p.226)".[4]

Unquestionably, British and Pakistani intelligence agencies and military establishment are in full control of the Tablighi Jamaat's Intelligence infrastructure, recruiting their educated young preachers in their intelligence centres then task them to collect political, economic, military and technological intelligence information from across the globe. In its annual congregation and gathering in Raiwand, Lahore Pakistan, expert of intelligence, terrorism, extremism, military generals, bureaucrats, political and religious scholars, and member of worldwide intelligence agencies, weapons experts, and technology experts participate to share their expertise with each other, designing worldwide strategies, planning jihad and financially sponsoring Terrorism. Pakistan army and the British intelligence agencies organize suchlike gathering every year and invite military and intelligence experts from Middle East, South Asia, Central Asia, Europe and Africa to their centres and recruit them to further Pakistan's Jihadist agenda. All participants retrieve new instructions, new programs, new guidance and return to their countries to undertake new jihadist programs. Pakistan's retired military generals and officers lead different groups in different states to further Pakistan's foreign policy objectives through the platform of Tablighi Jamaat.

Political, religious and military bureaucracy of the Tablighi Jamaat is consisted of retired military generals, bureaucrats and intellectuals. They have established separate military and intelligence commands for Europe, South Asia, Central Asia and South East Asia in order to establish contacts with intellectuals, government officials and intelligence stakeholders. The leadership train their agents in their intelligence schools. They are being sent to war zones in Europe and Asia to talk to jihadists and bring them close to their stakeholders. Several European intelligence agencies have prepared intelligence reports and papers about the clandestine activities of the Tablighi Jamaat, and its secret recruitment programme for Muslims and converted Christians. The groups have been recruiting and converting men and women for its extremist and intelligence networks in Europe since years, while European intelligence agencies missed the boat and recently recognised the other side of the mirror.

Members of Tablighi Jamaat are actively in contact with local population, building mosques, preaching centres, intelligence recruitment centres and collecting millions in EU currency to further expand its extremist and terrorist operations to Africa and Middle East. This author is witness to many faces of the Tablighi intelligence networks by visiting their centres times and again. Radicalization always emerges in specific places, and these places significantly shape the way people engage or disengage with extremist activities. The French authorities focus predominantly on Islamist radicalisation and jihadism, even though violent extremism is not bound by a certain ideology and neither is radicalisation. The government submitted, in December 2020, a bill to the parliamentarians with the purpose of tackling radicalisation. South Asia Democratic Forum in its research paper (Policy Brief 10–Tablighi Jamaat and its role in the Global Jihad. By South Asia Democratic Forum-11 December 2020) has uncovered investigation undertaken by EU intelligence agencies against the illegal activities of Tablighi Jamaat:

"The French intelligence agency, General Directorate for Internal Security in its 2018 report (state of the situation regarding the lodging of Islamic fundamentalism in France) described TJ28 as one of the four most active Islamist movements in the country–besides Muslim Brotherhood, Salafists, and the Turkish Movement–constituting 'the ultimate risk' in the form of 'an advent of a counter-society on national territory' (DGSI, 2018, p.3). The DGSI is particularly vigilant regarding TJ's growing influence within the educational system. More specific concerns regard the indoctrination of the teenager and parents by TJ supervisors, the influence of TJ imams on children education, and the immense difficulties faced by non-Muslim families (foremost Jewish ones) to get their children enrolled in public educational institutions where the majority of children are Muslims. European intelligence agencies have established several surveillance units to closely watch terrorist and secret business of Tablighi Jamaat in towns and cities. Italian and Brussels intelligence agencies have become vigilant to prevent radicalization and extremist activities of Tablighi Jamaat, while German BND supports other members and experts of the European intelligence community to adopt professional measures in controlling the illegal activities of Tablighi Jamaat.[5]

The Tablighi intelligence units are bound to trace addresses of government officials, intelligence workers and its sectarian opponents across Europe. Having reviewed the prevailing threatening situation and illegal activities of Tablighi Jamaat in the Netherlands, General Intelligence and Security Service of the Netherlands (AVID) have also identified a new phase of radicalization in the country. Tablighi Jamaat has also established an extremist and intelligence network in the Netherlands, where its workers have spread in towns and cities. The AVID stressed that Tablighi was a variant of radical Islam and 'manifest themselves in non-violent, radical-Islamic puritan groups'. In its report, South Asia Democratic Forum's paper (Policy Brief 10–Tablighi Jamaat and its role in the Global Jihad. South Asia Democratic Forum 11 December 2020) has reviewed concerns of Portugal intelligence agencies:

"Serviço de Informações de Segurança (SIS, Intelligence and Security Service). According to Maria do Céu Pinto, since 2001, the country's intelligence and law enforcing agencies have identified links 'between individuals residing in Portugal and radical Islamic operatives within the ideological network of Al Qaeda, as well as logistical and support activities for terrorism, namely of a criminal nature". This is an interesting, excruciating and gut-wrenching story of Tablighi Jamaat that preaches and delivers sermons across the globe, but secretly operates as an intelligence agency in India, Pakistan and Bangladesh. The group has been recently banned in some states, while it has changed its intelligence operational mechanism to dance with new tangos in South and Central Asia. The Tablighi Jamaat has been spying for some states since decades, collecting intelligence information from remote areas, terrorist nests, insurgent's centres and neighbouring states. Pakistan's Tablighi Jamaat has established different political and religious intelligence units in state institutions of India, Bangladesh and Pakistan, and appointed its own trained officers, bureaucrats, and political elements to collect money from every corner to facilitate its worldwide intelligence mission. The bureaucracy and leadership of the groups are composed of retired military generals and civil-military intelligence agencies. Experts who have established worldwide contacts with governments, intelligence agencies and extremist organisations are members of Tablighi Jamaat.[6]

The group has established its intelligence networks in all mosques of the EU member states, the United States, the Arab world and Africa. The group receive instruction from British and Pakistani intelligence agencies. The group traces addresses for wanted political workers and critics across EU and South Asia, and brings more young and educated people into its clandestine networks. Former intelligence experts, military generals and militant organizations are the main target of the Tablighi intelligence infrastructure. Every Pakistani and British government is bound to facilitate this group, participate in its mission, while civilian and military intelligence agencies of the two countries have been sending their spy agents with its groups to every town, city, and province to collect intelligence information, and trace addresses of political opponents, writers and militant organizations since years. The Tablighi Jamaat role under the leadership of former ISI Chief General Javed Nasir in Bosnia conflict was crucial by recruiting jihadists to fight the Serbian army. According to Vaibhav Singh's Tweet (04 April 2020), "Lt Gen Javed Nasir, former Chief of ISI was also a Patron of Tablighi Jamaat. Javed Nasir was the man who planned and organised "1993 Mumbai Bomb Blasts".[7]

The government of Imran Khan and the Military establishment have been financially supporting Tablighi Jamaat since 2019, while Punjab Assembly once passed a resolution in support of the group. In Britain, France, EU and the United States, the Tablighi Jamaat has appeared on the fringes of several terrorism investigations, leading some to speculate that its political stance simply masked fertile ground for breeding terrorism. The group is the best source of intelligence collection for some states and some western intelligence agencies. Hindustan Times (Pakistan stood in support of Tablighi Jamaat, is Imran Khan going against Saudi Arabia? 24 December 2021) reported Pakistan's resolution in support of Tablighi Jamaat: "Saudi Arabia's ban on Tablighi Jamaat was fiercely criticised in Pakistan. In the assembly of Punjab province, the most influential province of Pakistan, the legislators have even passed a resolution in support of the Tablighi Jamaat. All the legislators of the party and the opposition, in one voice claimed that Tablighi Jamaat has nothing to do with terrorism. At the same time, Saudi Arabia's Religious Ministry announced the ban, saying that this organization is an entry point of terrorism. Punjab Assembly Speaker Chaudhary Pervez Elahi called a special meeting of the House on Tuesday. During this, MLA Khadija Umar presented a proposal in support of Tablighi Jamaat. The Speaker read out the motion and said that the House agrees with the people promoting trust.[8]

There is hundreds of ISIS and IS-K recruited elements in France, Germany, Belgium, Netherlands and Italy who participated in holy wars against states and civilization time and again. Tablighi Jamaat is an old master of extremism and intelligence information collection in Asia and Europe that organizes such groups in Europe. In February 2020, counterterrorism operation in Moscow led to the dismantling of a terrorist cell directly affiliated to Tablighi Jamaat. The Russian Federal Secret Service arrested in fact seven people, both Russian and Central Asians, all actual members of the Tablighi. The cell, according to Russian intelligence, was engaged in various activities, including the search for new followers through a strong campaign of proselytising. In Pakistan, the Tablighi Jamaat has been discovered as the biggest intelligence information gathering group supported by a European state. "Despite warnings and entreaties to not hold the annual congregation in Raiwind, on the outskirts of Lahore, the ijtema (gathering) was held in the second week of March. Moreover, the EU today news report (Europe & US terror fears over Tablighi Jamaat Islamic group, 26 August 2020) also noted clandestine activities of Tablighi Jamaat in Europe and the United States. As of 2007, it was estimated that 10,000 Tablighi Jamaat members could be found in Kyrgyzstan, a presence largely driven by Pakistani migrants. The Group's activities in Kyrgyzstan are of particular interest: "The group is banned in a number of post- Soviet states, notably Russia, and Central Asian countries such as Uzbekistan, Tajikistan and Kazakhstan, where its puritanical preaching is viewed as extremist. As of 2007, it was estimated that 10,000 Tablighi Jamaat members could be found in Kyrgyzstan, a presence largely driven by Pakistani migrants. The Group's activities in Kyrgyzstan are of particular interest".[9]

Chapter 10

The Threat of Nuclear Weapons and the Jihadists use of Dirty Bomb, Chemical, Biological Weapons in France and the EU

The greatest threat to the national security of France stems from the business of nuclear smuggling and state sponsored terror groups operating in South Asia and Europe. The prospect of nuclear terrorism in Europe and possibly in France, is crystal clear as members of the Islamic State (ISIS) in Brussels tried to retrieve material for a dirty bomb. The risk of a complete nuclear device falling into the hands of terrorists will cause consternation in the country. Nuclear terrorism also remains a constant threat to global peace. Access of terrorist organizations to nuclear material is a bigger threat to the civilian population. The Edward Snowden leaks challenged policy makers and the public understanding and perspectives on the role of security intelligence in liberal democratic states. The persisting imbalance of power in the European Union states, intelligence war of foreign agencies on their soils, and the noticeably tilting power have made the continent feel vulnerable. National Security threat perception and countering foreign espionage strategies in every EU member state were diversified while their response to international terrorism flattered underwhelming. Over the past 20 years, growing national security controversies mostly revolved around the failure of intelligence cooperation among the EU member states, which resulted in mistrust and the emergence of major extremist organizations that threatened national security of the region. The introduction of Mass Surveillance programs of European intelligence services prompted anxiety and fear of warrantless information collection.

There are debates in some intellectual circles in London that foreign intelligence interference in France has established secret units in remote areas clean of CCTV and police visibility. The reason for this is that these agencies operate in cities with impunity. French intelligence agencies and parliamentarians have already warned that Chinese intelligence agencies were making things worse. French counter espionage Director, Mr. Nicolas Lerner, provided an overview of the current situation in front of a parliamentary committee of inquiry on foreign interference. Expert and writer, Jacques Follorou in his Le Monde newspaper analysis (Le Monde April 27, 2023) noted statement of the head of French Counter-Intelligence, Mr. Nicolas Lerner, in front of the parliamentary committee of inquiry into political, economic and financial interference by foreign powers: "This committee was established on 06 December 2022, chaired by MP Jean-Philippe Tanguy the head of the General Directorate for Internal Security (DGIS) was questioned behind closed doors. "Since I have been in charge of this service since 2018, we've detected efforts by certain intelligence officers to make approaches targeting the entire political spectrum," Mr. Lerner noted. He also stated that individual approaches are happening and some people have been able to enter into relationships not allowed under French law. He stated; "I do have some examples in mind." The head of the DGSI warned that once he had detected contacts with Russian intelligence officers under diplomatic cover."[1]

With the presence of Jihadist Groups and the ISIS members in France, the use of chemical, biological and nuclear weapons cannot be ruled out, the fact is, that the ISIS found these weapons in Iraq. Material of Dirty Bomb, the reason that biological and nuclear weapons material can be purchased from black market of India and Pakistan. There are possibilities that terrorists can acquire nuclear material or a complete warhead to use it against their targets. The risk of a complete nuclear device falling into the hands of terrorists will cause consternation in the EU. Over the past several years, the prospect of a terrorist group armed with nuclear and biological weapons has frequently been cited as a genuine and overriding threat to the security of Europe. Moreover, there are possibilities that Pakistan, Afghanistan and Africa based extremist and jihadist groups can purchase fissile material in black market or steal it from a military or civilian facility and then use that material to construct an improvised nuclear device.

The question of whether African and South Asian Muslim extremist groups pose a security threat to France which is complex and multifaceted. Extremist groups, such as Tablighi Jamaat, Lashkare-e-Toiba, Taliban, the ISIS and France based African groups constitute a great threat to Paris while as mentioned earlier, they can use chemical and biological weapons to inflict huge fatalities on civilian population in major cities and towns. African and South Asian Muslim extremist groups vary widely in their goals, capabilities, and reach. Some may focus primarily on local or regional issues, while others may have a more global agenda that could include targeting France. The French government has implemented various counterterrorism measures to address threats from these groups. The effectiveness of these measures can influence the level of threat these groups pose to France. Nuclear terrorism remains a constant threat to global peace. Access of terrorist organizations to nuclear material is a bigger threat to civilian population. Terrorist groups can gain access to highly enriched uranium or plutonium, because they have the potential to create and detonate an improvised nuclear device.

Information on how to manipulate nuclear material to produce an explosive device—an improvised nuclear device, which would produce a nuclear explosion and a mushroom cloud, or a radiation-dispersal device, which would spread dangerous radioactive material over a substantial area—is now available widely in parts of Europe and South Asia. Pakistan has also been heavily dependent on outside supply for many key direct-and dual-use goods for its nuclear programs. It maintains smuggling networks and entities willing to break supplier country laws to obtain these goods. Many of these illegal imports have been detected and stopped while the Khan Laboratory networks exposed in South East Asia, Africa and Middle East. These illegal procurements have led to investigations and prosecutions in the supplier states, leading to revelations of important details about Pakistan's complex situation to make nuclear explosive materials and nuclear weapons. According to some reports, weapons-grade and weapons-usable nuclear materials have been stolen by terrorist groups from some nuclear sites of Pakistan in 2009 and 2011. Once a crude weapon is in a country, terrorists would transport it in a vehicle to city and then detonate it in a crowded area.

In a democratic state, intelligence and the police play a vital role in strengthening institutions and law and order management. If intelligence is competent, reformed, organized and impartial, its role will be more clear and professional in protecting national security, and its role in combating terrorism and extremism will be more effective. The security sector is responsible for protecting the nation from internal and external threats and the threat of foreign interference in the affairs of the state. Its objective is to maintain peace and stability so that the public institutions can function properly and in accordance with the fundamental principles of a democracy. In order to effectively further their mission, intelligence and policing agencies are often invested with special powers enabling them, for instance, to gather otherwise inaccessible information. The question of how parliament can utilise its legal powers to oversight policing and intelligence agencies, it is clear that parliament is supreme and can monitor function of law enforcement agencies. Thus, while reforming the structure of the political system to increase a parliament's constitutionally given oversight capacities may not always be feasible, in some instances, parliaments can improve their oversight capacities by reforming their own rules.

The important thing is maintaining legislative framework for monitoring system and for managing law enforcement agencies. Such frameworks must be compatible with international obligations and universal human rights. The monitoring powers of parliament viz-a-vize oversight of intelligence agencies and their operations, is a vital component of democratic governance of the security sector. Parliaments have powers and responsibility for shaping public policy and law making. In a democracy, public power comes from the people and the exercise of executive power must, directly or indirectly, be answerable to the representatives of the people. According to European Parliament, oversight is comprised of verifying compliance by security sector actors with general policy and established laws and regulations governing their operation, as well as scrutinising effectiveness and efficiency of security sector institutions. Whereas the accountability of the intelligence services to the Executive and Parliament is strong, the accountability of the services and the intelligence oversight and control bodies to the public is less strong. Expert Dick Toornstra (Parliamentary oversight of the security sector. OPPD Publisher: An OPPD publication on topical parliamentary affairs. European Parliament–OPPD, 2013) in his research paper for European Parliament noted practices in exercising parliamentary oversight of intelligence:

"Best practices in exercising parliamentary oversight of the security sector are not born overnight. Rather, they constitute the accumulated wisdom from more than 150 years' experience in trying to establish, and refine, the democratic governance of the sword and shield of the state. Starting with the liberal revolutions which introduced parliamentary democracy in most European states from 1848 onwards, the elected representatives of the people and governments have interacted to evolve generally accepted principles and ground rules aimed at safeguarding the responsiveness of the security sector to the views of the people. This interaction has by no means been a straightforward process: more often than not, the executive and parliament have had to go through successive contentious rounds before settling on a cooperative relationship based on a clear division of responsibilities and agreed patterns of accountability. This evolution has culminated into today's broad consensus that real security cannot be achieved without the acceptance of democratic values and institutions and the observance of fundamental human rights - the notion of democratic security. Even so, today's fast changing security environment leaves no room for complacency: as security services are constantly challenged to respond to new demands, so are the rules and practices shaping parliament's prime role in exercising democratic oversight of the overall security sector. For best practices to remain true to their name, they must remain relevant and, therefore, must be adaptable to changing circumstances".[2]

In a democratic state, intelligence and police agencies play crucial roles in maintaining law and order, which is fundamental for the functioning of a democracy. The primary role of police is to prevent and investigate crimes. This ensures a safe and secure environment for citizens to exercise their democratic rights. Police enforce laws, which are democratically enacted. They ensure that everyone adheres to these laws, thereby maintaining social order. Intelligence agencies gather information that is vital for national security. This helps in pre-emptively identifying and mitigating threats that could disrupt societal peace or democratic processes. Both intelligence and police units work to prevent acts of terrorism that can undermine the security and stability of a democracy. Their effectiveness in these roles greatly depends on their adherence to the principles of democracy, such as respect for human rights, rule of law, transparency, and accountability. Misuse of power or lack of accountability in these institutions can lead to erosion of public trust and democratic values. Expert Mr Aidan Wills (Democratic and effective oversight of national security services. Issue paper published by the Council of Europe Commissioner for Human Rights. Council of Europe,. February 2019) in his paper highlighted democratic oversight and its importance for police and intelligence agencies:

"Democratic oversight is important because security services (and related executive departments) provide a public service to and on behalf of the public and therefore elected representatives should be involved in ensuring that this service is provided effectively, efficiently and lawfully. The "democratic" aspect of oversight is primarily achieved through the involvement of parliament, including by: ensuring that national laws provide for comprehensive oversight of security services; allocating the necessary budgetary resources to non-parliamentary oversight institutions; overseeing the work of expert oversight bodies; keeping under review the efficacy of oversight institutions; and conducting both ongoing scrutiny and ad hoc inquiries into security service activity. Most security services have growing capacities to collect, share and receive information and use increasingly complex systems for doing so. Accordingly, recourse to independent technical expertise has become indispensable for effective oversight. Intelligence collection and storage systems have become more complex and their human rights implications cannot easily be assessed without recourse to specialist expertise".[3]

Indeed, a competent and reformed intelligence agency plays a crucial role in combating terrorism, which is a significant challenge for modern societies, including democracies. A competent intelligence agency can effectively gather and analyse data to identify potential terrorist threats before they materialize. This proactive approach is key in preventing attacks. Terrorism often has cross-border elements. Reformed intelligence service can better collaborate with international counterparts, sharing vital information and resources. Competent intelligence agency can develop more effective counterterrorism strategies based on thorough research, analysis, and understanding of terrorist networks and their methods. Terrorism evolves rapidly, with new methods and tactics. Reformed intelligence agency is more adaptable and responsive to these changing threats. The competence and reform of intelligence agencies directly impact their effectiveness in combating terrorism. It's not just about being better equipped but also about being more strategic, adaptable, and respectful of democratic principles and human rights. Research scholar and expert, Franklin De Vrieze (Independent oversight institutions and regulatory agencies, and their relationship to parliament Outline of assessment framework. Westminster Foundation for Democracy, February-2019) in his paper argued that accountability is a vital condition for the effectiveness of intelligence agencies:

"Independence and accountability are both vital conditions for the effectiveness of regulatory agencies, but there is a trade-off between them: too much independence from the Government exposes the agencies to capture by the industries they oversee and regulate, and too little independence exposes the agencies to political interference that runs contrary to the economic and technical fundamentals of the industries or sectors concerned. For instance, a frequent pattern of political interference in some countries is to squeeze these companies by simultaneously raising their production costs, e.g. through overstaffing or staffing with less qualified clients, whilst pressuring these companies to sell goods at a price point below cost, which undermines their long-term financial viability. Moreover, independence depends on the institutional design of the oversight institution or agency (in particular the governing structures and powers), the financial and human resources available, political independence and independence from regulated industries. Accountability can be achieved through a proper system of checks and balances, a set of control instruments (reporting, public consultation and access to information, performance evaluation) and the possibility of judicial appeal. In addition, clearly defined objectives, transparency and public participation can enhance accountability without compromising the institution or agency's independence".[4]

Nuclear trafficking in Europe and South Asia was a key concern while the nuclear black marketing networks of Pakistani generals and some mafia scientists were uncovered in Libya, Syria, Malaysia and Afghanistan. Recent media reports identified Moldovan criminal groups that attempted to smuggle radioactive materials to Daesh in 2015. Analyst and expert, Muhammad Wajeeh, a Research Associate at Department of Development Studies, COMSATS Institute of Information Technology, Abbottabad Pakistan in his research paper (Nuclear Terrorism: A Potential Threat to World's Peace and Security-JSSA Vol II, No. 2), has reviewed a consternating threat of nuclear terrorism in South and Central Asia: "ISIS is believed to have about 90 pounds of low grade uranium (which was seized from Mosul University in Iraq were the invasion of the city in 2014) that can be used in the Dirty Bomb's to create serious panic among the public. In 2015 and 2016, ISIS became the leading high profile jihadist group in Iraq and Syria. Moreover, ISIS carried out attacks in Paris on November 13, 2015, killing 130 civilians and injuring more than 100 people. The ISIS carried out three coordinated suicide attacks."[5]

Terrorist groups will prefer to use biological weapons against their targets with low visibility, and this type of attack can be accomplished from a remote area. Extremists and jihadists could have up to two weeks of undetected operational lead time before local governments caught up with them. Research scholar and writer, Charles D. Ferguson has also spotlighted the same concerns of the international community that if Jihadists used biological weapons against civilian population, the crisis would be much bigger than the present-day Covid-19, States wouldn't be able to defeat the agents used by terrorists. Nuclear and biological weapons experts have also identified the insider help in stealing materials of dirty bombs from a secured facility. In 2015, Pakistan removed 1200 employed from different nuclear sites due to their links with terrorist organizations. They might have deliberately unauthorized transfer by a government official, or a facility custodian, looting during coups or other times of political turmoil. Analyst Charles D. Ferguson in his paper (Assessing Radiological Weapons: Attack Methods and Estimated Effects. Defence against Terrorism Review Vol. 2, No. 2, fall 2009) spotlighted clandestine relationship of terrorist groups with insiders within the government departments:

"The radioactive material in a radiological weapon can come from many sources. Nuclear power plants, research reactor facilities, hospitals, blood banks, universities, food irradiation centres, oil well sites, and shipbuilding and construction sites are many of the major places where radioactive materials are used and stored. Some of these places are more vulnerable than others to terrorists obtaining radioactive material. Of the places listed above, nuclear power plants would probably have the most rigorous security and would have radioactive materials that are too radioactive to handle without thick shielding and too heavy to carry without special equipment. At nuclear power plants, spent nuclear fuel is highly radioactive and could give a lethal radiation dose in a few minutes without adequate shielding. Moreover, a spent nuclear fuel assembly at power plants typically weighs many tons. Spent fuel from research reactors, on the other hand, may not contain nearly as much radioactivity as spent fuel from nuclear power plants because many research reactors operate at power levels much lower than nuclear power plants. Also, a spent fuel assembly at a research reactor can weigh much less than a spent fuel assembly at a power plant and thus might be more susceptible to transport by thieves. Of course, a terrorist group would have to surmount the barrier of finding out where the spent fuel is located within a facility".[6]

The speculation about extremist groups potentially using dirty bombs or nuclear explosive devices is a significant concern in global security discussions. A dirty bomb, or radiological dispersal device, combines conventional explosives with radioactive material. It's designed to scatter dangerous and sub-lethal amounts of radioactive material over a wide area. While the explosion itself might cause casualties, the primary intent of a dirty bomb is to cause panic and disrupt society through the fear of radiation. The actual radiological risk from such a device is typically limited compared to a nuclear explosion, but the psychological and economic impacts can be substantial. These devices are significantly more dangerous than dirty bombs. They involve the use of nuclear reactions to cause massive destruction and loss of life, along with long-term environmental damage. However, the creation of a nuclear explosive device is extremely complex, requiring technical expertise, materials, and technology that are heavily guarded and difficult for non-state actors to acquire. For France, a country with advanced counterterrorism capabilities and nuclear expertise, the threat of extremist groups using these types of devices is a critical security issue. The French intelligence and security services are likely to monitor closely any indications of such threats. France's experience with terrorism, both domestically and internationally, would contribute to its preparedness and response strategies.

The acquisition of radioactive materials for a dirty bomb or the highly enriched uranium or plutonium need for a nuclear device is a significant barrier for extremist groups. Such materials are closely monitored and protected. Nonetheless, the smuggling of radioactive materials remains a concern for global security agencies. While the threat of dirty bombs and nuclear explosive devices is a serious concern for any nation, including France, there are substantial barriers that make the execution of such attacks by extremist groups challenging authority of law enforcement. Continuous vigilance and international cooperation are key to mitigating these threats. The claim about jihadist groups from Central Asia and South Asia and Africa seeking nuclear material in the EU black market to retaliate against French law enforcement is a serious and complex issue. In terms of the jihadist threat, France has been a significant target in Europe due to various factors, including its large Muslim population, and its strong stances on freedom of expression. These factors have sometimes been interpreted by radical Islamist groups as provocations.

However, recent cases of nuclear proliferation and attacks on nuclear installations across the globe have further exacerbated the concern about the threat of nuclear attacks in France cities. The threat of chemical and biological jihad has raised serious questions about the security of European states nuclear and biological weapons. Experts have warned that the Central Asia, Pakistan and Afghanistan based jihadists, and the Taliban pose a great security threat to all European states. Improvised explosive devices and chemical and biological weapons are easily available in Asian and European markets and can be transported to the region through human traffickers. The influx of trained terrorists and extremist groups from several Asian, African and European states has raised concerns that those who sought asylum through fake documents in France could pose a threat to the country. The fear of such attacks still exists in Europe because thousands of European nationals joined ISIS's military campaign in Syria and Iraq. If terrorist groups such as ISIS or Lashkar-e-Tayba and Tablighi Jamaat determine to go nuclear, what will be the security preparations in

Europe to intercept these groups? These and other EU based groups can attempt to manufacture fissile material needed to fuel a nuclear weapon— either highly enriched uranium or plutonium, and then use it. Moreover, there are possibilities that France based extremist and jihadist groups can purchase fissile material in black market or steal it from a military or civilian facility and then use that material to construct an improvised nuclear device. Yet today, with France rising again as a military power, the grim logic of nuclear statecraft is returning.

Chapter 11

Transformation of State Security and Intelligence Services in Poland: A Job Still Unfinished

Agnieszka Gogolewska

Abstract

Since 1989, the Polish intelligence sector has been undergoing a democratic transformation which has turned into a continuous institutional change. In the process, the old communist services were abolished and new ones established in parallel with setting up executive and legislative oversight structures. But while the intelligence institutions and the oversight structures, on the whole, meet democratic standards and do not appear to threaten the constitutional system or citizens' rights in any systemic way, the more recent developments in the sector demonstrate that democracy in Poland has not in fact been consolidated. The state proved incapable of forming any dependable and effective model of control over the security sector in the sense of exercising both political guidance and democratic oversight. The intelligence services and some security institutions continue to enhance their prerogatives in the realm of covert operations, democratic control mechanisms are not sufficiently effective, and the issues of the communist past continue to be a disruptive factor. Under the circumstances, it is hard to single out good practices; rather, one should speak of lessons learned.

Keywords: civil watchdogs, intelligence oversight, judicial control, Poland, post-communist transition, Transformation

The Lonesome Transformation in Poland

After the fall of communist systems in 1989-1990, the reforms of civilian and military security services in the emerging democracies of Central Eastern Europe were imminent. Introducing democratic control was one of the most significant transformation challenges, not the least because the very concept was unfamiliar to politicians and political scientists alike. But while there was abundant literature on the theory and practice of past democratic transformations of civil-military relations, the theory of security sector reform was just emerging, and the post-communist transitions turned to be its main testing ground. In Poland, the post-1989 democratic reforms of the military enjoyed strong external institutional and financial support: lectures by prominent politicians and academics visiting the country, foreign fellowships available to Poles, and networking activities available and funded within the framework of Partnership for Peace throughout the 1990s. Above all, the reforms supported the ultimate political goal—full-fledged membership of Poland in NATO—and the democratic control over armed forces was a *sine qua non*.

No such backing was available to the reformers of post-communist security and intelligence services. The history of security sector reforms could not provide much background knowledge or tools for introducing intelligence oversight. There was no external, NATO-like institution that could propel reforms in anticipation of future political gains. Moreover, the security services had traditionally been the mainstays of communist power, enveloped deep in secrecy and notorious for oppressing opposition activists. More importantly, the fall of communist systems did not immediately lead to the collapse of those secret structures in Poland, nor did it instantly cut off the functionaries from their covert resources. Hence the incumbent democratic governments, still weak and besieged by political and economic problems, were reluctant to move in aggressively and to formally abolish the communist security services in their entirety, fearing possible consequences. The approach to the security sector was initially lenient and took place in several small steps, thus involuntarily laying the foundations for a number of future problems. This cautious approach might have also contributed to the lack of clarity in the institutional design of the sector and power overlaps characterizing the post-communist security and intelligence services in Poland.

Conceptual Problems

Conventionally, there is a clear distinction between intelligence-gathering responsibilities, typical of intelligence services, and policing/law enforcement functions, characteristic for the police, border guards, and customs. This distinction is reflected in the literature on the subject, for example, the toolkit for intelligence oversight published by DCAF.[1]Unfortunately, the Polish civilian services have never even come close to such a clear-cut division of tasks. Despite several conceptual and legislative attempts to clarify the division, the post-communist intelligence services have never let go of their policing and law enforcement prerogatives. Many experts have criticized the lack of clarity in this respect over the years. Both functionaries [2]and academic researchers[3]have stressed overlaps of tasks and powers between the security and intelligence services and pointed to the purely arbitrary distinction drawn between them, lacking conceptual premises.

The duty to gather, analyse and share intelligence is not a distinctive feature of the intelligence sector in Poland since similar duties are performed by several other security institutions in their respective fields. Law enforcement duties cannot be treated as an indicator of the type of service either due to the overlaps and similarities between security and intelligence services. The same is true for the right to carry out covert and intrusive surveillance operations vested in several agencies in Poland.[4]So the fact that any given agency is authorized to interfere covertly with private property or use intrusive surveillance techniques does not place this agency in the intelligence sector in Poland. Since the conceptual lines of division are so blurred, the only way to identify and delineate the intelligence sector is by following the practical approach taken by the executive authorities and reflected in the wording of the laws, both existing and projected. The laws point to five currently existing services as the so-called "special services," i.e., representing the intelligence sector. These are:

1. Internal Security Agency, in Polish Agencja Bezpieczeństwa Wewnętrznego, ABW, i.e., civilian counterintelligence;

2. Foreign Intelligence Agency, in Polish Agencja Wywiadu, AW, responsible for the information gathering abroad;

3. Central Anticorruption Bureau, in Polish Centralne Biuro Antykorupcyjne, CBA, the main organ for monitoring the implementation and effectiveness of countercorruption regulations and investigating breaches of legal provisions in that respect, mostly (but not exclusively) concerning companies and public entities or state functionaries;

4. Military Counterintelligence Service, in Polish Służba Kontrwywiadu Wojskowego, SKW, responsible for counterintelligence in Poland and protection of military operations abroad;

5. Military Intelligence Service, in Polish Służba Kontrwywiadu Wojskowego, SWW, in charge of military intelligence and covert operations abroad.

Security and Intelligence Sector under the Communist Regime

In terms of institutional design, the security and intelligence sector in the final stage of the communist regime in Poland was relatively simple. The civilian part was composed of the main police force called People's Militia (Milicja Obywatelska, MO), the intelligence service called Security Service (Służba Bezpieczeństwa, SB) and several minor police-like formations with anti-riot functions. Legally, all those services were covered by one bill [5] and were subordinated to the Minister of Interior. However, the real subordination was along political lines, as the Minister of Interior was always a high-ranking member of the Central Committee of the Communist Party. In the late 1980s, the Security Service (SB) numbered 24.3 thousand functionaries and had over 90 000 agents registered as secret operatives. SB was tasked with safeguarding the internal and external security of the state; however, the term 'security' was mainly understood in terms of political compliance. Therefore, the Service was primarily engaged in surveillance of the political opposition both in Poland and abroad.

Regarding the military sector, the post-WW2 military intelligence was organized into separate structures within the MoD. Before 1990, by order of the Minister of National Defense of November 15, 1951, the military intelligence was embedded in the Ministry of National Defense structures as the Second Directorate of the General Staff of the Armed Forces, subordinated to the Minister. Military intelligence officers were part of the repressive political apparatus of the communist regime. However, their focus was more abroad, especially concerning the Vatican policies and opposition emigrants in Europe. Additionally, military intelligence was a statutory intermediary in the Polish foreign arms trade and controlled the state-owned company CENZIN, tasked with the sales of armaments. It was a highly profitable source of operational funds and one that often bordered on criminal activity. Additionally, military intelligence operatives were often placed in management positions in Polish foreign trade companies, which resulted in several criminal affairs in the later period of transformation. From 1957 until 1990, counterintelligence was embedded in the Ministry as the Military Internal Service, responsible for counterintelligence but also for political compliance of the military and hence was much despised by the members of the Armed Forces at large. There was no separate legal bill to regulate its functioning; instead, their structures and functions were regulated by the minister's internal orders.[6]

Transformation of the Civilian Intelligence Services

Reforms of civilian and military intelligence services in post-communist Poland did not follow the same paths. In the civilian sector, the old communist Security Service SB managed to survive the first (partially) free elections of June 4, 1989, and the inception of the non-communist government. Former members of the opposition were dragging their feet in taking over the Ministry of Internal Affairs. Initially, the Ministry of Internal Affairs remained within the purview of the high-ranking communist regime representative, General Czeslaw Kiszczak, and his officers, while the security service SB continued to function largely unhindered. Consequently, the first reorganization of communist security services was introduced by the very communist general and mainly served to facilitate the process of concealing the crimes and abuses of the communist service from the new government.

The first non-communist Deputy Minister of Internal Affairs, Krzysztof Kozłowski, was appointed on March 7, 1990. Ultimately, the last communist representatives left the government in July 1990. Only then the opposition really took over internal affairs and initiated the post-communist transformation in the civilian security sector. Unfortunately, the timespan between the creation of the non-communist government in the autumn of 1989 and the takeover of the internal affairs in March 1990 gave the communist functionaries plenty of time to destroy or remove to private lockers a considerable part of the archives. It was a reason why many former opposition activists claimed that the communist security services were offered impunity which became a source of many political troubles in the years to come. At the outset of reforms, there were plans to establish a parliamentary commission to investigate the communist Security Service crimes and make them known to the public. Such an extraordinary parliamentary commission was set up early on after the free elections of June 1989, perhaps too early, because it failed to deliver substantial results.

Milestone # 1: Bill of April 6, 1990, Creating the First Post-communist Civilian Intelligence Service

On April 6, 1990, the parliament adopted a ground-breaking set of reforms initiating the democratic transition of the civilian security sector. The package included the following acts:

- Bill on the Post of the Minister of Internal Affairs;

- Bill on the Police;

- Bill on the Office for State Protection, in Polish *Urząd Ochrony Państwa*, UOP.

Based on art. 131 of the Bill on the Creation of the State Protection Office *UOP*,[7] the old Security Service SB was formally abolished, and all former functionaries were discharged from service. Subsequently, based on Resolution # 69 of the Council of Ministers (government) of May 21, 1990, the former members of the communist services could apply for work in the newly created Office for State Protection UOP or the new Police, pending a positive outcome of the vetting process by the special governmental commission.[8] The process is commonly known as "the verification of the functionaries of the Security Service *SB*." All former officers were given the application forms and had to submit their applications until July 04, 1990. Only officers under 55 were eligible to apply; anybody over 55 was automatically retired. The same verification procedure was mandatory for the candidates to the Office for State Protection and the Police. It was a matter of an individual decision whether the candidate applied. The commission declined applications in cases when an officer was suspected of brutal surveillance and persecution of former opposition activists, a member of the senior leadership of the Security Service before 1989, or known for alcohol abuse. Anybody who was disqualified could first appeal to the same regional commission that took the original decision and then to the Central Vetting Commission. The subsequent decision of the latter was final and binding.

The verification was conducted in July and August 1990. All but 14, 5 thousand former functionaries of the communist Security Service SB submitted their applications and underwent the vetting procedure. This number amounted to approximately 60% of the former staff of the communist service. Of those, 10,439 people were assessed positively. It is worth noting that only 8,681 officers were positively appraised at the first round of verification; the remaining staff was qualified as a result of their successful appeal. Importantly, a positive decision of the commission did not equal automatic acceptance in any of the new services. The ultimate decision was to be taken by the respective regional commanders of the Police and the Chief of UOP.[9] As consequent events demonstrated, many of those officers should not have been positively appraised. The rather weak hold of the former opposition on the Ministry of Interior, their limited knowledge of the field or the archives, and the haste could all account for the imperfect vetting process. Therefore, it is not surprising that the process was criticized as insufficient in delivering justice.[10] The acceptance of so many former regime officers into the new service was also the primary source of distrust that many former opposition activists demonstrated towards the post-communist intelligence sector, although often the accusations were not supported by documentation.[11]

The First Post-communist Intelligence Service UOP, 1990-1996

The new Office for State Protection UOP was formed within three months following the passing of the founding Bill of April 6, 1990. By the decision of the Minister of Internal Affairs, UOP initially numbered 5,522 officers, organized in one central structure in Warsaw and 14 regional offices. The Office for State Protection was subordinate directly to the Minister of Internal Affairs and was on a par with other security services, such as the Police, Border Guards, Firefighters, or Office for Government Protection. It was a two-in-one structure – UOP was responsible for intelligence and counterintelligence functions, and the division of duties was purely internal. The Chief of Service was appointed by the Prime Minister upon the motion of the Minister of Internal Affairs and following the positive opinion from the Political Advisory Committee to the Minister of Interior. Effectively, the Chief of UOP was one of the closest collaborators of the Minister, and any vital information would be passed on via the Minister to the Prime Minister and elsewhere. The Bill of April 6, 1990, defined the scope of duties of the new intelligence service in a rather traditional way, protecting state security and the constitutional order. More specifically, UOP was responsible for:

- surveillance and monitoring of threats to national security, defense, sovereignty, integrity, and international position of the state;

- preventing and detecting crimes of espionage and terrorism and other crimes against the state security as well as prosecuting the perpetrators;

- protection of classified information, monitoring as well as preventing any breaches of such information;

- gathering intelligence and preparing analyses essential for national security and sharing information with the highest state authorities and the central administration.[12]

The first intelligence service in democratic Poland can be defined as essentially a counterintelligence service with a mixture of intelligence gathering and policing functions, working in new structures but banking on knowledge and, to a degree, on procedures derived from the old communist service.[13]The founders of the democratic intelligence service lacked the knowledge or experience to propagate intelligence-gathering missions or even to aptly use and share the acquired intelligence.[14]Article 11 of the Bill on UOP only stated that the Office is under obligation to inform the Prime Minister and the Minister of Internal Affairs about any issues essential to the security of the state.

Milestone # 2: Reorganization of the Office for State Protection, 1996. Nascent Executive Oversight of the Intelligence Service

In 1996 came the first democratic reform of the security sector in post-communist Poland. The reform was the corollary of the changing security situation both in Poland and in the region. With the fall of the last communist regimes in Central and Eastern Europe and the onset of technological revolution came the era of organized crime transcending borders and challenging traditional security structures. Another incentive for the change was purely internal. It concerned the growing power of the Ministry of Internal Affairs, which was quickly becoming a supreme security institution with the powers of control over all the law enforcement, police, and intelligence services and hardly controllable itself.

Based on those premises, the parliament introduced a package of legislative changes. Regarding the Office of State Protection UOP, three important changes were introduced.[15] First, its scope of duties and responsibilities was substantially amended. Secondly, the service became directly subordinated to the Prime Minister. The Chief of UOP was now accountable to the Prime Minister. Last but not least, to aid the supervisory function of the Prime Minister, a special advisory and consulting institution was established within the structure of the Prime Minister's Office, called "College for Intelligence and Security Services."[16] This was the first such institution dedicated to the oversight of the intelligence sector in Poland. Despite its inherent limitations and deeply political character, it contributed to the development of executive oversight practice in Poland. In the aftermath of the legislative change, the responsibilities of the Office of State Protection shifted further away from classic intelligence-gathering towards investigative and counterterrorist functions, keeping intact the counterintelligence and classified information protection duties. A number of new investigative functions were added to the scope of duties of UOP in the field of economic crimes, adding to the already existing overlap between the Police, undergoing similar reforms at that time.[17] Namely, the reformed UOP was now responsible for:

- conducting reconnaissance and countering threats to national security, defense, sovereignty, integrity, and the international position of the state;

- preventing, countering, and disrupting acts of espionage and terrorism;

- preventing, detecting, and investigating economic crimes, including corruption, and prosecuting their perpetrators;

- conducting surveillance, investigating, and countering transnational crimes, including the illegal production, possession, and sale of weapons, ammunition and explosives, narcotics, psychotropic drugs, and nuclear and radioactive materials and prosecuting their perpetrators;

- protection of classified information, including encryption of classified and sensitive information, exchanged between governmental institutions;

- information and analyses.

In the aftermath of the changes, the Office started to widely employ covert methods of surveillance, investigation, interception of communication, etc. Also, after 1996 UOP was undergoing constant internal structural changes.[18] The seemingly never-ending internal transformations were accompanied by personnel reassignments and relocations and were perceived by most intelligence officers as disruptive to professional conduct.

Milestone # 3: Dissolution of the Office for State Protection UOP and Establishment of Separate Civilian Intelligence and Counterintelligence Agencies

The last few years of the workings of the Office for State Protection were wrought with controversies and marked by increasing politicization of the service. The biggest scandal came at the end of 1995, when the then Chief of UOP, Andrzej Milczanowski, gave a speech at the Lower Chamber of the Parliament (Sejm) and publicly accused the Prime Minister in office, Mr. Józef Oleksy, of being the Russian spy nicknamed Olin. A huge political scandal followed, with Mr. Oleksy stepping down (though not immediately). Still, the Prime Minister denied being the spy and a subsequent investigation failed to produce unquestionable evidence of such activities.[19] The Olin scandal instilled deep distrust of UOP in post-communist political forces. Another major reform of the intelligence sector followed the scandal. In 2001, the post-communist coalition won the election and formed a Government. Subsequently, on May 24, 2002, the parliament adopted the new Bill on the creation of the Internal Security Agency, ABW and the Intelligence Agency AW.[20] Thus, the Office for State Protection UOP was by a counterintelligence service (ABW) and the entirely new foreign intelligence service (AW). In theory, the goal was to separate counterintelligence and internal security duties from foreign intelligence. Hence ABW was to be the main institution responsible for the protection of the internal security and constitutional order in Poland. Its range of activities was very similar to that of its predecessor UOP:

- protection of national integrity, sovereignty, and independence, and countering threats to national defines;

- detection, surveillance, and countering the threats of espionage and terrorism;

- detection, reconnaissance, and countering economic crimes;

- surveillance and investigation of acts of corruption by public functionaries, posing a threat to national security;

- investigation and prevention of illegal sales of weapons and ammunition, the proliferation of WMD, drugs, and transnational crimes of similar nature;

- protection of classifies information;

- gathering and analysing information vital for protecting internal security and constitutional order and sharing it with relevant government institutions.

The new Intelligence Agency numbered 1,000 people and was designed as an intelligence service of a more traditional outlook, tasked with the protection of external security of the state and gathering, analysing, and sharing intelligence with relevant institutions on issues essential to the national security and international position of Poland as well as its economic and defense potential. Further to this, the AW was responsible for:

- reconnaissance of external threats to the sovereignty, integrity, and security of the state;

- protection of diplomats, diplomatic institutions, and Polish representatives working abroad from the activities of foreign intelligence services;

- provision of encrypted communication between Polish diplomatic institutions abroad and relevant institutions in Poland;

- reconnaissance of international terrorism and transnational organized crime;

- reconnaissance and countering of illegal international sales of weapons, ammunition, WMD, drugs, etc.;

- gathering of intelligence on international hot spots, conflicts, and crises abroad that may affect national security;

- electronic counterintelligence.

Both newly created services were subordinated directly to the Prime Minister. However, the change aimed not only to reform the scope of duties and prerogatives of the civilian intelligence sector but, perhaps, and equally importantly, it was a political act of retaliation against the now-defunct UOP post-communist politicians perceived as inimical and prejudiced. Soon after the new Bill came in force, the newly appointed Chief of ABW, Andrzej Barcikowski, hastily discharged 420 former UOP officers.[21] The redundancies were mainly for political reasons.

The final act of the intelligence sector reform of 2002 took place four years later under the successor right-wing government with the creation of the third and so far last civilian intelligence service, the Central Anticorruption Bureau (in Polish, *Centralne Biuro Antykorupcyjne, CBA*). The law was adopted on June 9, 2006.[22] CBA is responsible for monitoring, surveillance, detection, investigation, and countering corruption and bribery among public functionaries (whose list has constantly been growing since then) and for investigating and countering economic crimes that may cause substantial financial loss to the State Treasury, local government budgets or public finances. In parallel, those duties were withdrawn from *ABW*, albeit not completely. CBA was created in a form resembling a police force, without the internal system of ranks typical for other services, with the police-like investigative and covert surveillance powers, and with the type of mission that would invite controversies in any democracy due to its potential edge against opposition parties. It numbers slightly over 800 functionaries, mostly deriving from the Police or investigative directorates of ABW.[23] Not surprisingly, it was not long before such controversial operations were made known to the public in the form of scandalous, covert operation against former President Aleksander Kwasniewski (unsuccessfully) aimed at detection of his secret funds, as well as arresting the opposition party local government politician Beata Sawicka who was later acquitted of charges by the court.

Prospective Milestone # 4: Projected Reform of the Civilian Intelligence Services Sector, 2018

Despite seemingly never-ending reforms, politicians continue to express their dissatisfaction with the intelligence services in Poland. With the radical right-wing government now in power in Poland, the next round of reform was announced. The government adopted the project for an amended bill on ABW and AW to transform the sector again.[24]

Paradoxically, in organizational terms, the project partially puts the sector back into the 1990s, as it plans to subordinate the Internal Security Service ABW back to the Minister of Internal Affairs. The reform will also disrupt the institutional design of the intelligence sector as the Intelligence Agency AW will continue to be subordinated directly to the Prime Minister. It is not clear at the moment where the Central Anticorruption Bureau CBA would go. Furthermore, the College for Special and Intelligence Services will be abolished, and the new Committee of the Council of Ministers (i.e., the Government) for the Security of the State will be created to replace the College. It will have a similar composition and advisory role as the College; however, its controlling powers will be more limited. Also, given the projected law, the overlap in the scope of duties of services will only grow. According to the project, ABW will be in charge of investigating financial/ corruption crimes exceeding 16 mln PLN (3.8 mln Euro). Effectively, CBA will be reduced to investigating lesser corruption and financial crimes, below the 16 mln PLN threshold. Furthermore, ABW will be assigned to pursue the most serious economic crimes, acts of organized crime, illegal sales of drugs, weapons, and WMD proliferation. Those activities should be carried out in coordination with the Police and other security institutions. At the same time, lesser crimes in this domain will be passed over to CBA, the Police, and the remaining institutions of the security sector.

Transformation of the Military Intelligence Sector

The reform of military services took a different path. The military counterintelligence structures were disbanded by the order of the Minister of National Defence on April 22, 1990. Based on the structures of the

Second Directorate of General Staff and three directorates of the former Internal Military Service, the new military intelligence was formed, first in the form of a new Directorate of Intelligence and Counterintelligence embedded in the General Staff by the Order on July 27, 1990. Then, on July 22, 1991, the new Inspectorate of Military Intelligence Services was created. In terms of legal regulations, until August 2003, the Inspectorate was legally based on Article 15 of the amended Law on universal military service.[25]The Inspectorate was subordinated to the Minister of National Defense (except for the period 1994-1995, when it was under the Chief of the General Staff). However, it was not until July 9, 2003, that the separate Bill on Military Intelligence Services [26]was adopted. According to the Bill, the Military Intelligence was responsible for tactical and reconnaissance operations that would provide intelligence on defines planning, the organization, armaments, and technology of foreign armies, as well as for the tasks in the field of military counterintelligence and the protection of classified information in international activities of the Polish Armed Forces.

The Military Intelligence Services (Wojskowe Służby Informacyjne, WSI) were strongly criticized because they never underwent any vetting procedures, even to the limited extent found in the civilian sector.[27]Instead, the Service was formed as a result of internal reorganization. But while it is true that military intelligence WSI did not experience any institutional verification of the personnel, certain informal, internal vetting procedures had been implemented during the first transformation of 1990. According to various sources,[28]around 1,000 officers were discharged from service or left voluntarily. This amounted to approximately 40 % of the original personnel strength. Further, about 70 % of the former officers in commanding positions either left or were discharged even before the new military intelligence WSI was formed. Still, from the formal point of view, the post-communist service was essentially a simple continuation of the former communist service, burdened with either undesirable people or practices from the past. The military intelligence was never fully trusted by the post-Solidarity governments, despite the apparent need for their professional involvement with the deployment of Polish troops in Iraq and Afghanistan. When the right-wing Government took office in 2005, the dissolution of WSI was imminent. The overwhelming majority of 367 MPs (out of 460) adopted the presidential legislative project to dissolve the existing Military Intelligence Services WSI and form two new services. Only 44 MPs from the post-communist party opposed the bill. The new law was adopted on June 9, 2006,[29] providing for:

- dissolution of the Military Intelligence Services WSI by September 30, 2006;

- creation of the Liquidation Committee led by the right-wing politician Antoni Macierewicz;

- formation of two new military services replacing WSI: Military Intelligence Service *SWW and Military Counterintelligence Service SKW*.

The professionalism of the new military services was often questioned as the recruitment was largely closed to any seasoned professionals. At the same time, in February 2007, the Liquidation Commission, headed by Macierewicz, published a report in which the former Military Intelligence Service WSI was declared a criminal organization, alienated from the intelligence sector, engaged in illegal operations, and evading civilian control. The report claimed that Russian agents saturated WSI throughout the 1990s, and the Polish military intelligence service was fully aware of the fact and tolerated the agents. The so-called Macierewicz's second list was subsequently made public and proved to be highly disruptive to polish military intelligence. It revealed its structures and working methods and, worse still, published the non-verified and error-strewn list of secret agents of the communist military intelligence, many of them still active many years later. This action resulted in the weakening of Polish military intelligence for many years to come, libel suits from the unjustly accused (most won in courts), and, worst perhaps, dismantling the counterintelligence protection of Polish soldiers on missions in Iraq and Afghanistan.[30] The Minister of National Defense Radosław Sikorski initially demanded the instant dismissal of Antoni Macierewicz from his subsequent position of the Chief of Military Counterintelligence. When Prime Minister Jarosław Kaczyński refused, Sikorski himself resigned.

Democratic Oversight of Intelligence Services

As any nascent democracy, Poland experienced difficulties in establishing democratic oversight of the security sector. The oversight institutions have been established in Poland, but the control mechanisms have never been properly consolidated. On the contrary, since the transformation of 2002, the civilian intelligence sector has managed to increase its independence and decrease the degree of democratic oversight, among other things, taking full advantage of European antiterrorist directives but also fostering informal ties with political parties.

Legislative Oversight

The legislative oversight is carried out mainly by the Parliamentary Commission for Intelligence Services. Its composition and prerogatives are regulated by the Rules of Procedure of the Sejm [31](lower chamber of the Polish parliament). The Commission's role is mainly to scrutinize the most important documents pertaining to intelligence sector institutions and their operations and give opinions. Among the documents, routinely scrutinized by the Commission, are projects of relevant legislative acts, guidelines for annual activities of the services prepared by the Prime Minister and Minister of Defense for civilian and military services respectively, annual plans of service activities and subsequent annual reports, and last but not least, projected state budgets in the part related to the intelligence and reports on the execution of those budgets. The Commission is also to be informed and consulted on candidatures for chiefs of the intelligence services and the deputies. It gives an opinion in the case of any planned dismissal. It merits a mention that while the issuance of the formal opinion from the Commission is a necessary condition for taking further steps in the legislative or executive processes pertaining to the intelligence organizations (approving laws, budgets, appointments, or dismissals), it is not, however, necessary to acquire a positive opinion from the parliamentary Commission for the legislature or the executive to go ahead with the scheme.

The Commission is entitled to demand complete information or relevant documents from the services, particularly if the MPs acquire information about possible irregularities in the service operations. There is a caveat here, however, which may hinder effective control. According to the Law on the protection of classified information, all the MPs (with the sole exception of chairpersons of both chambers of the parliament) have to obtain personal security clearances to gain access to classified information. The screening procedure is carried out and the clearances are issued (and possibly revoked) by the Internal Security Service ABW. The whole process of issuance is obscure, and the appeal procedure complicated (Prime Minister, then the courts), which leaves ABW an option to deny the clearance or revoke it if any MP is particularly 'difficult' from the point of view of the intelligence officers. There were such cases in the past concerning opposition politicians. One such case involves Zbigniew Wasserman, who subsequently became Minister-Coordinator of Intelligence Services in 2005 but had been earlier denied security clearance while being a member of the parliamentary opposition.

Another potential impediment to effective legislative oversight is that the Commission always has a majority of governing party representatives. As a result, the MPs are usually reluctant to hold the executive branch to account and seldom issue controversial opinions. For example, the only registered activity of the Commission in 2018 was the positive opinion on dismissals of previous and appointments of new chiefs of intelligence services following the Prime Minister's decision to change the heads of services. The register of 2017 activities looks similar. Furthermore, the upcoming reform of civilian intelligence services planned by the present government was not discussed in the documents processed by the Commission. The Commission's activities are limited to statutory duties and respond to the demands of the executive, without playing any role in substantial monitoring of the operations of the services and striving to correct the system of oversight. The weakness of the legislative oversight was vividly demonstrated in the dramatic events related to the 2007 botched ABW operation of arresting Barbara Blida, former minister of construction in the preceding government, suspected of corruption. The operation ended with Mrs. Blida committing suicide in the course of arrest by shooting herself in her own bathroom. Subsequent investigations by many institutions showed that the arrest was politically motivated and that the operation was ill-prepared, and the ABW officers did not follow the procedures. At the end of 2007, a special parliamentary investigative commission was created to investigate the case. Yet, despite the change of government in 2008 and three more years of existence, it never came to any substantial conclusions.[32]

Executive Oversight

The executive leg of intelligence oversight is represented by the institution originally established in 2002. Its composition and rules of functioning were defined by the Resolution of the Prime Minister of July 2002.[33] Uncharacteristically for the Polish political scene, the College's institutional design was left largely intact until 2018, when the Government revealed plans for its abolition. The College is an institution chaired by the Prime Minister and includes the following members of the Government:

- Minister of Internal Affairs
- Minister of Foreign Affairs
- Minister of National Defense
- Minister of Finance

- Head of National Security Office (presidential institution)

- Minister Coordinator of Intelligence Services (if appointed).

Chiefs of the intelligence services (ABW, AW, CBA, SWW, SKW) participate in the meetings, but the Bill makes it clear that they are not members of the College. The Chairperson of the parliamentary Commission for Intelligence Services is also entitled to participate in College sessions and is notified for each upcoming meeting. The College's role is to give opinions on all documents pertaining to intelligence, starting with appointment and dismissal of the chiefs of services, through projects of legislative acts, budgets, guidelines for annual planning, annual plans and reports, to the issues of coordination of intelligence activities with any other security service. The College also commonly puts current matters on the agenda, taking advantage of the obligatory presence of all relevant decision-makers in the field of state security. If used properly, the College could become a powerful instrument of intelligence control and might facilitate the sharing of intelligence with government members. However, it did not become a robust oversight institution, primarily due to the lack of focus on effective oversight and sharing intelligence among the politicians.

The composition of the College makes it an appropriate body for substantive discussion on important matters, and the presence of the Prime Minister and all the chiefs of services facilitates control and coordination. The College meetings are classified and take place in the special safe room in the Prime Minister's Office, protected from interception of any kind. Over the years, a minor information leak to the media occurred only once, making it an impressive record compared to the parliament or other government institutions. Therefore, the idea that a new round of intelligence reform is coming, the College will be disbanded, and some new body created is rather disturbing. Finally, there is the position of the Minister-Coordinator of Special Services. However, his appointment is optional for any Prime Minister. Such a minister without portfolio (or recently just undersecretary of state) does not have independent powers or an institutional place of his own in the government structures. His actual importance strongly depends on the support of the Prime Minister. For that reason, he is hardly a controlling authority; rather, he serves as a liaison between the services and the government and is used as an expert in internal government workings.

Judicial Control/ Civil Watchdogs

In discussions on intelligence oversight in Poland, one cannot but notice the weakness of the judicial control of the intelligence sector and the scarcity of citizens' watchdogs. The judicial branch does not have any specially designated role in the systemic oversight of the intelligence sector. Similarly, there is no specified procedure for complaints against the services. Often, the court proceedings are stalled by problems with access to classified information or lack of experience with security issues on the part of the judges. There is a degree of irony in the fact that it was the judicial sector, after all, that managed to curtail the growing powers of the intelligence services to carry out covert, intrusive operations. That was achieved against the background of the utterly inert executive and legislative oversight bodies. The Constitutional Tribunal abolished some controversial prerogatives of the security and intelligence services and forced legislative changes in this respect.[34] More information on that subject can be found in the subsequent section discussing the operational powers of intelligence services.

Regarding the civil watchdogs, it seems that, after the initial extensive development of civil society in the 1990s, the process has stalled, and civil activities in the security area are now few and limited. That does not mean, however, that they are non-existent. At least two professional watchdogs carry our systematic oversight of legislative regulations and covert activities of the intelligence and security services and deliver public reports. These are the Panoptykon Foundation [35]and the Helsinki Foundation for Human Rights,[36] both actively monitoring the sector and providing invaluable insights.

The Problem of Covert Surveillance Powers

At the heart of the problems with democratic control of the intelligence sector in Poland lies the unsolved and unregulated issue of how to control the use of covert surveillance and intrusive investigative methods without jeopardizing the assets and putting intelligence operations at risk. From the start of the democratic transformation in Poland, the mix of police, law enforcement, and intelligence-gathering powers vested in the intelligence services opened the way to their heavy reliance on using covert, intrusive methods of investigation and surveillance. With time, this reliance only grew stronger. Since the early 1990s, several legislative attempts were made to regulate the covert powers of investigation and surveillance by a separate bill, the disclosure of such information, and its ultimate disposal. The first semi-complete legislative project was created in 2008 by the parliament. It included the definition of covert surveillance and the investigations linked to the goal of such activities.[37]The works on that project were abandoned though, and the same happened to several other attempts. Consequently, the term "covert surveillance and investigation activities" [38]has been widely used in several legislative acts pertaining to security and intelligence services and their activities. Yet, none of them gives a legal definition or sets limitations to such activities. As a result, the scope of powers and the constraints have been defined by the services' practice and their internal regulations.[39]

The enhancement of covert powers began in 2003 when Polish intelligence services (and the Police) obtained the right to request telecommunications data (granted by the law on the telecommunications sector, not the intelligence bills). Paradoxically, the arrival of the European directive on data retention [40]and its incorporation into the Polish law gave the services almost unlimited and uncontrolled access to telecommunication data and provided a strong incentive to augment their powers of direct surveillance. In parallel, it limited the opportunities for control over the secret intelligence operations. But while the European directive aimed at countering terrorism, the Polish law did not provide for such limitation with regard to requesting telecom data. Effectively, the right to obtain individual telecommunication data was granted to the intelligence services unreservedly, without imposing any restriction or additional requirement for justification. Before long, it became the favorite method of any investigation carried out by the intelligence services (or the Police, for that matter), without considering its proportionality to the potential threat or a requirement that it be a genuine threat to national security. In the record year 2014, the services asked for disclosure of telecommunication data 2.35 million times.[41]

The indiscriminate right to demand telecommunication data helped deepen the intelligence services' secretive culture and weaken external controls. The services were reluctant to disclose even the exact number of requests for information they lodged with telecom providers within a given period. In 2009, the Helsinki Foundation for Human Rights in Warsaw asked ABW for such statistics for 2002-2009, and it was denied information. The Internal Security Service ABW claimed that the information was secret and could not be disclosed as public information. The Foundation appealed to the administrative court against the decision. After several years of going back and forth, the court ruled in favor of the Foundation. However, the law had changed in the meantime, and the whole case could not be used for further reference or as a case of good practices.[42]

Looking back at the development of the intelligence sector's covert powers between 2003 and 2018, one can notice that, despite being better positioned to exert scrutiny and oversight, neither legislative nor executive institutions played any part in curtailing the growing independence and secrecy of the services. Instead, the judicial sector and some civic foundations played that role, proving to be more effective than designated control bodies. In 2005, acting on the motion of the Ombudsperson, the Constitutional Tribunal declared several regulations in the Law on Police unconstitutional. More specifically, the Tribunal abolished the articles that permitted the situation when data acquired by the services without prior judicial authorization (in the course of covert operations) could be stored indefinitely and could be used as legally sanctioned evidence in the criminal court proceedings. The corollary of the sentence was the amendment of legal regulations in all relevant bills, including the laws on the intelligence sector.[43]The second round of legal changes limited the covert powers of the services concerning the indiscriminate and disproportionate use of telecommunication data by the security and intelligence sector. Finally, on July 30, 2014, the Constitutional Tribunal, again acting on the motion of the Ombudsperson and several civil watchdogs, declared those regulations unconstitutional and allowed 18 months to make the relevant laws compliant with the Constitution. Unfortunately, the sentence did not indicate how precisely the legal regulations should be changed, leaving the problem entirely to the discretion of the politicians.

Ultimately, the parliament passed a separate bill, dealing collectively with the required amendments in relevant bills on all the security and intelligence services authorized to carry our covert activities. The Bill, adopted on January 15, 2015,[44] was immediately nicknamed "The Surveillance Bill" as it did more harm than good to curb the services' appetite for personal data acquisition. In the common opinion of watchdogs and independent experts, in fact, the new law facilitated the access of the services to certain categories of data while further diminishing the transparency of their covert activities. Specifically, in striving to regulate the data acquisition processes, the new Bill introduced a new category of data that can be disclosed to the services, namely the data on the use of the internet by individuals. Even more, if any intelligence service concluded an agreement to that effect with the internet service provider, the data will be disclosed through a dedicated link without even the provider knowing the content of the data disclosed.

Previously such arrangements were only possible with telecommunication companies; now, the security and intelligence sector won additional powers and further diminished oversight. The purpose of obtaining such data has been defined very widely in the new law as being in connection with "prevention and investigation of criminal acts as well as in order to save the life or health of natural persons." The Bill did establish some judicial control over acquiring such data, but the control is retrospective, information aggregated, and the present law does not provide any measures to stop such process before it happens. It is also practically impossible to judge whether the data was acquired in connection with legally authorized causes for such request, or it was legally dubious, as the new law allows for the gathering of data on the "just in case" basis, previously not allowed with the telecommunication data.[45]

In brief, one may say that intelligence services in Poland, supported by politicians, were very proficient in using the European directives aimed at improving the efficiency of counterterrorist activities in order to increase their covert surveillance and investigatory powers beyond justifiable levels—Poland not being precisely the terrorist hub of Europe—and to limit the effective oversight from any external institutions. Sadly, such an approach to European directives seems like a Polish 'trademark.' When the EU was debating the data retention directive, Poland postulated 15 years period of data retention, the longest proposed by any EU country. When the PNR Directive [46]came into force, it was incorporated into Polish national law in an all-inclusive manner so that the PNR regulations also cover domestic flights. Part of the fault may lie with the European legislators who never included any provisions for obligatory national checks on the data acquisition, allowing for national incorporation of the regulations in the manner exceeding the original cause of action. But more importantly, the situation is blatant proof of the weakness of all the state oversight and control institutions and their apparent inability to counter the increasing secrecy of intelligence services. To dot the 'i', the case of the so-called Police directive [47]should be mentioned here. This directive is supposed to provide a degree of protection of natural persons from excessive personal data processing practices. Yet, it is clear that the Polish government is dragging its feet in preparing the legislative regulations to adopt it to national law[48]

Tentative Conclusions in Lieu of Good Practices

Looking back at the history of democratic transformations of the intelligence sector in Poland, it is difficult to point to practices that had proved unequivocally successful in the course of reforms. Rather, it is the case for lessons learned, which may help with recommendations for avoiding certain mistakes and achieving higher success with less cost in the future. Dealing with the communist past of the services and vetting former communist officers appears to be the most important and most disruptive issue throughout the history of the post-communist transformation of intelligence. In post-1989 Poland, there were three options for dealing with the past: 1) the policy of "thick line," proposed by the first post-communist Prime Minister Tadeusz Mazowiecki and offering to close the past accounts on day one and never look back; 2) the so-called "zero option," consisting in getting rid of all the former functionaries of the communist regime and starting new services from scratch; and 3) the option of central vetting of former officers thus limiting the access of officers of the old regime to the new services. Each option had (and still has, for that matter) its supporters and opponents among the politicians. However, the problem was that each option was applied partially and to a limited extent in different places. There was never a binding decision taken by any government to apply one of those options in its entirety and end the discussion. Consequently, the debate on historical injustices is still ongoing. Politicians from the first post-communist government are accused of betraying the nation. The subsequent rounds of reforms of the intelligence sector always have had a backdrop of historical resentments. Those unsealed historical accounts have been partly the reason for the recurrent waves of institutional transformations of the services, which in the long run contributed to the politicization of the sector, had an adverse effect on the officers' professionalism, and hampered the relations between the politicians and the functionaries.

Secondly, the democratic intelligence sector in Poland has not been formed along any conceptual lines. Rather, it was affected by the existing security situation and current political priorities, combined with the traditional scope of responsibilities inherited from the communist period. Hence the inherent overlap of intelligence, policing, and law enforcement powers and responsibilities, particularly in civilian and military counterintelligence services. Given the combination of investigative and policing prerogatives, the services shifted the focus to enhance their powers of covert and intrusive operations. This, in turn, has led to increased secrecy of the intelligence sector and weakened the effectiveness of the oversight. Thirdly, the legislative and executive oversight institutions have been successfully established following commonly recognized democratic principles but were never properly consolidated in their functions. As a result, the oversight bodies have all the tools at their disposal necessary to exert their powers but remain reluctant to do so. Also, until recently, no special judicial authorities have been established to monitor the sector, although, in practice, the judicial branch proved to be most efficient in curtailing the undesirable processes of deepening secrecy in the services. Last but not least, the prolonged and complicated process of transforming the sector has resulted in highly dispersed legislative regulations pertaining to the security sector and the lack of definition or regulations of some key aspects of the functioning of the intelligence.

Still, the transition of the security sector in Poland should not be looked at too critically. The services, in general, accepted the civilian leadership and oversight of often inexperienced politicians and, with the dubious exception of the OLIN case over a decade ago, they have never appeared a serious threat to the sovereignty or integrity of the democratic state (notwithstanding some unsubstantiated accusations of certain politicians). The services were also reconciled with the successive rounds of institutional reforms and, in contrast to the military, never openly challenged the politicians. Finally, the post-1989 intelligence services did register some notable successes. All in all, it seems that the main problem of the Polish transformation is the impeded development of the democratic system, which was successfully established but failed to fully consolidate into a mature democracy with a robust civil society. This has led to certain alienation of the intelligence sector and permanent distrust between the politicians and the services. Based on those observations, the following recommendations for the democratic transitions of the intelligence sectors may be formulated:

1. Historical past should be dealt with knowingly, purposefully, and without undue delay. Politicians should hold some sort of national discussion in this respect and legitimize their decisions about the inheritance of the past regime and the functionaries of the predecessor institutions, whatever the decision might be. Leaving the historical resentments unresolved will inevitably lead to undermining the democratic legitimacy of the new intelligence institutions in the future;

2. The powers and responsibilities of the intelligence sector should be delineated as clearly as possible at the start of the transformation, with some conceptual underpinning of the institutional design to justify the division of prerogatives. It would be advisable to avoid excessive fragmentation of the sector and overlaps of powers as that will complicate control and coordination procedures, lead to intra-services rivalries and increase the budget for intelligence;

3. Covert surveillance prerogatives should be legally regulated early on, preferably through a separate bill or as part of laws on individual services; above all, the field of covert operations should not be left for the services to define and decide what can be done and what not;

4. While drafting new directives, European legislators need to take into account the possibility of undermining democratic oversight in transitional states and unduly enhancing the powers of intelligence services. Therefore, it is recommended to impose in the directives some obligatory constraints on the use of new powers, if only for educational reasons.

Disclaimer: The views expressed are solely those of the author and do not represent official views of the PfP Consortium of Defense Academies and Security Studies Institutes, participating organizations, or the Consortium's editors. **Acknowledgment.** *Connections: The Quarterly Journal, Vol. 20, 2021, is supported by the United States government. About the Author: Agnieszka Gogolewska is an e-learning consultant, scenario writer, academic lecturer, and author. Since 2010 she is a Senior Lecturer at the European University of Information Technology and Economics in Warsaw. Her main research interests are in democratic transitions and security sector reform, processes of democratization and de-democratization, intelligence and security studies. Connections: The Quarterly Journal is the official academic publication of the Partnership for Peace Consortium of Defense Academies and Security Studies Institutes(link is external), that brings together faculty members and researchers from 29 NATO and 21 partner countries in North America, Europe and Asia, and is open to authors beyond the Consortium. It facilitates dialogue, exchange of knowledge and experience, and dissemination of good academic practices. Connections is an open-access journal covering security, defense, armed forces, war and conflict, terrorism, trans-border and organized crime, intelligence, cybersecurity, emerging security challenges. A list of priority themes is defined annually by the journal's Editorial Board. The journal is published in English, and then translated and published in Russian, thus increasing its coverage and impact. Starting with the Summer 2018 issue, Connections is published by Procon Ltd.(link is external), based in Sofia, Bulgaria. Contact Us: Interested authors can submit their paper through the lead editors for a special journal issue or the Connections editorial office electronically at PfPCpublications [at] marshallcenter [dot] org. For other matters contact the Strategic Communications Manager of the PfP Consortium by phone: +49 8821 750 2256 or E-mail: pfpc [at] pfp-consortium [dot] org. Attribution statement & Disclaimer: Partnership for Peace Consortium (PfPC) of Defense Academies and Security Studies Institutes is a multi-national network of defense academies and security studies institutes strengthening democracy through education, est. 1999. The PfPC is funded & governed by Austria, Canada, Germany, Poland, Sweden, Switzerland, the United*

Chapter 12

Soviet and Russian Diplomatic Expulsions: How Many and Why?

Kevin P. Riehle

Abstract

Between 1946 and 1991, over 1,500 Soviet officials—mostly intelligence officers operating under diplomatic cover—were expelled from diplomatic and other government representations around the world. Expulsions often involved single or small groups of officials, but occasionally occurred en masse. Countries chose to expel Soviet officials for four reasons: in reaction to anti-Soviet regime changes and political reversals, in retaliation for Soviet covert activities and political manipulation, in reaction to Soviet intelligence officer defectors and intelligence obtained from penetrations of Soviet intelligence services, and, most frequently, in retaliation for espionage. Recent expulsions are modern adaptations of a method that was common during the Cold War with commonalities of purpose, but some variations, especially in scale and level of international cooperation.

Since February 2022, 34 countries, mostly in Europe, have expelled over 700 officials from Russian diplomatic establishments. That follows a wave of expulsions in the aftermath of Russia's attempt to assassinate Sergey Skripal in 2018, and the closure of Russian diplomatic establishments in the United States after Russia's manipulation of 2016 elections. These are modern adaptations of a method that was common during the Cold War but had become more sporadic in the post–Cold War era. Relying on a combination of press information, declassified intelligence reporting, and bulletins published by the U.S. Department of State, this article analyses the countries that applied that method, what Soviet activities prompted expulsions, what effects they had on the operational environment, and how they were similar to or different from their modern equivalent.

Based on international standards, diplomats enjoy immunity, which means that a person who holds diplomat status cannot be put in jail or prosecuted in court, no matter what they do. The only recourse for a host government that wants to protest the actions of a foreign diplomat is to declare the person persona non grata and expel them from the country for "activities incompatible with diplomatic status." There have been exceptions made to diplomatic immunity in rare cases when a diplomat is involved in an extreme crime, like a vehicular homicide. But even in such cases, exceptions are never automatic, and only the sending country can agree to waive immunity. For a charge of espionage, which is a political crime not a physical crime, an exception is never made.

The practice of diplomatic expulsions was institutionalized in the Vienna Convention on Diplomatic Relations of 1961, which gives countries the right to expel diplomats who violate host country laws or who interfere in the host country's internal affairs.[1] Both the United States and the Soviet Union frequently expelled each other's officials during the Cold War, and the United States also experienced similar treatment from left-wing governments in Latin America, as Andrew Jordan describes in his 2018 dissertation, "You're Out! Explaining Non-Criminal Diplomatic Expulsion." Nevertheless, Jordan notes, "[T]he practice of diplomatic expulsions, as well as expulsions of other foreign personnel by an executive, has received little attention in the field of international relations or in political science more broadly,"[2] although research has been done into some specific cases.[3]

The lack of focused research is true for expulsions of Soviet officials during the Cold War, which usually fell into two broad categories that aligned with the two reasons allowed under the Vienna Convention: retaliation for Soviet covert activities and political manipulation, leading to the closing or reduction in the size of a Soviet diplomatic establishment; and retaliation for espionage, which violates a country's laws. An expelling country weighed those purposes against the costs: as most Soviet officials expelled from embassies were intelligence officers, the inevitable reciprocal Soviet expulsion of an equal number of the expelling country's officials meant the loss of intelligence assets inside the Soviet Union. Many times during the Cold War and since, countries counted the benefit worth the cost.

Between 1946 and 1991, at least 79 countries expelled over 1,500 Soviet officials, not counting several mass expulsions involving unspecified numbers. The practice of expelling Soviet officials included those who were resident in a foreign country as well as countries barring the re-entry of officials who had travelled to Moscow. Expelled officials represented the full spectrum of Soviet establishments abroad. They were often embassy-based diplomatic personnel, but also included non-diplomatic employees, such as interpreters, maintenance workers, security guards, and technicians. They were assigned to consulates, commercial and trade offices, and many from military attaché offices. Soviet officials were also expelled from the United Nations (UN) secretariat and UN specialized agencies like the International Civil Aviation Organization, International Wheat Council, and International Cocoa Organization. Others represented Soviet commercial companies, like Amtorg, Aeroflot, Inturist, Sovexportfilm, and joint ventures with local companies, as well as Soviet newspaper, television, and radio news outlets.

The expelling countries included 22 in Africa, 21 in Asia (including the Middle East), eighteen in Western Europe, eight in South America, seven in North America (including the Caribbean), and three in Eastern Europe (Figure 1). The numbers of expulsions were small up to 1970, with most years under twenty worldwide. A mass expulsion from Great Britain in 1971 made that year stand out, followed the next year by another mass expulsion from Bolivia. The year 1983 was the most damaging of the entire Cold War for the Soviet Union, with over 200 officers expelled from 26 different countries, including four countries—Bangladesh, France, Grenada, and Iran—expelling nineteen or more, each for different reasons. Trend of Soviet expulsions in the Cold War. Database of expulsions compiled by the author based on press information, declassified intelligence reporting, and bulletins published by the U.S. Department of State. Not included are the countries that completely severed diplomatic relations, the 1963 and 1971 expulsions of Soviet diplomatic staff from Congo, and the 1981 expulsion from Equatorian Guinea, specific numbers for which were not announced.

About one-third of publicly expelled officials were announced publicly by quantity but without names. The remaining were named. In most cases, the expelled officials were officers from the Committee for State Security (KGB) or the Main Intelligence Directorate of the General Staff (GRU). Consequently, it is likely the names by which many were known outside the Soviet Union were fictitious. Nevertheless, in several cases, officers were dispatched to multiple countries using the same fictitious name, facilitating the identification of Soviet intelligence officers when they appeared elsewhere. Of the expelled officials, only eleven were women, most of them wives of expelled Soviet officers, reflecting the male-dominated Soviet intelligence and diplomatic system. A country that expelled a Soviet official could do so either quietly or publicly. In some cases, a government demanded that an official depart the country, but made no public statement, often in response to espionage cases. The expelling country's decision against making a public announcement was due to a combination of the sensitivity of a counterintelligence operation and to avoid inevitable political repercussions from the Soviet Union. The total number of quiet expulsions is unknown, although declassified records shed some light on them. For example, a 1984 Department of State analysis of diplomatic reciprocity with the Soviet Union and Soviet Bloc countries included a list of 94 Soviet officials expelled from the United States from 1946 to 1983, 24 of whom had not been announced publicly. The list was declassified in 2011.[4]

Reasons for Expulsion

In many cases, however, the expelling country did publicize the action, at times sweeping out large numbers of Soviet officials and naming them. These actions were based on two sometimes simultaneous reasons: to send a political message of dissatisfaction with the Soviet government's interference in internal affairs, and to punish the Soviet government for aggressive intelligence activities. When an expulsion received publicity, the expelling country often announced only that a Soviet official was engaged in "activities incompatible with diplomatic status." The Vienna Convention does not require the host country to articulate a reason. The lack of specificity afforded the Soviet Union the opportunity to claim that the charges were unfounded and unjustified, fuelling Soviet propaganda about capitalist aggressiveness and lack of diplomatic propriety, which the Soviet Union could then contrast with its own supposed peaceful motives. Other times, a little more detail was made public, such as claims that the individual committed espionage, was caught in possession of classified information, or was recruiting spies. Nevertheless, in many instances, the expelling government cited specific details of the activity that precipitated the expulsion.

Anti-Soviet Regime Changes and Political Reversals

A large portion of public expulsions of Soviet officials during the Cold War came in connection with coups that overturned Soviet client regimes. Expulsions were a tool that a small state could use against a superpower with minimal risk. The Soviet Union lost more influence within the expelling state than the converse after a regime change that precipitated expulsions. Jordan argues that expulsions "increase in value to states on the weaker end of a power disparity."Footnote5 While that may not always have held true, especially in U.S.–Soviet tit-for-tat expulsions, it aligns with many instances of small states expelling Soviet officials during the Cold War. This was a uniquely Cold War type of expulsion founded in bipolar superpower competition with no analogy in the post–Cold War world. The Soviet government's reputation and relationships repeatedly suffered during the Cold War from reversals of countries' cooperation with the Soviet Union or coups that removed Soviet-friendly governments and replaced them with pro-Western ones, often with U.S. sponsorship. A country could respond to an anti-Soviet coup in a spectrum of ways: reduce the size of the Soviet diplomatic presence to a level that aligned with the new, less cooperative relationship; close a Soviet consulate or military mission; or at the most serious level, sever diplomatic relations altogether.

These events were often the result of Cold War proxy battles. For example, in November 1963, during the Congo crisis, the Congolese government expelled the entire Soviet embassy staff, claiming the right to approve any Soviet diplomats who were sent to replace them. In March 1966, Ghana expelled 22 Soviet embassy officials along with over 200 non-diplomatic Soviet technicians and advisors. The action followed a Central Intelligence Agency (CIA)–sponsored coup that removed the president of Ghana, Kwame Nkrumah, who had become close to the Soviet Union.Footnote6 Bolivia acted similarly in March 1972, after a right-wing junta took over the government from a Soviet-friendly one. The Bolivian government demanded that the Soviet Union remove 119 officials from the embassy in La Paz, leaving less than ten.[7] In August 1979, a pro-Western coup removed Francisco Macías Nguema as president of Equatorial Guinea. Nguema had come to power in 1968 and expanded his country's ties with Cuba, China, and the Soviet Union. In 1981, the pro-Western regime that removed him ordered the Soviet embassy to reduce its size from 195 personnel to an unknown but much smaller number. Some of the expelled advisors were undoubtedly intelligence personnel, as the new regime also closed a signals intelligence (SIGINT) collection base on the Gulf of Biafra from which the Soviet Union had supported interventions in other African countries. Footnote8 As of 2022, Russia still did not have a resident embassy in Equatorial Guinea, covering the country from neighboring Cameroon.

In August 1980, the Iranian revolutionary regime instructed the Soviet Union to close one consular office in Iran and reduce its diplomatic staff in

Tehran. The move came after the Iranian foreign minister publicly accused the Soviets of interfering in Iranian internal affairs and refusing to agree to a natural gas export deal. The Soviet consulate in Isfahan was subsequently closed, and the staff in Tehran cut back. This came just a year following the Iranian revolution, which Soviet leaders initially greeted with hopefulness because it removed a U.S. ally from the Soviet border. It also followed the Soviet Union's invasion of Afghanistan, which Iran viewed with suspicion. The Soviet Union's inability to take advantage of regime change in Iran led to the revolutionary Iranian regime expelling Soviet diplomats.[9]

Egypt was a particularly thorny partner during the Cold War for both the West and the Soviet Union. In 1972, Anwar Sadat's government expelled thousands of Soviet non-diplomatic advisors. Then, in September 1981, the Egyptian government expelled the Soviet ambassador and eight other named officials, all of which were identified as KGB officers and accused of exploiting religious strife and coordinating leftist elements in the country. The Egyptian government shut down the Soviet military mission in Cairo and closed its own military office in Moscow. The 1981 expulsion also extended to over 1,000 non-diplomatic Soviet technicians working on infrastructure and industrial projects in Egypt.Footnote10 Similar political reversals led to Soviet expulsions in Pakistan in 1980, Costa Rica in 1982, Grenada in 1983, and Liberia in 1983 and 1985. In other cases, anti-Soviet regimes severed diplomatic relations with the Soviet Union altogether, such as in Brazil (1947), Colombia (1948), Venezuela (1952), Israel (1967), and Côte d'Ivoire (1969), leading to the complete closure of Soviet embassies. These anti-Soviet coups and reversals sent political messages to the Soviet Union, often inspired by a U.S. covert action, such as in Ghana in 1966, or overt military invasion, such as in Grenada in 1983.

Retaliation for Covert Activities and Political Manipulation Operations

During the Cold War, countries around the world regularly accused the Soviet Union of political manipulation, organizing coups, and interfering in internal affairs. These allegations were reminiscent of Soviet covert operations in the 1920s designed to remove capitalist governments and install Bolshevik regimes in places like Bulgaria, China, Estonia, Finland, Germany, and Hungary. Russian political interference also forms a foundation for similar allegations against the Russian government in the twenty-first century in places like Libya, Montenegro, and North Macedonia. Beginning early in the Cold War, at least 25 countries expelled Soviet officers in retaliation for political interference. Japan became the first when it expelled a Soviet embassy official in 1951, accusing him of controlling communist party activities in the country. Both Argentina and Mexico accused the Soviet Union in 1959 of employing covert operations to foment communist agitation. The U.S. Department of State's 1987 annual summary of expulsions listed a range of allegations levied against Soviet officials from 1971 to 1986:

Plotting to foment religious and sectarian strife (Egypt: September 1981). Maintaining contact with and financing leftist rebel movements, communist parties, and other local opposition groups (Bolivia: April 1972; Liberia: April 1979; New Zealand: January 1980; Bangladesh, November 1983). Complicity in antigovernment coup plotting (Sudan: August 1971; Liberia: November 1983). Disseminating hostile propaganda (Pakistan: August–September 1980). Manipulating local media and financing local peace and antinuclear movements (Denmark: October 1981; Switzerland: April 1983; West Germany: May 1983). Maintaining contact with suspected terrorist and other "extra-paramilitary" organizations (Spain: February 1980 and March 1981). Infiltrating and influencing local exile communities and ethnic emigré groups (Sweden: April 1982). Manipulating local agrarian reform movements, fomenting local labor strikes, and helping to organize demonstrations against food price increases (Ecuador: July 1971; Liberia: April 1979; Costa Rica: August 1979; Portugal: August 1980).[11]

Additionally, in April 1983, the Swiss government ordered the closure of the Soviet Union's Bern-based Novosti press bureau, charging that it was a center for "political and ideological indoctrination" of young members of Swiss peace and antinuclear movements and for planning street demonstrations. Swiss authorities said that the Novosti bureau had "served as a center for disinformation, subversion, and agitation" rather than as a news agency. The director of the bureau, Aleksey Dumov, was expelled.[12] Expulsions following covert manipulation activities were founded on anger and disillusionment toward the Soviet Union, even among some countries that would normally be inclined to ally with Moscow. One anomalous event occurred in 1957, when the Polish government expelled Soviet press attaché Nikolay Maslennikov. Maslennikov had expressed support for a tightly controlled press system and clashed with outspoken and independence-minded Polish journalists. He reportedly attributed the conflicts to Jews holding positions of authority in the Polish government.[13]Romania, another Warsaw Pact country, also expelled a Soviet military attaché, Aleksandr Musatov, in 1972, probably to confront Moscow's "Brezhnev Doctrine" and in relation to Romania's refusal to follow Moscow's lead in the Sino–Soviet split.[14]

Since the dissolution of the Soviet Union, analogous cases arose in several countries. The Greek government expelled two Russian diplomatically covered individuals in 2018, accusing them of trying to persuade the population along the northern border of Greece to oppose a solution to the long-simmering naming issue for what was then referred to as the Former Yugoslav Republic of Macedonia. The Russian officials allegedly tried to bribe local Greek leaders to disrupt the agreement by which the territory would become formally named the Republic of North Macedonia.[15] The naming issue had been an obstacle to North Macedonia acceding to the North Atlantic Treaty Organization (NATO), and Russia's attempted, albeit failed, disruption would have delayed accession. The most prominent post–Cold War expulsion for political manipulation occurred in the United States in two consecutive presidential elections. In January 2016, President Barack Obama expelled 35 Russians officials in retaliation for election interference, and then in April 2021, President Joe Biden announced the expulsion of ten officials in reaction to allegations of Russian intelligence services attempting to interfere in the 2020 U.S. elections.[16] Although there have been numerous additional reports of Russia manipulating elections, for example in France, Montenegro, Spain, and the United Kingdom, the reactions to those events did not elicit public diplomatic expulsions.

Reaction to Defectors and Penetrations

Another catalyst for expelling Soviet officials came when Soviet intelligence personnel defected or cooperated with Western intelligence and revealed their colleagues' names and activities, sometimes resulting in large-scale expulsion actions. Defectors' revelations provided firsthand knowledge of the identities of intelligence officers within a Soviet embassy, giving the receiving country grounds to reduce that intelligence presence. Knowledge gained from defectors at times precipitated immediate expulsions, while other times it sparked investigations that led to expulsions over the following year. Although defections of Russian intelligence officers did not end with the Cold War, the use of defectors' information to prompt expulsions has not been a post–Cold War phenomenon. The first such incident occurred in May 1946, when the Canadian government ordered the departure of seventeen Soviet officials named by Igor Gouzenko. The expulsions came eight months after Gouzenko's defection and three months after the Canadian government initiated a royal commission to investigate Gouzenko's revelations.[17] The next occurred in 1954, when the Soviet Union severed diplomatic relations with Australia. Although the severance of relations was the Soviet Union's initiative, not Australia's, it led to the closure of the Soviet embassy in Canberra for the next five years. It came after publicity surrounding the defection of Vladimir Petrov, and a few weeks later, his wife Yevdokiya Petrova, in April 1954. The Petrovs' detailed information about Soviet intelligence operations directed against Australia and launched from Australian territory sent political ripples around the world.[18]

The United Kingdom issued the largest ever defector-related expulsion order in September 1971, called Operation "Foot," when it expelled 90 Soviet officials and barred the reentry of fifteen others. That order was executed three weeks after the defection of Oleg Lyalin, a KGB officer responsible for collecting intelligence about potential sabotage targets that the Soviet Union would attack in case of war. Lyalin's revelations went beyond his personal operations and included information about numerous KGB officers and activities in general, and the UK government took the opportunity of Lyalin's defection to send a retaliatory message to the Soviet Union. The British government did not immediately name the expelled officials publicly. However, their names appeared three years later when U.S. author John Barron published a list of nearly 1,600 Soviet intelligence officers in his book KGB: The Secret Work of Soviet Agents.[19] The level of detail in his book suggests unacknowledged government support. According to Mitrokhin, the KGB was caught completely off guard by the mass expulsion but was more worried about Lyalin's revelations regarding Soviet preparations for sabotage operations in case of war.[20] Kalugin similarly claimed that the Lyalin defection inflicted a crippling blow on KGB activities, both because of the expulsions and because of Lyalin's revelations.[21]

Two other defectors resulted in expulsions in 1971, although not on the scale of Lyalin's. In March 1971, Mexico expelled five KGB officers accused of supporting guerilla groups that opposed the Mexican government. These expulsions came a year after the defection of Raisa Kiselnikova, an administrative employee at the Soviet embassy in Mexico City, whose revelations provided details of KGB covert operations in Mexico. She claimed, with CIA prompting, that Soviet influence had stimulated unrest in 1968 that resulted in over 100 deaths in Mexico.[22] Kiselnikova's revelations spurred a yearlong investigation that identified embassy-based officers.

Another expulsion order occurred in October 1971, a few weeks after Lyalin's. The Belgian government ordered the departure of nine Soviet officials based on the revelations of Anatoliy Chebotarev, a GRU officer assigned to the Soviet embassy in Brussels who defected in early October.

The Belgian government initially planned to keep the order quiet, but it was soon leaked that Chebotarev had identified 37 intelligence officers at the embassy. Nevertheless, the Belgian government did not publicize the names of the expelled Soviet officials and did not expel all 37.[23] several of the names, although not all of them, appeared in Barron's 1974 published list. Ironically, Chebotarev himself requested to redefect to the Soviet Union only two months after defecting. No public information is available about how he was received after his return to Moscow, but the damage he did to Soviet operations in Belgium likely weighed into his reception.

The year 1983 saw a particularly large number of expulsions due to defectors and penetrations. Iran expelled and publicly named eighteen Soviet personnel in May 1983 based on investigations of the Tudeh Party following the defection of KGB officer Vladimir Kuzichkin the previous year. As in Mexico a decade earlier, the expulsions came over a year after the defection and were based on similar allegations of Soviet meddling in Iranian internal affairs.[24] A month before the Iranian expulsions, France expelled 47 Soviet officers, naming all of them publicly. The names came from over 4,000 pages of documents that detailed KGB science and technology intelligence collection operations and personnel around the world. KGB officer Vladimir Vetrov, codenamed FAREWELL, provided the documents to the French counterintelligence service in 1982, leading the French government to the mass expulsion on the grounds that the Soviets were "engaged in a systematic search on French territory for technological and scientific information, particularly in the military area."[25] France also shared the identities of Soviet officers internationally, and over the next several weeks, Austria, Australia, Belgium, Italy, Japan, Norway, Switzerland, the United States, and West Germany expelled nearly 150 intelligence officers accused of collecting science and technology intelligence.[26] Initial public statements from various governments implied that the expulsions were related to Kuzichkin's defection to draw attention away from Vetrov, leading newspapers to compare the case with Great Britain's mass expulsion in 1971. Despite the attempted misdirection, Vetrov was arrested in Moscow in 1982 on unrelated charges and executed in 1985.[27]

In July 1985, the British responded quickly to Oleg Gordievskiy's defection by declaring 25 Soviet officials persona non grata. Gordievskiy had been an MI6 penetration of the KGB for over ten years before his defection, so the British government had ample time to process his information and prepare an expulsion order, even before the defection. After the Soviet

Union reciprocated with an equal number of expulsions of British officials, the British government expelled six more Soviets. Unlike the 1971 mass expulsion, the British government published the names of all 31 Soviet officials expelled in 1985.

Just a few weeks after Gordievskiy's defection, Vitaliy Yurchenko defected to the U.S. government in Italy and revealed the existence of two Soviet penetrations of U.S. intelligence services: Ronald Pelton at the National Security Agency and former CIA employee Edward Lee Howard. Although Yurchenko redefected only three months later, those espionage cases, along with others that broke in 1985, such as the Jonathan Walker spy ring, compounded by the Soviet expulsion of U.S. journalist Nicholas Daniloff, prompted the U.S. government to expel 25 Soviet intelligence officers in September 1986 in Operation "Famish." When the Soviet Union responded with reciprocal expulsions, the U.S. government expelled 50 more in October, and then five more after that, totaling 80. Mikhail Gorbachev reportedly stated at a Politburo meeting, "We cannot let this hostile action go unanswered. ... This is important not only from the point of view of Soviet-American relations, but international relations as well. If they are talking with the Soviet Union in such a manner, one can imagine how they will act with other countries."[28]The Politburo meeting did not mention Yurchenko's defection or Soviet espionage activities.

Two additional defections in the late Soviet period led to expulsions. GRU officer Yuriy Smurov defected in Canada in May 1988 while working as a Soviet employee at the International Civil Aviation Organization in Montreal. From Smurov's revelations, the Canadian government identified the Soviet case officers handling agents inside a defense contractor firm, prompting the expulsion of eight Soviet officials, likely all GRU officers, in June 1988. Canada also barred nine others who had previously served in Canada from reentering the country. When the Soviet government reciprocated, the Canadian government expelled two more Soviet officers. The final defector-related Soviet expulsions during the Cold War occurred in October 1991. The Norwegian government declared eight Soviet officials persona non grata following the defection in May 1991 of KGB officer Mikhail Butkov. Norwegian government spokespersons provided few details of the reasons for the action; however, press reports indicated that one of the expelled officers, Boris Kirillov, had been a case officer responsible for contact with Norwegian prime minister Jens Stoltenberg.[29]

Defectors and penetration agents thus accounted for over 200 Soviet expulsions during the Cold War, not counting the complete closure of the

Soviet embassy in Canberra in 1954. In some cases, the expelling country used public defections as a pretext to sweep out Soviet officers about which they already knew. The speed with which the British government identified and expelled large numbers of Soviet officials both in 1971 and 1985 suggests foreknowledge of their existence. The CIA assessed the week following the 1971 expulsion that the British had planned the move months before it actually took place, but that Lyalin's defection "strengthened the government's resolve."[30]Similarly, a Belgian expulsion order came just a few weeks following Chebotarev's defection in 1971, and a Canadian order that came just a short time after Smurov's defection in 1988 included officers who had departed Canada years earlier. In other cases, the expelling country used defector revelations as the starting point for counterintelligence or counterinsurgency investigations, sometimes waiting over a year to issue the order, such as in Mexico and Iran.

Retaliation for Espionage Cases

Espionage cases are the most frequent reason for expulsions, both during the Cold War and since. Unlike defectors, which sometimes led to mass expulsions, espionage cases usually led to smaller numbers per incident, often one or two. The expelling government frequently does not reveal the nature of the espionage, stating publicly only that the officer was caught with classified information or clandestine communication devices. The evidence in many cases is based on sensitive counterintelligence operations, and thus the expelling government is sometimes loath to make those operations public. In other cases, the expelling country has announced details, even revealing sensitive offensive counterintelligence operations. The U.S. Federal Bureau of Investigation (FBI) occasionally announced publicly that a Soviet officer was caught in a double agent operation. For example, GRU officer Yuriy Leonov was expelled from the United States in August 1983 after a two-year double agent operation involving Armand Weiss, a technical editor and government consultant. Weiss publicized his own role in the case after the expulsion.[31]KGB officer Gennadiy Zakharov was expelled from the United States in August 1986 after receiving "three classified documents from an undercover informant."[32]Those cases often involved targeting military-related or science and technological information. Others were not as clear but stated more vaguely that the official was expelled after "trying to obtain" defense or classified information.

When a recruited agent was arrested or when the Soviet officer was caught publicly, the expelling country often publicized the specifics of the espionage. Arrests in these cases were timed to catch the handler in the act of meeting the source to support a prosecution and to gain the most public visibility possible. The first such cases appeared in the 1950s, when espionage-related public expulsions of nearly 100 Soviet officials occurred in 25 different countries during the decade. The United States led the pack by far with 27 expulsions. Justifications for expulsions were mixed, but military-related espionage was the most common. Several prominent espionage cases in the 1950s prompted expulsions, including the arrests of Judith Coplin in 1950, Kurt Verber and Otto Ponger in 1953, and Jack Soble in 1957 in the United States. Three separate espionage cases in Sweden led to expulsions in the 1950s: Ernst Hilding Andersson in 1951, radar expert Anatole Ericson in 1956, and Bedros Zartaryan in 1957, each related to military information. Iran expelled GRU officer Anatoliy Kuznetsov in March 1956 for recruiting an Iranian air force warrant officer who was tasked with providing intelligence on Iranian military logistics and fuel supplies. The 1950s also saw the first expulsions of Soviet officials from the United Nations in New York, usually for military-related espionage.

Military personnel were often the targets of Soviet operations targeting sensitive military plans, equipment, or technology. The Italian government expelled two Soviet officials in 1970 a week after arresting an Italian noncommissioned officer for espionage. Indian police expelled a Soviet military attaché in February 1984 after catching him meeting with a junior Defence Ministry officer. In 1986, the French government expelled four GRU officers after the arrest of a French Air Force officer who was tasked with tracking French naval and nuclear submarine movements at strategic ports near Brest. Other major espionage cases that resulted in expulsions were the Ivan Rogalsky case in 1977 in the United States involving National Aeronautics and Space Administration information; multiple cases in 1983 and 1984 in Belgium, in which Soviet officers tried to acquire NATO and Belgian government information; and the 1985 arrest in India of nineteen Indian officials in multiple government ministries who provided military and economic information to Soviet handlers. The Norwegian government expelled nine Soviet officials after a multiyear investigation that culminated in the January 1984 arrest of Arne Treholt, who had provided the KGB with Norwegian defense information.

Espionage-related expulsions were most common in NATO and technologically advanced countries, reflecting the information available to steal, the military threat those countries posed to the Soviet Union, and the more hostile counterintelligence environment for Soviet officers. The

United States led the way in espionage-related expulsions. In the 44 years from 1946 to 1989, there were only eight years in which the United States did not expel at least one Soviet official. Most years the United States expelled five or fewer; Operation "Famish" in 1986 was the lone exception of a U.S. mass expulsion. Beginning in 1976, France also began to take more public action against Soviet espionage. The Farewell Dossier expulsions in 1983 were the most extreme example, but every year from 1976 to 1987 saw at least one Soviet expulsion from France. Western European countries, such as Denmark, Italy, the Netherlands, Norway, Switzerland, and West Germany employed expulsions frequently to remove Soviet intelligence officers caught conducting espionage.

In addition to military-related espionage, some Soviet officials also were expelled for counterintelligence-related operations, such as attempting to penetrate a counterintelligence service or pursuing Soviet defectors abroad. For the KGB, persuading a Soviet defector to return home was a counterintelligence mission, and several officers were expelled for approaching defectors, especially in the 1950s. For example, the U.S. government expelled two KGB officers in 1956 for trying to coerce members of the crew of the Soviet merchant ship Tuapse, who had defected in Taiwan in 1954, to return to the Soviet Union. The next year, the U.S. government expelled KGB officer Gennadiy Mashkantsev for trying to coerce defector Soviet Air Force pilot Petr Pirogov to return. In 1956, Petr Kashtanov, a former Soviet officer who emigrated to the United States after World War II (WWII), reported having been approached by officials based at the Soviet mission to the United Nations. Kashtanov testified in a congressional hearing that the officials knew who he was even though he was using a pseudonym. They told him that the United States would lose the battle against communism in the end, so the sooner Soviet emigres returned home, the better off them would be. The Soviet UN officials were expelled soon after their approach to Kashtanov.[33]One other expulsion in 1956 even allegedly involved a Soviet officer forcing the repatriation of a Soviet citizen whose child had been born in the United States.[34]

Soviet officers were caught trying to penetrate foreign counterintelligence services as well. The first post-WWII Soviet officer expelled from the United States, Valentin Gubichev, was arrested receiving documents from Judith Coplin, a Department of Justice employee who provided information about U.S. counterintelligence investigations of Soviet individuals. In 1971, the Ghanaian government expelled Gennadiy Potemkin after he was caught with police special branch documents in his possession. Most prominently, in February 1978, the Canadian government expelled or barred the reentry of thirteen officers who had tried to penetrate the Royal Canadian Mounted Police. Although not as common as military targets, counterintelligence targeting was not unusual among Soviet expulsions.

Russian espionage slipped from countries' priorities after the dissolution of the Soviet Union, which, along with efforts to encourage democratization and reform in Russia, led to fewer espionage cases in the 1990s and early 2000s. However, it did not disappear altogether, with Russia running prominent cases like Aldrich Ames and Harold Nicholson after 1991. The first post-Soviet mass expulsion occurred in 2001, when the United States expelled 50 Russian officials after the arrest of Robert Hanssen.[35]However that was an exception for most of the post–Cold War era. Isolated expulsions occurred in the first decade of the 2000s. After Russia's annexation of Crimea in 2014, the practice returned in greater force, with Russia's own actions making states less hesitant to accuse Russian officials of espionage, sabotage, and assassination operations. Between 2014 and 2018, multiple countries, mostly in Europe and North America, expelled Russian officials, climaxing in 2018, when 30 countries expelled nearly 150 Russians in retaliation for the attempted assassination of Sergey Skripal in the United Kingdom.

The 2018 Skripal case was an unusual event in the history of diplomatic expulsions. The Russian activity that precipitated the expulsions occurred on the soil of one country, but nearly 30 other countries expelled Russian officials in sympathy. A sympathetic expulsion had occurred only once during the Cold War after the Farewell case in France (see above) and has occurred only a few times since. It occurred again in 2021, after the Czech government reduced the size of the Russian embassy in Prague to parity with its embassy in Moscow in retaliation for the 2014 sabotage of weapons warehouses in Czechia. Estonia, Latvia, and Lithuania soon announced expulsions in solidarity with Prague.[36]The largest sympathetic expulsion in history occurred within six weeks after Russia's invasion of Ukraine, when nearly 500 Russian officials were expelled from 29 countries, mostly in Europe; over 200 additional expulsions occurred over the following year. Never during the Cold War did such an intense reaction come from an event involving a single country, which, like the Skripal assassination attempt, demonstrated a level of diplomatic unity not seen previously.

Effects of Expulsion

Expulsions of Soviet officers could accomplish two simultaneous operational goals: reduce the Soviet espionage threat and provide propaganda opportunities. Those benefits came with costs, especially related to Soviet reciprocal actions that reduced the expelling country's intelligence access to the Soviet Union, and the replacement of known Soviet intelligence officers with unknown ones.

Reduce the Soviet Threat

The expulsion of intelligence officers temporarily lowered the Soviet intelligence threat by reducing the opportunity factor of the threat equation, threat intent, capability, opportunity.[37] When a Soviet officer was expelled, the Soviet service's access to the target eroded, restricting Soviet intelligence reach. The other two factors of the threat equation did not change as much: expulsions did not affect Soviet intent to conduct intelligence or covert operations; that was driven by Soviet ideological rivalry. Overall, Soviet intelligence capabilities did not necessarily change, unless an inexperienced officer replaced a more seasoned one. Expulsions did, however, limit opportunities for Soviet services to contact recruited sources or to operate embassy-based SIGINT platforms. Expulsions shrank the number of Soviet officers, temporarily reducing the opportunity factor.

That threat reduction was mitigated by the fact that when a known officer left, a Soviet service replaced him with another officer. Expulsions may have delayed Soviet intelligence services' activities, but they did not stop dispatching officers abroad. Over the months and years following an expulsion, Soviet services found new officers or new cover positions in which to place them. It then took time and counterintelligence resources to identify the new officers. Expulsions, especially en masse, set the expelling country's counterintelligence back to the starting point in identifying who among the Soviet embassy staff was an intelligence officer.

Over time, the threat returned. For example, the 1983 Farewell Dossier expulsions resulted in severe damage to the KGB's science and technology collection in industrialized countries, causing "the collapse of Line X (science and technology collection) operations in Europe."[38] In relation to collection of intelligence on high-performance computers, the expulsions caused "the collapse of a crucial program just at the time the Soviet military needed it," according to Weiss.[39] However, in 1991, two other KGB science and technology collection officers defected in European countries—Sergey Illarionov in Italy and Vladimir Konoplev in Belgium—revealing that the

KGB had replaced expelled officers and reconstituted the collection effort. Konoplev's defection led to the first post-Soviet expulsions for espionage in April 1992, including officers who had handled an asset who had been recruited as early as 1967.[40]Although the Farewell Dossier expulsions had a significant effect, the effect was temporary, because the Soviet Union's need to collect science and technology intelligence and to handle assets did not end. Kalugin further claimed that KGB officers expelled from Western countries received assignments in East Berlin, which gave them opportunities to travel to West Germany, partially mitigating the lost access.[41]

Additionally, the Soviet government almost invariably reciprocated by ordering an equal number of expulsions from Moscow, so the expelling country paid for the action by losing access in the Soviet Union. The Department of State stated in its 1984 assessment of reciprocity with Soviet diplomatic representations, that since the 1950s, Most U.S. PNG [persona non grata] actions have been based on evidence of espionage—in contrast to Soviet PNG actions against our diplomatic personnel, which have often been retaliatory in nature. The Soviets have proven less likely to retaliate when the U.S. PNG action has been based on hard evidence and when the case is not publicized.[42]

Countries that posted intelligence officers to the Soviet Union were forced to weigh the prospect of reciprocity when deciding to expel officers, and then whether to do so publicly or quietly, which was undoubtedly a major reason why the Soviet government persisted with that policy. Expulsions thus required extensive coordination between intelligence, counterintelligence, diplomatic, and political equities, because one or more of those equities was likely to lose access in Moscow. After initial Operation "Famish" expulsions in September 1986, the Department of State and CIA reportedly had misgivings about the risk that the United States could lose more than it gained in continuing tit-for-tat expulsions.[43]One U.S. intelligence commentator even stated that the expulsions produced "no net long-term gain to U.S. security."[44]U.S. President Ronald Reagan decided to proceed anyway, mostly for political reasons.

In other cases, governments chose the opposite course of action specifically to avoid losing their visibility on the existing Soviet intelligence presence or their access in Moscow. When Great Britain expelled 25 officers after Gordievskiy's defection in 1985, the Danish government faced a similar choice. Gordievskiy had operated under diplomatic cover in Copenhagen in the 1960s and 1970s, and his cooperation with MI6 and

Danish intelligence began during his second posting in Denmark.[45]When Gordievskiy defected, the Danish Security and Intelligence Service (PET) recommended that Denmark expel eleven KGB officers from Copenhagen. The Danish government had expelled Soviet officers several times before, including as recently as 1984, although never enmasse. However, this time the government decided to allow them to stay. According to Danish Minister of Justice Erik Ninn-Hansen, it was wiser to maintain the known presence but to employ counterintelligence operations to monitor and obstruct their operations.[46]

The same dynamic continued past the end of the Cold War, especially after mass expulsions following the 2022 Russian invasion of Ukraine. In July 2022, MI6 chief Richard Moore assessed publicly that expulsions of over 400 diplomatically covered Russian intelligence officers had "reduced [Russia's] ability to do their business to spy for Russia in Europe by half."[47]However, some states have weighed the value of expelling or not, and if so, to publicize or not. In February 2023, Australia announced that it had detected and disrupted a major spy network and expelled an unspecified number of Russian diplomatic personnel over the previous six months, providing few details.[48]The United Kingdom, which has held a strong line against Russia's invasion, has not publicly expelled any Russian officials, possibly both to monitor known officers in the United Kingdom and to protect British intelligence operations inside Russia. Russia's practice of reciprocating for diplomatic expulsions has continued unchanged since the dissolution of the Soviet Union, forcing countries to make the same choices that they faced during the Cold War.

Propaganda Benefit

Part of the decision to proceed with expulsions was likely due to the recognition that, parallel with reducing the intelligence threat, expulsions also provided propaganda benefit for the expelling country and for the anti-communist West in general. Western countries, especially the United States, faced relentless Soviet propaganda that accused them of spying on the Soviet Union. One method that Western countries could use to counter those allegations was to expose Soviet intelligence officers caught conducting espionage operations and publicize the reasons for their expulsions. The more specificity in the announcement, the more ammunition Western states had to drive the propaganda message.

Up to the early 1980s, the Department of State and FBI frequently issued press releases naming Soviet officers expelled around the world and identifying their espionage and covert activities. Those statements made the threat of Soviet intelligence front-page news, but brief press coverage quickly faded from view. In May 1960, less than three weeks after a U.S. U-2 surveillance aircraft was shot down over the Soviet Union, the U.S. House of Representatives Un-American Activities Committee tasked the Legislative Reference Service of the Library of Congress to compile an inventory of Soviet espionage cases worldwide. The list included 65 cases, beginning with the Gouzenko case in Canada, and included 21 expulsions of Soviet officials up to 1960. U.S. Senator Karl Mundt had the list read into the Congressional Record on 18 May 1960. The shootdown of a U.S. U-2 surveillance aircraft in Soviet airspace had elicited sharp accusations from Soviet leader Nikita Khrushchev against the United States for conducting illegal intelligence activities. To counteract those allegations, Mundt stated, referring to an international meeting in Paris, which U.S. President Dwight Eisenhower and Khrushchev were scheduled to attend, but which collapsed after the U-2 incident,

"This week in Paris, Mr. Khrushchev engaged in a global blasphemy by raising his right hand and swearing before the God in whom he does not believe that his hands were clean from the standpoint of international espionage."[49]The U.S. Intelligence Community created the Active Measures Working Group in 1981 to counter Soviet propaganda and disinformation operations. Less than a year later, in February 1982, the Working Group published the first Department of State "foreign affairs note" that detailed Soviet expulsions and identified Soviet officers' names. These notes, which were produced annually until 1988, became regular public reminders that the Soviet Union was under diplomatic pressure globally for its intelligence and covert operations.[50]

Part of the motivation behind these annual notes was likely the works of disaffected former CIA officer Philip Agee, who exposed over 2,000 CIA officers in his two volumes, Dirty Work: The CIA in Western Europe and Dirty Work: The CIA in Africa in 1978 and 1980.[51]The KGB fed many of the names to Agee, who unabashedly exposed CIA officers and accused them of assassinations, bribery, and coup plotting, some real and some fabricated. The difference between Agee's publications and the U.S. response was that the United States published "foreign affairs notes" overtly as government documents, taking advantage of the Department of State's authoritative voice. Soviet support to Agee, on the other hand, was covert and even Agee was sometimes unaware of the KGB hand behind the data he published.[52]However, the KGB covert supply of information to

Agee may have been retaliation for previous U.S. covert leaks, especially after John Barron's publication of a list of nearly 1,600 Soviet officers, along with their career histories, in 1974.[53]

The first edition of the Department of State's foreign affairs notes, titled "Expulsion of Soviet Representatives from Foreign Countries, 1970–81," covered the previous decade. Successive annual reports were published in January each year until 1988 and covered the previous year, while maintaining a running alphabetical annex of all the names published to date. The note published in 1987 provided both a list of expulsions for the previous year and a review of expulsions since 1970. By 1988, the alphabetic annex included 367 names (including several misspelled duplicates), over 100 of which had never appeared in any of the previous annual notes, suggesting that the annex included declassified material that had not appeared elsewhere in public.

The foreign affairs notes were far from comprehensive. Another list, published by journalist John Barron in his 1983 book KGB Today: The Hidden Hand, contained the names of 197 Soviet officers who had been expelled or withdrawn between 1974 and 1983, 44 of which had never appeared in a Department of State note. Barron's 1983 list, which was read into the Congressional Record on 18 June 1987, also included full patronymics for most officers, which seldom appeared in the foreign affairs notes.[54]The Department of State notes also contained many mis-transliterations of Soviet officers' names, which Barron corrected in most cases. Barron apparently had other sources besides foreign affairs notes. Department of State notes and other public revelations served both to counter Soviet propaganda and to inform other countries of the names of Soviet intelligence officers. Some countries shared the identities of Soviet officers through intelligence liaison relationships even if an expulsion action was taken without publicity. The CIA declassified in 1999 a document dated mid-1959 that listed Soviet officials exposed publicly over the preceding decades, including some who had been declared persona non grata. The list was translated into French, presumably for sharing with Francophone liaison partners.[55]

The foreign affairs notes gave public notice of the expulsions, not just for a U.S. audience, but also as an overt intelligence sharing method, which served simultaneously as threat reduction and propaganda. However, sharing was not universal. At least seventeen Soviet officers reappeared in a new country after having been expelled elsewhere, either because the latter country had not received information about the previous expulsion or had chosen to disregard it. For example, Gennadiy Potemkin was expelled from Congo in 1963 and then again from Ghana in 1971. Yevgeniy Fedorovich Ivanov was expelled from France in 1976, and then from Portugal in 1978. Yuriy Churyanov, one of the 47 Soviet officials expelled from France in 1983, was expelled from Zaire in 1987. Dmitriy Dyakonov was expelled three times: from Argentina in 1959, Brazil in 1963, and Mexico in 1971. A British newspaper report in 1979 listed an individual named Nikolay Vasilyev who had also reportedly been expelled three times, from France in 1939, Sweden in 1946, and Ghana in 1966.[56]

At least one post–Cold War instance of an expelled officer reappearing in another country was reported in 2017, when an individual using the name Eduard Shirokov was named in Montenegro in connection with an attempted coup. Polish officials recognized Shirokov as a former Russian military attaché who used the name Eduard Shishmakov, who was among four Russians expelled from Poland in 2014 for conspiring to recruit Polish government officials.[57] In this case, Shishmakov/Shirokov's latter mission was not under diplomatic cover, and he disappeared from Montenegro without being arrested. Russian officers from among the over 700 expelled from European countries in response to Russia's 2022 invasion of Ukraine could also appear elsewhere in the world, most likely in non-European countries. If this has occurred, it has not become public. However, an increase in nonpublic international counterintelligence information sharing since the Russian invasion may make it more difficult.

Conclusion

The over 1,500 public expulsions of Soviet officials between 1946 and 1991 were a Cold War tool to weaken the Soviet intelligence threat and publicize its hypocrisy about espionage. Soviet intelligence services operated aggressively throughout the Cold War but were not invulnerable. Hundreds of Soviet officers were caught meeting with agents—bona fide and double—clearing dead drops, or communicating in other ways. They also suffered from defections from among their own. That allowed the expelling country to impair Soviet operations by publicly expelling officers and countering Soviet propaganda. Expulsions tapered off toward the end of the 1980s, with only Great Britain, Norway, and the United States taking public action after 1988, and no public expulsions reported in 1990 at all, the only year since 1946 in which there were no announced expulsions.

Expulsions of Russian officials have continued since the dissolution of the Soviet Union, although more sporadically, with the first mass expulsion occurring in 2001 after the arrest and conviction of Robert Hanssen in the United States.[58] The return of that method in force since 2014 shows both commonalities and differences from the Cold War era. Countries' retaliation for Russian espionage and covert operations have continued to yield expulsions to reduce Russian intelligence reach, while simultaneously propagandizing Russia's aggressive operations. However, the Cold War phenomenon of anti-Soviet coups has disappeared. Additionally, although defections of Russian officers still occur—over 40 Russian intelligence and state security officers have defected publicly since 1992, with others likely not publicized—defections have not resulted in mass expulsions since the Cold War.

Another difference lies in execution. During the Cold War, the majority of expulsions were done by a single country based on a specific Soviet action within that country. Collective and collaborative expulsions were rare, with the 1983 expulsions following Vladimir Vetrov's Farewell Dossier being an exception. Since 2018, there have been three collective expulsion actions, two of which were enmasse—following the 2018 Russian assassination attempt on Sergey Skripal in the United Kingdom and since early 2022 to protest Russia's actions in Ukraine. The number does not count the complete closure of all Russian government establishments in Ukraine, which had been reduced to small staffs over the preceding years anyway. Although at least 79 countries publicly expelled Soviet officials over the whole course of the Cold War, the extent of sympathetic diplomatic actions and the numbers of officials expelled in 2022 far exceeded any one-year period during the Cold War.

Both during and after the Cold War, expulsions have been a reaction to Soviet/Russian aggressive actions, most often espionage and covert activity, through which Russia has brought diplomatic expulsions on itself. But Russia has never given up, using reciprocal expulsions to punish other states and gradually replacing expelled officers back to previous levels. Although expulsions have resulted in a short-term reduction of the threat from Russian intelligence services, the propaganda effect has caused even greater pressure on the Soviet Union and Russia because of its ability to expose Soviet/Russian aggressiveness and hypocrisy in the international environment.

Disclosure statement: No potential conflict of interest was reported by the author(s). Additional information. Notes on contributors. Kevin Riehle is a Lecturer at Brunel University London. He spent over 30 years in the U.S. government as a Counterintelligence Analyst and as an Associate Professor of strategic intelligence at the National Intelligence University. He received a Ph.D. in War Studies from King's College London, an M.S. of Strategic Intelligence from the Joint Military Intelligence College, and a B.A. in Russian and Political Science from Brigham Young University. His next book, The Russian FSB: A Concise History of the Federal Security Service, will be published by Georgetown University Press in early 2024. The author can be contacted at kevin.riehle@brunel.ac.uk. Print ISSN: 0885-0607 Online ISSN: 1521-0561, 4 issues per year. Abstracted/indexed in: America: History & Life; CSA; EBSCOhost Online Research Databases; ESCI; Historical Abstracts; OCLC; PAIS International; Periodicals Index Online; Scopus; The Lancaster Index; and Ulrichs Periodicals Directory. The International Journal of Intelligence and CounterIntelligence serves as a medium for professionals and scholars to exchange opinions on issues and challenges encountered by both government and business institutions in making contemporary intelligence-related decisions and policy. At the same time, this quarterly serves as an invaluable resource for researchers looking to assess previous developments and events in the field of national security. Dedicated to the advancement of the academic discipline of intelligence studies, the International Journal of Intelligence and CounterIntelligence publishes articles and book reviews focusing on a broad range of national security matters. As an independent, non-partisan forum, the journal presents the informed and diverse findings of its contributing authors, and does not advocate positions of its own. Peer Review Policy: All papers submitted to the International Journal of Intelligence and CounterIntelligence undergo initial editorial screening. Once deemed suitable, research articles are sent out for double-anonymous peer review by at least two independent referees. Soviet and Russian Diplomatic Expulsions: How Many and Why? Kevin P. Riehle. To cite this article: Kevin P. Riehle (06 Dec 2023): Soviet and Russian Diplomatic Expulsions: How Many and Why?, International Journal of Intelligence and CounterIntelligence, DOI:10.1080/08850607.2023.2272 216.

Appendix-1

A Detailed Review of Some Books of Prominent Author Musa Khan Jalalzai

Professor Jandad Jahani and Dr. Jabeen. J

Hazob Magazine. Journal of Afghan Academic Forum, Berlin Germany-December 2023

Musa Khan Jalalzai is a journalist and has written extensively for various newspapers. His work has been featured in multiple publications including Daily Outlook Afghanistan, The Post, Daily Times, and The Nation. Jalalzai's extensive writing covers topics such as Afghanistan, terrorism, nuclear and biological terrorism, human trafficking, drug trafficking, and intelligence research and analysis. Musa Khan Jalalzai is indeed regarded as an expert in intelligence analysis. His extensive body of work, including numerous books and articles, focuses on topics such as intelligence research, terrorism, nuclear and biological terrorism, and security issues in various regions. His background as a journalist and research scholar, coupled with his in-depth studies on these subjects, contribute to his expertise in intelligence analysis.

Musa Khan Jalalzai, in his recent works, delves into the complexities of intelligence challenges in Europe and the UK, specifically addressing the presence and operations of foreign espionage networks within the UK. His books, such as The UK Big-3: The French and German Intelligence Reforms, Intelligence Diversity and Foreign Espionage and Spying with Little Eye: Complexity of Intelligence Challenges in Europe, and the UK, Interference of Russian, Chinese and Iranian Intelligence, Oversight of Intelligence Infrastructure and Post Snowden Reform, explore the nuances of how foreign intelligence agencies have established espionage, terrorist, and extremist networks to influence policymaking, target critics, and promote subversive activities . Indeed, Musa Khan Jalalzai deserves recognition for his in-depth analysis and exposure of foreign intelligence agencies' activities in Europe and the UK. Through his investigative work, he sheds light on the intricate web of espionage, highlighting how these agencies operate within foreign territories to influence policy, target dissidents, and engage in subversive activities. His contributions provide valuable insights into the challenges of national security and intelligence oversight, fostering a greater understanding of international espionage's impact on domestic and foreign policy.

Musa Khan Jalalzai's work on French intelligence also underscores his expertise in exposing foreign intelligence operations, this time focusing on France. In this context, he meticulously details how foreign espionage networks have infiltrated and operated within France, mirroring his investigations into the UK and broader Europe. By doing so, Mr. Jalalzai contributes significantly to our understanding of international intelligence dynamics, emphasizing the pervasive nature of espionage across national borders. His analysis not only highlights the specific challenges faced by France in countering these operations but also contributes to the broader discourse on national security, sovereignty, and the complexities of global intelligence warfare. Through his scholarly and investigative efforts, Jalalzai offers a critical perspective on the implications of foreign espionage for national security policies and the need for robust intelligence reform and oversight mechanisms.

Afghanistan is a cauldron boiling with terrorism, extremism, suicide bombings, drone attacks, civil war, warlords, private militias, and Taliban insurgency. In the backdrop of all these burning issues, the book of Musa Khan Jalalzai (Civil War and the Partition of Afghanistan, Royal Book Company-Pakistan) provides a comprehensive account of the past, present and the future of Afghanistan. With the imminent withdrawal of the US troops, there is a growing perception in the world that the end game is being played in Afghanistan. How this great game unfolds, what will be the fate of Afghanistan, and what will be the impact of the 'final solution to the Afghan problem' on the regional and global security have been analysed threadbare by Musa Khan Jalalzai.

Will Afghanistan finally see peace after decades of civil war, or will it relapse into total chaos and anarchy after the withdrawal of the US/NATO forces? Will the partition of Afghanistan along the ethno-geographic north-south divide, as advocated by western analysis, ultimately solve the Afghan problem, or sow the seeds of a perpetual conflict, engulfing not only

Afghanistan but also its neighbouring countries? These and other questions agitating the minds not only of the Afghans but also of the thoughtful, conscientious people of a globalised world have been answered in Musa Khan Jalalzai's book, which is a treatise on contemporary Afghanistan and its inevitable fate, which has ramifications not only for Afghanistan and the region but also for the global peace and security.

Author Musa Khan Jalalzai's book on nuclear terrorism in Pakistan (Prospect of Nuclear Jihad in Pakistan: The Armed Forces, Islamic State, and the Threat of Chemical and Biological Terrorism, India, 22 August 2015) presents a concerning scenario regarding the security of Pakistan's nuclear facilities. He highlighted the potential threats from terrorist groups like the Tehrik-i-Taliban Pakistan (TTP), and the ISIS, and their ability to infiltrate and attack these critical sites. These threats include commando-style attacks, aircraft crashes into reactors, and cyberattacks, any of which could result in the dispersal of radioactivity and have disastrous consequences. Mr. Jalalzai pointed out that past terror attacks on Pakistan's nuclear facilities like Wah, Kamra, Dera Ghazi Khan, Karachi and Sargodha demonstrate the vulnerability of these nuclear sites. The extremist groups' access to nuclear facilities, potentially aided by radicalized individuals within the armed forces of Pakistan, raises significant security concerns. Further complicating the situation.

The information the author shared about the Pakistani army allegedly transferring nuclear weapons in a passenger wagon from the Khyber Pakhtunkhwa (KP) province to Punjab in 2013, is quite alarming. Such a method of transportation for nuclear weapons seems highly unconventional and risky, given the immense security risks involved with the handling and movement of nuclear materials. This situation, as described by author Jalalzai, raises serious questions about the security protocols and measures in place for the transport of Pakistan's nuclear arsenal. Typically, the movement of such sensitive and potentially dangerous materials is expected to be conducted with the highest level of security, often involving heavily armoured and guarded convoys.

The use of a passenger wagon would not only be inadequate in terms of security but also increases the risk of theft, sabotage, or accidental detonation. It's important to consider the context and implications of such actions, especially in a region with complex geopolitical dynamics and the presence of various extremist groups. The security of nuclear materials is a critical issue that has global implications, given the potential for catastrophic consequences in the event of a nuclear incident. Mr. Jalalzai's report underscores the need for robust, transparent, and effective security measures in the handling of nuclear weapons, not just in Pakistan but worldwide. The author's revelations suggest a precarious situation regarding the security of Pakistan's nuclear arsenal and facilities, highlighting the need for stringent measures to prevent potential nuclear incidents. Musa Khan Jalalzai warned that nuclear power plants, research reactors and uranium enrichment plants of Pakistan may, at any time, come under potential attack from the TTP and ISIS as they have already established a strong network within the headquarters of the armed forces.

Musa Khan Jalalzai's recent book, "Nuclear War in Europe: War in Ukraine, Intelligence and Prospect of Nuclear and Biological Terrorism in Europe and Central Asia," discusses the governance and protection of radioactive materials in conflict zones like Ukraine. It examines the challenges faced by governments and the United Nations in managing such threats, especially in states with large stockpiles of weapons. The book also explores modern military technologies, including artificial intelligence, robotics, and cyber warfare, and their impact on national security, particularly in the EU, Ukraine, Afghanistan, Pakistan, and Central Asia. Mr. Jalalzai, known for his extensive work on various security issues, provides an in-depth analysis of these critical topics in his book

The Taliban's intelligence services, one notable book is "The Taliban Intelligence: Intelligence Services in a Non-Democratic State". By Musa Khan Jalalzai. This book provides an in-depth analysis of the collapse of the Afghan state, the shortcomings of Afghan leadership, and the establishment of the Taliban's General Directorate of Intelligence (GDI). It discusses the challenges faced by the GDI in establishing itself amid Afghanistan's complex security situation. Musa Khan Jalalzai, the author, is a journalist and research scholar with extensive experience in writing about Afghanistan, terrorism, and intelligence research. This book is available in hardcover and paperback editions, and it covers various aspects of the Afghan state's collapse, the role of the US in Afghanistan, and the internal dynamics of the Taliban's intelligence services.

I encountered some difficulty accessing detailed lists of books by Musa Khan Jalalzai from online bookstores and databases. However, based on his profile and previous works, Musa Khan Jalalzai is known for writing extensively on topics related to Afghanistan, terrorism, nuclear and biological terrorism, human trafficking, drug trafficking, and intelligence research and analysis. Author Musa Khan Jalalzai is indeed recognized as a specialist in the field of intelligence, among other areas. He has written extensively on topics related to Afghanistan, terrorism, and intelligence research and analysis. His background and expertise are reflected in his writings, which often delve into geopolitical issues, security, and intelligence operations within the context of Afghanistan and the broader region. His book "The Taliban Intelligence: Intelligence Services in a Non-Democratic State" is a clear example of his work in the field of intelligence. This book provides an analysis of the intelligence services within the Taliban regime, offering insights into the operations and challenges of intelligence in a non-democratic state. Musa Khan Jalalzai's work is well-regarded for its depth and insight, particularly concerning the complex dynamics of terrorism, warfare, and intelligence in South Asia.

For those interested in intelligence studies, especially in relation to Afghanistan and its regional dynamics, his books can be a valuable resource. Musa Khan Jalalzai's book, "The Taliban Misrule in Afghanistan: Suicide Brigades, the IS-K Military Strength and its Suicide Vehicle Industry," explores the mechanisms of terror marketing and the use of suicide bombers in regions like India, Pakistan, and Afghanistan. The book discusses the strategies used by terrorist organizations such as ISIS and the Taliban to recruit and employ suicide bombers as tools in their campaigns of fear and violence. It delves into the evolving techniques of these groups and their impact on civil society and military infrastructure. Musa Khan Jalalzai's book likely addresses the presence and operations of the Daesh Khorasan branch in Afghanistan, uncovering various hidden aspects of their activities. This branch is known for its violent extremism and has been a significant concern in the region.

While specific details of the secrets revealed in the book are not provided in the summary, it is clear that Mr. Jalalzai offers deep insights into the tactics and strategies of such terrorist groups. For a comprehensive understanding of the book's contents, it would be best to read it directly. Musa Khan Jalalzai is a journalist and research scholar with extensive writing on Afghanistan, terrorism, and related topics. His expertise includes nuclear and biological terrorism, human trafficking, drug trafficking, and intelligence research. Mr. Jalalzai has been involved with several publications and has received notable educational credentials from various institutions in the United States. His broad research and writing scope suggest a deep understanding of regional issues, particularly concerning Afghanistan. Musa khan jalalzai in his book (is Britain becoming a failed state?) has claimed that Britain is becoming a failed state and highlighted the causes of failure.

Mr. Jalalzai, explores the idea that Britain may be on the path to becoming a failed state. He delves into various causes that he believes are contributing to this decline. These causes could range from political instability, economic challenges, social unrest, to issues in governance and public policy. Mr. Jalalzai's analysis likely includes examining historical trends, current events, and potential future implications, providing a comprehensive overview of the factors that might lead a country like Britain towards such a precarious situation. He has asserted that the British intelligence community (MI5, MI6, GCHQ and Menwith Hill) have failed to manage the political and economic security of the state. He likely critiques the effectiveness and strategies of British intelligence agencies in safeguarding national interests. This could involve analysing their roles in political decision-making, economic stability, handling of internal and external threats, and their overall impact on the security and wellbeing of the United Kingdom. Mr. Jalalzai's perspective might offer insights into the complexities and challenges faced by intelligence agencies in a rapidly changing global landscape.

Recently, author Musa Khan Jalalzai published an excellent book, "The French Intelligence: The Yellow Vests, the CNCTR and G10 Commissions and the EU Next Frontier for Intelligence", a comprehensive book that delves into the complexities of intelligence, security, and law enforcement mechanisms in Europe, with a focus on France. The book discusses how France has undergone significant political, social, and economic transformations, particularly in the context of intelligence and security. Mr. Jalalzai explores various themes, including the radicalization of the young generation in France by jihadist groups since 2001, the operations of African and South Asian jihadist groups in France, and the potential threats posed by the presence of ISIS in the country. He raises concerns about the possibility of terrorists acquiring nuclear materials or even complete warheads from black markets in India and Pakistan, and the consequent risks to European security.

The book also examines how France has managed its internal security in light of the Yellow Vest movement and recent terrorism incidents. Musa Khan Jalalzai highlights the professional approach of French intelligence in managing national security crises and emphasizes the importance of security sector reforms for maintaining law and order. This book is a significant contribution to the field of intelligence studies, providing insights into the challenges and strategies of French intelligence in navigating the evolving security landscape of Europe. His other notable book, "Spying with Little Eye" examines the complexities of intelligence challenges in Europe, the UK, and the involvement of Russian, Chinese, and Iranian intelligence.

The book delves into the assessment of intelligence agencies in the context of the Ukraine war and the miscalculations by major powers about Ukrainian and Russian military power. It highlights the issues of intelligence sharing among EU states, the diversity of national security threat perceptions, and the challenges in countering foreign espionage and terrorism. The book also discusses the interference of foreign intelligence in UK politics, exemplified by cases like Alexander Litvinenko and Sergei Skripal. Mr. Jalalzai, an experienced journalist and research scholar, offers an insightful analysis of these intelligence-related complexities.

Professor Jandad Jahani is the Chief Executive of Translation at the Department of ATR, Afghanistan. He is teaching Economics at Paktia University, Afghanistan based in Berlin, Germany. Dr. Jabeen. J is a retired professor of International Affairs, Kabul Afghanistan.

Appendix-2

The ISI War Crimes and Murder of Civilian Culture of Intelligence in Pakistan

Musa Khan Jalalzai, (Vij Publishing, New Delhi, 2021). pp. 236.

Reviews By: Wankhede Rahul Bhojraj. The Defence Horizon Journal. August 15, 2023

The ISI War Crimes and Murder of Civilian Culture of Intelligence in Pakistan presents a comprehensive examination of Pakistan's Inter-Services Intelligence (ISI). Established in 1948 to safeguard national security, the ISI holds considerable influence over the defense and foreign policy decisions in Pakistan, which often results in conflict with other national intelligence agencies. Numerous accounts have claimed that the ISI supports global terrorist activities, particularly against India and Afghanistan. Musa Khan Jalalzai, an experienced journalist with insider contacts, explores the origins and evolution of the ISI in 11 chapters supported by references and primary sources. The book traces the rise of the ISI and its entanglement in civil administration since Pakistan's independence. The agency's role in manipulating domestic and foreign policies has resulted in conflict with other intelligence agencies, further politicizing its activities with the support of politicians (in power and in opposition).

From the 1970s till the 1990s, the "critical years" played a significant role in shaping the ISI's intelligence culture, as it gained strategic experience training the mujahideen against the Soviets and later the Taliban against the U.S. This period was marked by the ISI's expansion into neighbouring countries like Nepal, which were then used as bases to launch attacks on India. Said expansion marginalized other intelligence agencies in Pakistan, granting the ISI dominance. Although Western spy agencies consider the ISI superior to its Indian counterpart, the Research and Analysis Wing, the ISI does not possess the professionalism found in organizations like the CIA or Britain's MI6. It suffers from the same inefficiencies and corruption prevalent in the rest of the Pakistani state. The ISI has repeatedly lost control over its most dangerous assets. Additionally, its analytical capabilities have been questioned, including its tendency to interpret information based on predetermined ideological biases.

The book sheds light on the ISI's involvement in extrajudicial killings, war crimes, human rights violations, and covert operations against India and Afghanistan. Double dealings with the U.S. and other countries are also explored, revealing the ISI's self-serving nature and its "miltablishment" apparatus. Its role in managing both internal and external affairs in Pakistan is noted, with journalists, activists, and minority leaders becoming targets of human rights violations. The book sheds light on the ISI's involvement in extrajudicial killings, war crimes, human rights violations, and covert operations against India and Afghanistan.

It concludes with an analysis of Pakistan's internal political situation, highlighting Baloch nationalism, the rise of the Tehreek-e-Taliban Pakistan, and other social movements. Despite the current internal turmoil in Pakistan, the ISI and the Pakistan Army maintain control, ensuring the country remains intact. The ISI's functioning, overseen by influential generals and army officers, remains unchecked, while civilian oversight remains superficial. In summary, this book offers valuable insights into Pakistan's intelligence culture and the dominance of the ISI. Musa Khan Jalalzai's work presents a compelling account of the agency's actions, making it a significant read for both general audiences and subject experts seeking to understand the ISI's role within Pakistan's intelligence landscape.

Wankhede Rahul Bhojraj is a research scholar at the JNU Special Centre for National Security Studies. The Defence Horizon Journal. He previously worked as an assistant professor at Savitribai Phule Pune University. His previous publications include web articles, book chapters and journal articles. The views contained in this article are the author's alone.

Appendix-3

My Pain in the Neck

Those who awaken communities and young generations about new developments, human rights and injustice are punished, or roasted like Gallus-Gallus. The Story of my awakening of communities and the young generation about the hidden things has been so painful during the last ten years when I decided to bring things to light. I discovered injustice in my books, articles and research papers and exposed things under the carpet. My anecdote has been indeterminately excruciating, and harrowing since 2018, while my literary and intellectual journey became full of suffering and pain. The fact is, I am an author of many books-published in Pakistan, the UK, India, Germany, the United States, Moldova, and Afghanistan, but some of these books put my life at stake, and some evoked my anxiety and pain. These books enraged British intelligence agencies and attempted to kill me. I have been receiving death threats from different terrorist organizations, suchlike Tablighi Jamaat, the ISIS terrorist group, Taliban and the British intelligence agencies since 2021, and lingered under different types of intelligence led surveillance at home, high streets and markets.

I reported all these death threat letters received and cases of harassment to the local police stations, office of MI5 and Home Office time and again, but unfortunately no legal action was taken against these sarcastic elements. I remained vulnerable and threatened. My human rights; right to life, privacy and freedom of expression was violated by agencies. I understand that "Article 8 of the UK Human Rights Act 1998" protects my right to respect for private life, my family life, home and my correspondence (letters, telephone calls and emails, for example), but in my case the picture was underwhelming and gloomy. I was not feeling safe in my flats (322-Wellington Road South Hounslow London-38-Meadowbank Garden Cranford, Hounslow London, TW5 9TU), streets, towns and cities due to my analysis and writing against the weak approach of the British intelligence agencies to counter-extremism and foreign espionage. My privacy and communications were contravened, breached and stolen. While Article-8 gives me the right to live my own life privately without the interference of intelligence agencies, police and government, I experienced immeasurable interference, uncontrollable surveillance and powerful Facial Recognition technological spying.

My articles, research papers, intelligence analyses, and books radically exposed plans and strategies of the successive British governments. Over the past 10 years, I documented growing national security controversies of the UK governments that mostly revolved around the failure of the state to extend hands of intelligence cooperation to the EU member states. I am well-aware of the Universal Declaration of Human Rights, the European Commission of Human Rights, and the European Court of Human Rights and the Committee of Ministers of the Council of Europe. The European Convention on Human Rights is an international convention to protect human rights and political freedoms in Europe. The EU Charter of Fundamental Rights Article 2-Right to life defines that everyone has the right to life. Paragraph 1 of this Article is based on the first sentence of Article 2(1) of the ECHR that elucidates that everyone's right to life shall be protected by law? In the UK, human rights are protected by the Human Rights Act 1998, but governments have been accused of perpetrating and being complicit in torture and inhumane or degrading treatment, notwithstanding ratification of several international conventions. The UK has also ratified a number of international treaties that provide further protection against torture and ill-treatment.

The UK Human Rights Act 1998 gives effect to the human rights set out in the European Convention on Human Rights. Article 2 defines the right to life as one of the rights protected by the Human Rights Act: "Article 2 protects our right to life. The right to life means public authorities have the duty not to end life except in very limited situations". Article 2 is often referred to as an absolute right. Absolute rights are rights which can never be interfered with by the state. While Article 3 of the European Convention on Human Rights provides that: "No one shall be subjected to torture or to inhumane or degrading treatment or punishment". Article 8 of the European Convention on Human Rights protects private and family life, home and correspondence. I have been critically discussing all security related issues for years and pointed to the fact that the present security infrastructure cannot secure the lives of citizens. The issue of foreign espionage once more reverberated in British newspapers in 2022 after the arrival of my book (The UK Big-3: The French and German Intelligence Reforms, Intelligence Diversity and Foreign Espionage. Musa Khan Jalalzai, July 10, 2022) in market.

In my recent book (The Intelligence War in Britain: Public Perceptions of the UK Intelligence Agencies, Foreign Espionage, the Tory Party and its Response to the Salisbury Attacks. Musa Khan Jalalzai. Vij Publishers India, 2022) I highlighted the intelligence war in Britain because foreign intelligence agencies in the UK have established different espionage, terrorist, and extremist networks to influence policy making and target their critics. In this book, I discovered public perception of MI5, MI6 and GCHQ, and internal war in different perspectives. Russian, Pakistani, Indian, Bangladeshi, Chinese, and some African states have been exhibiting their power every year in different forms-including extremist and sectarian fight in cities and towns. My book has addressed all espionage issues in the UK, but some circles didn't like my perception about the failure of British intelligence. In my book, (The UK Big-3: The French and German Intelligence Reforms, Intelligence Diversity and Foreign Espionage. Musa Khan Jalalzai, July 10, 2022) I documented interference of Iranian, Chinese and Russian intelligence agencies in Denmark, Norway, Sweden and Baltic States, and also highlighted intelligence surveillance reforms in France and Germany. I criticised the British intelligence's dirty business of harassing critics.

These challenges debilitated the voice of Britain on international forums, and incapacitated its enforcement capabilities to energetically respond to the waves of terrorism, foreign espionage, and extremism. External interference damaged the state's fundamental institutions. There have been several types of interference in the UK that complicated the security of citizens. To control society and political opponents, British Intelligence has been using technology and abusing power which threatens freedoms and the very things that make us human. When I wrote an article in the Daily Times about the country's Snooper Charter Surveillance in 2017, I was threatened of dire consequences. Later on, I wrote a book (Intelligence in Vex-2018) in which I documented the failure of British intelligence on all fronts. The introduction of Mass Surveillance programs by the British authorities prompted nationwide debate on the rights of civilians to be protected from illegitimate or warrantless collection, and analysis of their data and metadata. The Home Office Web-Spying Powers and its collaboration with Internet Providers who helped the Home Office and National Crime Agency in tracking websites-visits was a matter of great concern in 2022.

Statewatch, monitoring the state and civil liberties in Europe, (11 March 2021) in its report noted the covert human intelligence sources (Criminal

Conduct Act). Covert Human Intelligence agents might be secret police officers, informers and state agents. In my new book, (The UK Big-3: The French and German Intelligence Reforms, Intelligence Diversity and Foreign Espionage. Musa Khan Jalalzai, July 10, 2022) my fault was to critically discuss all the above-mentioned failures of British intelligence. In January 2024, the government announced a new Counter Espionage Unit (CEU) to deal with the risk of foreign espionage and intelligence war in the UK. In these circumstances, I wrote a letter to the Commissioner of London Metropolitan Police and shared my pain in the neck:

1. Commissioner of Police of the Metropolitan

6th Floor Fry Building, 2 Marsham Street SW1P 4DF.London

Honourable Sir Mark Rowley

I want to share my pain in the neck with you as I have been under threat from intelligence agencies and their private partners in Hounslow Borough since 2019. I have often been intimidated, consternated, followed and harassed in streets, markets and on my way to home. Now, I am thinking on different lines about whether to leave this country. All these consternating incidents were gradually reported to the police, MI5, and investigatory Power Commissioner by post, but unfortunately, I received no encouraging response from the police, in order to authenticate who is harassing me, who follows me and why? On 24 October 2019, I registered a complaint with the Hounslow Police Station that I was being spied on by unauthorized persons of different nationalities, the police response was underwhelming to find a reasonable panacea to my intensifying pain, or consider my screech and yell accordingly. Consequently, this posterior letter automatically updates you about the evolution of my physical threat-reported to the law enforcement authority's months ago. Recent development in my physical security threat is more consternating. From February 2022, one of the UK Pakistani spy (B. Ramazan of Heston area, cell-07915609296, Office cell: 07946867182) spied on me and followed me during my walk time, and on my way to home.

On 23 April 2022, he and his colleagues had parked a vehicle (Jeep) opposite to my house on sander road (the Mosque Street) to spy on me. On 25 April 2022 (1:15 PM) he followed me from my house (Wellington Road South Hounslow) to Hounslow West Tube station, and finally shamefully approached me and said: "Sorry I was following you from your house, but I had parked my car here in Hounslow West Tube Station Park." I want to ask who this man is and what his intentions are. Is he spying for the UK intelligence agencies? I need the answer first, and this is a moral obligation of the police to investigate him. I am an author of over 80 books (My CV Attached) and expert of Geospatial Intelligence and Mind Control Intelligence (telepathic intelligence). I have written 5 books on EU intelligence challenges and interoperability.

However, on 25 April, 2022, in a Treaty Centre restaurant (Hounslow High Street), a masked man disguised as a cleaner came to our table looking and watching me for 10 minutes. One of my friends, Imtiaz Shah, intimated and spotlighted me that the man was very dangerous and looked at me and said he was not a cleaner. As I have already reported these unauthorized and illegal individual surveillance and espionage against me in the Hounslow area by different people, I over-and-above want to inform the MET Police Headquarters-London that my life is under serious threat. In Hounslow Borough, particularly in the Treaty Centre, foreign intelligence spies are operating illegally in case of camera, car and mobile surveillance against me. I have had a depressing experience of this unauthorized intelligence directed at my flat since 2018, and 2021, I have mentioned my pain in my recent book (Stop Spying on Me). These espionage masters have already killed over a dozen people in different states because headquarter of the Killer Unit is based in Pakistan's High Commission London. On 01 May 2020, Balochistan Times reported the killing of a Baloch journalist & editor Balochistan Times, Sajid Hussain who went missing from Sweden was found in a river Upsalla, Sweden. The Pakistan intelligence agencies based in London have been constantly following their critics, writers and journalists. In Pakistan's high commission in London, a killer unit was established by Pakistan's army chief General, Qamar Javed Bajwa during his official visit to Pakistan High Commission in London in June 2019 to kill and intimidate Pakistani critics and writers. Pakistani and Indian intelligence agencies are using targeted killers to eliminate their opponents and critics. In 2022, a London based British Pakistani terrorist Gaohir Khan was arrested by our police and sentenced to life in prison. The Nation weekly reported a 31-year-old British Pakistani man Muhammad Gaohir Khan was hired by Pakistani intelligence agency for £100,000 to kill Netherlands-based journalist and blogger Ahmad Waqass Goraya. Our Police uncovered more than 2,000 WhatsApp messages exchanged between Muhammad Gohir Khan and Pakistani intelligence agency (ISI). I trust our MET Police, and hope my pain will be realized."

Sincerely

Musa Khan Jalalzai:

322-Wellington Road South,

Hounslow, Middlesex,

TW4 5JU, 27 April 2023

Email, journalistn4@gmail.com

Cell: 07447522293

On 15 November 2023, I wrote another letter to the office of Investigatory Powers Commissioner and requested to consider my yell against intelligence agencies:

2. Investigatory Powers Commissioner's Office

PO Box 29105, London SW1V 1ZU

Dear Sir

I want to share with you my pain in the neck and I am living through severe pain of harassment and metal torture. I need your help in saving my life. I have been in a critical situation due to intelligence surveillance and spying games after the arrival of my book (The Intelligence War in Britain: Public Perceptions of the UK Intelligence Agencies, Foreign Espionage, the Tory Party and its Response to the Salisbury Attacks, November-2022). I have received different types of verbal abuse and threats in streets and towns. Intelligence agencies are behind me to torture me. Your office oversees the use of covert investigatory powers by more than 600 public authorities, including the UK's intelligence agencies, law enforcement agencies, police, councils and prisons. This means that you independently review applications from public authorities to use the most intrusive of these powers and check that all the powers are used in accordance with the law. You are kindly requested to please consider me screech and yell.

In all conscience and earnestly

Musa Khan Jalalzai

38-Meadowbank Garden

Cranford Hounslow Middlesex

TW5 9TU, 15 November 2022

In August 2023, on my way to high street, four vandals harassed me and tortured me. Later on, I published two articles in Global Security Review-

USA about the deteriorating security situation in the UK, I further received extra threat letters by unknown groups remonstrating that they could translate their anger into a violent action. I posted and emailed all these letters in July 2023 to the UK Foreign Ministry in order to protect me from a possible terrorist attack, but FCO never responded to my yoo-hoo and screeching. Secret forces started harassing me through private intelligence and surveillance agencies in 2022 and 2023. Some vilified me, some slapped me on the face and some terrified me by different humiliating means in Richmond and Hounslow Boroughs in 2023, but I never relinquished. I wrote a book (Is the UK becoming a failed state? Musa Khan Jalalzai-2022 India), in which I highlighted power centralization and so called power devolution in Wales and Northern Ireland. Funds were unequally distributed in Wales and Northern Ireland. More than £400 billion was stolen and taken for oneself, and in 2023, £370 billion disappeared. I strongly criticized the deficiencies of the British intelligence agencies National Security Council (NSC) and Parliamentary Intelligence Committee, which lacked professional capacity to investigate these cases. I received mixed threatening messages, chain of surveillance and uncontrollable secret police watchdog and faced the wrath of MI5. Intelligence and policing agencies pointed at me the gun of Facial Recognition Technology and several other types of surveillance technologies were used against me to intimidate me and bring me to their streak. I refused and said: "I am unable to dance to your tango". In my letter to intelligence commissioner, I stated:

3. Investigatory Powers Commissioner's Office

PO Box 29105, London

SW1V 1ZU

Dear Sir,

I want to share my pain in the neck with you as I have been under threat from different British intelligence agencies and their private partners since 2020. I have often been intimidated, consternated, followed and harassed in streets, markets and on my way to home. Now, I am thinking on different lines either to do suicide, or leave this country. All these consternating incidents were gradually reported to the Hounslow police station, MI5, Metropolitan Police Department, and investigatory Power Commissioner by post, but unfortunately, I received no encouraging response in order to authenticate who is harassing me, who follows me and why? On 24 October 2019, I registered a complaint with the Hounslow Police Station that I was being spied on by unauthorised persons of different nationalities-working with private agencies, the police failed to find a reasonable panacea for my intensifying pain, and considered my yell. Attitude of the London Borough of Hounslow has also changed as intelligence gives me pain by different means.

Consequently, this posterior letter automatically updates you about the evolution of my physical threat-reported to the law enforcement authorities from 2018-2022. Recent aggrandisement in my physical security threat is more consternating. From February 2022, a Pakistani (B. Ramazan of Heston area, cell-07915609296, Office cell: 07946867182) spying on me and following me during my walk time, and on my way to home. On 23 April 2022, he and his colleagues had parked a vehicle (Jeep) opposite to my house on sander road (the Mosque Street) to spy on me from their car surveillance camera. On 25 April 2022 (1:10 PM) he followed me from my house (Wellington Road South Hounslow) to Hounslow West Tube station, and finally approached this scribe and said: "Sorry I was following you, but I had parked my car here." I want to ask who this man is and what his intentions are, is he spying for the Hounslow police station based intelligence networks, or is he barking for the Pakistani intelligence killer unit based in Pakistan's Embassy in London. I need the answer first, and this is a moral obligation of the police to investigate him.

As I have authenticated by my deep research efforts that foreign espionage in the UK has been a bigger challenge since 2001. Intelligence agencies of South Asian States in London have been reported by newspapers for years but successive governments have been helpless to counter their subversive campaign. Pakistani and Indian intelligence agencies are using targeted killers to eliminate their opponents and critics. In 2022, a London based British Pakistani terrorist Gaohir Khan was sentenced to life in prison. The Nation weekly reported that a 31-year-old British Pakistani man Muhammad Gaohir Khan was charged for conspiring to kill Netherlands-based journalist and blogger, Ahmad Waqass Goraya on behalf of Pakistani Inter-Services Intelligence (ISI).

Musa Khan Jalalzai: 322-Wellington, Road South,

Hounslow, Middlesex, TW4 5JU, 12 April 2022

My letters to the Police, Surveillance Commissioner London

4. Dear commander Hounslow Police Station

Honourable, this is my fourth complaint. I am going to register with the Hounslow Police Station about my vulnerability and harassment by different fashions. Sometimes, I am being spied on by spy agencies, including Pakistani secret agencies, and sometimes, Pakistanis (UK Based) belonging to their military establishment and political parties threaten me through different channels. Unfortunately, the police have failed to protect me. The fact is, I am an author-writing on terrorism, law enforcement agencies and intelligence analysis, which highlights the whole process critically. Now, I have become exasperated. This is my last complaint to register with you, if considered accordingly that's ok, otherwise I will be leaving this country.

Sincerely

Musa Khan Jalalzai-10 May 2023

322-Wellington Road South

Hounslow Middlesex London UK. TW4 5JU

5. Honourable Chief London Borough Hounslow

I am not going into the details and debate of civil rights, human rights and citizen rights in the British constitution, I just want to complain about my consternation and trepidation I have been suffering from since last year. As I have already registered several complaints with the local police and the council against foreign suspicious people, and their cronies dancing in Hounslow with impunity. I am going outside in consternation, and coming home through different streets with fear. When I go upstairs to my flat, I feel myself under threat from unknown people coming into Hounslow Central Mosque (opposite to my flat).

These spy agents are women, men belonging to houses No-56,7,8, and more importantly, in my neighbourhood, queer-looking men and women are visiting the house. People from house No_ 346 also spy on me every morning. In Treaty Centre Hounslow High Street, every day, I come across new people with their eyes on me. I am now in a state of distress and fright-embroiled in different negative thinking. I requested the police to help me in moving me out of London, or provide me reasonable protection, requested the council to shift me out of London, nothing positive happened. Finally, I wrote a letter to the in charge of the diplomatic section in FCO last year. Now I am writing to inform you about my saga, and would like to request you to help me solve my problems.

In all conscience

Musa Khan Jalalzai

322-Wellington Road Hounslow

London, TW4 5JU. 20 June 2023

6. The Investigatory Powers Commissioner's Office

PO Box 29105, London, SW1V 1ZU

Dear Sir,

Please find my new paper (attached), and my torment and consternation. I have been experiencing an irksome situation since 2018. Surveillance of the local police is consternating. Facial recognition surveillance is making things worse. On 22 June 2019, I had intended to write an article on the UK surveillance mechanism, and collected information from different sources that the file was removed by invisible people from my desktop immediately. Please address my concerns according to the freedom of expression law.

Sincerely

Musa Khan Jalalzai

322-Wellington Road South

Hounslow TW4 5JU-30 June 2023

7. The Surveillance Camera Commissioner

2 Marsham Street, 1st Floor, Peel London

SW1P 4DF, United Kingdom

Dear Sir,

Please address my concerns and my torment and consternation. I have been experiencing an irksome situation since 2018. Surveillance of the local police is consternating. On 22 June 2019, I had intended to write an article on the UK surveillance mechanism-collected information from different sources that file was removed by invisible people immediately. Please address my concerns according to the freedom of expression law.

Sincerely

Musa Khan Jalalzai

322-Wellington Road South

Hounslow TW4 5JU

23 June 2022

The UK police and intelligence agencies were given full power to crush my computer without the permission of information and intelligence commissioners. I experienced a bitter taste in 2023, when I was investigated before going to France at Heathrow Airport. By arriving in Paris, they also booked a room next to me in the same hotel near to the Eiffel Tower. I was under full surveillance in Paris unfortunately. I started feeling excruciate and realized that I have become more vulnerable. I am under constant threat from agencies and different religious and political circles. I need protection and security to continue my struggle against injustice. I was tortured by masked men on several occasions, harassed, vilified and my email and computer was hacked, my data was destroyed and important files were eliminated by agencies. Two assassinated attempts were made in September 2022, and 28 June 2023 after the enactment of the Covert Human Intelligence Sources (Criminal Conduct) Act 2022. However, journalist Lara Keay (MI5 'really does have a licence to kill.

Mail-online, (06 November 2019) reported the MI5's authorization of its agents to commit serious crimes, potentially including murder, kidnap and torture. Human rights organizations initiated legal action against the agency's illegal assassination campaign. They argued that this illegal assassination policy was kept secret for decades. On 28 January 2023, Daily Mail noted Big Brother Watch concerns regarding the army Brigade-77 controversial role. Secret units operation in British Cabinet Office and in the Department of Digital, Culture, Media and Sport are spying on politicians. The agency killed innocent opponents and critics and kidnapped people of its choice. Tortured writers and journalists. Spy agency has secretly allowed informants to murder, kidnap and torture for decades, tribunal hears: Four human rights organisations are taking legal action against UK Government. Claim policy allows MI5 agents to commit crimes and get immunity from justice.

Human rights organizations initiated legal action against the agency's illegal assassination campaign. They argued that this illegal assassination policy was kept secret for decades. Privacy International, Reprieve, the Committee on the Administration of Justice and the Pat Finucane Centre were asking the Investigatory Powers Tribunal to declare the policy unlawful and grant an injunction 'restraining further unlawful conduct'. Four human rights organisations have claimed that MI5 informants employed by the spy agency have been illegally committing crimes for the intelligence services for decades. The MI5 agency has been weak and controversial throughout 21st century-demonstrating intransigence, irresponsibly managing controversial security measures. Never demonstrated as a professional agency according to its historical roots. The agency killed innocent opponents and critics and kidnapped people of its choice. Tortured writers and journalists. Spy agency has secretly allowed informants to murder, kidnap and torture for decades, tribunal hears: Four human rights organisations are taking legal action against UK Government. Claim policy allows MI5 agents to commit crimes and get immunity from justice. I became the first victim of this law that authorised MI5 to hire a private agent and kill me. I am in pain and vulnerable due to my critical writing and agencies are behind me to eliminate me. Policing agencies have been following me in streets and markets since 2022. In 2023, I told my son if anything happened to me the intelligence and the policing agencies would be responsible for my death. After two assignation attempts against me, I become weak and my body has broken. I need justice and protection and an environment free of harassment.

Musa Khan Jalalzai

London-20, 02, 2024

Notes to Chapters

Chapter 1: The Post-Cold War Intelligence Mechanism and Dynamic of Britain's National Security Threats: Foreign Espionage, Extremism and Hostile States.

1. Warren Chin (Technology, war and the state: past, present and future: International Affairs, Volume 95, Issue 4, 01 July 2019.

2. Dr. Kristi Raik (Deputy Director and Head of the Foreign Policy Programme of the International Centre for Defence and Security) and Eero Kristjan Sild in their research paper (Europe's broken order and the prospect of a new Cold War Authors. International Centre for Defence and Security. October 2023.

3. Dr. Mazzola Stephanie in her PhD thesis (Intelligence services in Post Conflict State Building a comprehensive study of Iraq and Afghanistan Mazzola, Stephanie. War Studies Department, King's College London, July 2021.

4. Dovydas Vitkauskas in his research paper, (The Role of Security Intelligence Services in a Democracy- North Atlantic Treaty Organization: Democratic Institutions Fellowships Programme 1997-1999.

5. Larry L. Watts in his research paper (Conflicting Paradigms, Dissimilar Contexts. Intelligence Reform in Europe's Emerging Democracies, New Democracies, Studies in Intelligence, Vol. 48, No.1.

6. Mikael Lohse, Chief Specialist and Deputy Intelligence Ombudsman at the Office of the Intelligence Ombudsman in Finland in his paper (Finnish intelligence overseers' right of access supersedes Originator Control. About Intel.

7. Mikael Lohse (The Intelligence Process in Finland. Scandinavian Journal of Military Studies. 19 June 2020.

8. Hager Ben Jaffel and Sebastian Larsson in their research analysis (Why Do We Need a New Research Agenda for the Study of Intelligence? International Journal of Intelligence and Counterintelligence. 06 July 2023.

9. David Anstiss, Dr. Cemal Dikmen, and Kevin McTiernan, (Global Lawful and Location Intelligence Outlook: 18 January 2024/

10. Daniela Richterova and Natalia Telepneva inn their paper, An Introduction: The Secret Struggle for the Global South–Espionage, Military Assistance and State Security in the Cold War-18 Jun 2020.

Chapter 2: The British Intelligence Remained Imbalanced in National Security Strategy Contents: Lack of Coordination among British Intelligence Agencies and the Police is a Challenging Quiz.

1. Vanessa Thorpe, Arts and Media correspondent, 31 Dec 2023-Guardian

2. Karen Lund Petersen and Kira Vrist Rønn in their research paper (Introducing the special issue: bringing in the public. Intelligence on the frontier between state and civil society- Intelligence and National Security 2019, vol. 34, NO. 3. Routledge, 12 Feb 2019.

3. Journalist Nazia Parveen in her news analysis (MI5 didn't trust black people with secrets in the 1960s, files show. The Guardian, 30 October, 2018.

4. George Kassimeris and Oliver Price in their paper (How the rise of Militant Tendency transformed MI5's perception of Trotskyism's ability to pose a threat to the British state. LSE British Politics and Policy, a multidisciplinary academic blog run by the London School of Economics and Political Science. 15 November 2021.

5. Journalist Lara Keay (MI5 'really does have a licence to kill': Spy agency has secretly allowed informants to murder, kidnap and torture for decades, tribunal hears: Four human rights organisations are taking legal action against UK Government. Claim policy allows MI5 agents to commit crimes and get immunity from justice. Mail-online, 06 November 2019.

6. Journalist Claire Ellicot in his Daily Mail article discovered the ex-wife of agent Harry Houghton had informed his employers that he was 'divulging secret information to people who ought not to get it. The MI5 spy leader, (Security Minister Ben Wallace) in an interview with daily Mail newspaper painted a disturbing picture of Russian aggression, and Islamic extremism. The inability of MI5 to protect its secret files led to the risk of 600 police experts. 2024,

7. Integrated Review Refresh 2023: "Responding to a more contested and volatile world-16 May 2023.

8. The UK Big Three, Musa Khan Jalalzai, 2022

9. Ibid

10. Ibid

11. 31 January 2023, Forces-Net

12. Ibid

13. Paul Knaggs. 77 Brigade: The British Army spied on its citizens during lockdown-January 30, 2023, Labour Heartland

14. 28 January 2023, Daily Mail

15. The UK Big Three, Musa Khan Jalalzai, 2022

16. Ibid

Chapter 3: The CONTEST, PREVENT and the Troubled and Challenging European Union's Intelligence Cooperation with the United Kingdom

1. The New CONTEST-2023

2. 13 January 2022, Al Jazeera

3. 25 July 2022, Human Rights Organization Liberty

4. Xinhua News Agency. British security tactics proved ineffective, outdated. March 1, 2015

5. Chief Minister of Wales, Mark Drakeford expressed concern over the attitude of Whitehall towards provinces and the future of the Union. In his commentary in the foreword of the report of his administration (Reforming our Union: Shared Governance in the UK-2021.

6. BBC reported, 25 January 2021

7. Former Prime Minister Gordon Brown statement, Al Jazeera-25 January 2021

8. Intelligence and Security Committee (Diversity and Inclusion in the UK Intelligence Community Presented to Parliament pursuant to section-3 of the Justice and Security Act 2013, 18 July 2018.

9. Daniel W. B. Lomas. ForgetJamesBond: diversity, inclusion and the UK's intelligence agencies, Intelligence and National Securit.

10. In July 2018, the Intelligence and Security Domestic Governance, Intelligence Diversity, and Surveillance Committee reported on Diversity and Inclusion in the UK intelligence Community".

11. Daniel W. B. Lomas, ForgetJamesBond: diversity, inclusion and the UK's intelligence agencies, Intelligence and National Security.

12. Deputy Digital Editor of Wired, Matt Burgess (The UK is secretly testing a controversial web snooping tool-11.03.2021).

13. 30 January 2023, Liberty and Privacy International won landmark case against MI5's unlawful handling of millions of people's data.

14. 13 February 2020, Liberty Human Rights organization lawyer, Megan Goulding

15. 11 April 2022, Arab News

16. Gavin Mortimer (How much longer will MI5 cloak its incompetence in secrecy? The Spectator, 3 March 2023.

17. 31 January 2023, Joshua Rozenberg (MI5 and Home Office acted unlawfully: But tribunal rules that a public finding of 'serious failings' is punishment enough-A Lawyer writes

18. 20 December, 2023, the Guardian newspaper's Legal affairs correspondent, Haroon Siddique reported some legal aspects of a Palestinian national, Abu Zubaydah's pain inflicted by MI5 and the CIA agents.

19. As the Covert Human Intelligence Sources (Criminal Conduct) Bill 2019-2021 generated debates in domestic and international forums, analyst and expert Joanna Dawson noted that the Covert Human Intelligence Sources (Criminal Conduct) Bill 2019-2021 would 'introduce a power in the Regulation of Investigatory Powers Act 2000 to authorize conduct by officials and agents of the security and intelligence services, law enforcement, and certain other public authorities, which would otherwise constitute criminality.

20. Ibid

Chapter 4: Failure of British Intelligence to Counter Foreign espionage, Murder by Poisons, Viruses and Firearms.

1. Daniel Salisbury and Karl Dewey. (Murder on Waterloo Bridge: placing the assassination of Georgi Markov in past and present context, 1970–2018, Contemporary British History, Volume 37, 2023-issue 1.18 Jan 2023.

2. Joshua Stewart. (Responding to Security Threats, the Grey Orchestra: Elastic Communications and the UK's Response to Salisbury, the RUSI Journal. Volume 167, 2022 - Issue 231 May 2022

3. December 2018, the Guardian

4. Kevin P. Riehle. (Ignorance, indifference, or incompetence: why are Russian covert actions so easily unmasked? Intelligence and National Security, 30 Jan 2024

5. Intelligence in a constitutional Democracy: Ministerial Review Commission on Intelligence, Republic of South Africa, 10 September 2008

6. 23 January 2024, writer and analyst, Paul Medina. (To Ten Scandal with British Intelligence-23 January, 2024

7. 29 October 2023, the Guardian reported, Second investigation to open into role of British spies in torture of Guantánamo detainee. Lawyers for Abd al-Rahim al-Nashiri claim UK intelligence was 'complicit in his ill-treatment' by the US, Guardian Sun 29 Oct 2023

8. The Guardian newspaper on 01 August 2023 reported (UK spy agencies want to relax 'burdensome' laws on AI data use: GCHQ, MI6 and MI5 propose weakening safeguards that limit training of AI models with bulk personal datasets- Harry Davies, The Guardia Tue 1 Aug 2023.

9. The Guardian newspaper on 01 August 2023 reported (UK spy agencies want to relax 'burdensome' laws on AI data use: GCHQ, MI6 and MI5 propose weakening safeguards that limit training of AI models with bulk personal datasets- Harry Davies, The Guardia Tuesday 01 August, 2023

10. Ibid

11. Manchester Arena Inquiry: Volume 2: Emergency Response. Volume 2-II. Report of the Public Inquiry into the Attack on Manchester Arena on 22nd May 2017. Chairman: The Hon Sir John Saunders. Presented to Parliament pursuant to section 26 of the Inquiries Act 2005, ordered by the House of Commons to be printed 3 November 2022.

12. Ibid

13. Karen Lund Petersen and Kira Vrist Rønn. (Introducing the special issue: bringing in the public. Intelligence on the frontier between state and civil society- Intelligence and National Security 2019, vol. 34, NO. 3. Routledge, 12 Feb 2019.

14. George Kassimeris and Oliver Price. (How the rise of Militant Tendency transformed MI5's perception of Trotskyism's ability to pose a threat to the British state. LSE British Politics and Policy, a multidisciplinary academic blog run by the London School of Economics and Political Science. 15 November 2021.

15. Intelligence and Security Committee of Parliament on page 31 and 36 of its China report (1918).

Chapter 5: Collective Expulsion of Russian Diplomats from the US and EU Member States, Hostile States and the Chinese and Iranian Intelligence Networks in Britain

1. The Guardian, 26 March 2018

2. 07 December 2023, Guardian

3. 08 January 2024, Al Jazeera

4. Journalist Jill Lawless (MI6 spy chief says China, Russia, Iran top UK threat list-November 30, 2021

5. Asian Lite International (UK government taking poll interference threats seriously-23 January 2024

6. 15 January 2024, British Defence Secretary, Grant Shapps, speech at Lancaster House in London

7. Kyle S. Cunliffe. Cyber-enabled tradecraft and contemporary espionage: assessing the implications of the tradecraft paradox on agent recruitment in Russia and China-Intelligence and National Security Volume 38, 2023-Issue 7. 02 Jun 2023

8. Kevin P. Riehle in his research paper (Soviet and Russian Diplomatic Expulsions: How Many and Why? 06 Dec 2023

9. Express and Star.com on December 20, 2023

10. The Global Times. 24 January 2024

11. Andrew Macaskill and Kylie Maclellan-Reuter, September 14, 2023

12. 08 January 2024, Al Jazeera

13. Ibis

14. Ibid

15. 18 October 2023 the Independent

16. BBC Security Correspondent, Gordon Corera. Has the UK woken up to the China spy challenge? 11 September 202

17. British Intelligence Shines Light on Chinese Spy 'Hiding in Plain Sight-VoA, January 14, 2022, Jamie Dettmer.

18. 08 January 2024, Chinese spy agency

Chapter 6: The UK Security Challenges, Democratic Transition and Security Sector Reform in Eastern Europe.

1. Larry L. Watts (Conflicting Paradigms, Dissimilar Contexts: Intelligence Reform in Europe's Emerging Democracies. Larry L. Watts- Studies in Intelligence, New Democracies, Vol. 48, No. 1

2. Ibid

3. Aidan WILLS, Mathias. Hans Born, Martin Scheinin, Micha Wiebusch and Ashley Thornton (Parliamentary Oversight of Security and Intelligence Agencies in the European Union- European Parliament, Brussels, 2011

4. Larry L. Watts (Conflicting Paradigms, Dissimilar Contexts: Intelligence Reform in Europe's Emerging Democracies. Larry L. Watts- Studies in Intelligence, New Democracies, Vol. 48, No.

5. Dan Sabbagh Luke Harding and Andrew. Guardian-21 Jul 2020

6. Dan Lomas. The Russia Report: Intelligence Expert Explains How U.K. Ignored Growing Threat. Conversation, 21 July 2020

7. BBC Reality Check (Russia report: The unanswered questions-21 July 2020

8. Home Office in its recent Policy paper on Espionage and National Security Bill factsheet-08 September 2022

9. The Chinese Global Times (21 January, 2024

10. Ibid

11. Ibid

12. BBC April 2023

13. 21 January 2024, the Press United

14. 21 January 2024, Agency France Persse

15. The Intelligence and Security Committee of Parliament annual report for 2022–2023.

16. Mazzola Stephanie in her PhD thesis (Intelligence services in Post Conflict State Building a comprehensive study of Iraq and Afghanistan King's College London- July 2021

17. FRA report, Surveillance by intelligence services: fundamental rights safeguards and remedies in the EU Volume II: field perspectives and legal update- European Union Agency for Fundamental Rights, 2017

18. Julia Tinsley-Kent. 26 January 2024

19. Ibid

20. Byline Times analysis (Tens of billions in Government and Council pandemic spending unaccounted for as local authority auditing scandal worsens. David Hencke. 26 January 2024

21. Emma DeSouza (How long can the UK Government ignore the collapse of Governance in Northern Ireland? Rather than adapting to a new political landscape, leaders are laying roadblocks in place. Byline Times, 19 January 2024

22. Jeanine de Roy van Zuijdewijn and Edwin Bakker (Twenty years of countering jihadism in Western Europe: from the shock of 9/11 to 'jihadism fatigue', Journal of Policing, Intelligence and Counter Terrorism-26 Apr 2023

23. Victoria E. Bonnell, Centre for Slavic and East European Studies. University of California at Berkeley

24. Intelligence and Security Committee of Parliament China-2023.

Chapter 7: The France's National Security Challenges, the Fight against Foreign Espionage, Radicalization, and Extremist Organizations

1. James J Giordano and Bert Gordijn (Possibilities, limits, and implications of brain-computer interfacing technologies. Cambridge University Press: 07 May 2010.

2. Intelligence in a constitutional Democracy report, (Ministerial review commission on the intelligence Republic of South Africa, in its final report-10 September 2008

3. Al Jazeera (02 Jul 2023

4. Christiaan Menkveld. Understanding the complexity of intelligence problems-08 Feb 2021

5. Felix Treguer in his paper (Major oversight gaps in the French intelligence legal framework. 25. March 2022

6. Ibid

7. The report-Intelligence in a constitutional Democracy, Ministerial review commission on the intelligence in the Republic of South Africa (10 September 2008.

8. An Associate Researcher at the CNRS Centre for Internet and Society and postdoctoral fellow at CERI-Sciences. Professor Félix Tréguer in his recent research paper (Overview of France's Intelligence Legal Framework. December 2021.

9. (Rise of the Reactionaries: Comparing the Ideologies of Salafi Jihadism and White Supremacist Extremism. Alexander Meleagrou-Hitchens, Blyth Crawford, Valentin Wutke, the Program on Extremism, George Washington University, December 2021).

10. Laurence Bindner, Hugo Micheron, Aaron Y. Zelin (Policy Analysis, Policy Watch 3400. Terrorism in France: New and Old Trends in Jihadism. The Washington Institute for Near East Policy, 13 November 2020).

11. The EU's response to terrorism: Fighting terrorism is a top priority for the EU. Member states work closely together to prevent terrorist attacks and ensure the security of citizens. Council of the European Union

12. Jacques Follorou (Intelligence-gathering: French oversight board alarmed by the rise in requests concerning political activism: In its annual report, the secret services watchdog stated that it increased disciplinary warnings and requests for additional information. The commission warned of the weakness of its oversight measures, which are ill-adapted to 21st-century technology. Le Monde, June 16, 2023.

13. Surveillance by intelligence services: Fundamental rights safeguards and remedies in the EU–2023

14. The 2017 FRA report

15. Ibid

16. The Euronews on 09 July 2023

17. Ibid

18. Alina Clasen (Intelligence reform and the transformation of the state: the end of a French exception German intelligence services point to increased hybrid security threats. EURACTIV.de-19 July 2023

19. Were the Paris attacks a French intelligence failure? Al Jazeera November 17, 2015

20. 23 December 2022, BBC

21. 28 October 2020, Paris based Le Monde Newspaper

22. 05 July 2016, Associated Press

23. 05 July 2016, New York Times

24. Jacques Follorou. France's tepid intelligence reform, 07 June 2021, About Intel

25. Griff Witte and Loveday Morris (Failure to stop Paris attacks reveals fatal flaws at heart of European security-Washington Post, 28 November 2015

26. Anne Lise Michelot (Reform of the French Intelligence Oversight System-30 November 2028

Chapter 8: The French Intelligence Reform, the Charlie Hebdo Assassination Attacks, Foreign Espionage, CNCTR and Democratization of Post-Cold War Intelligence in Europe.

1. James J Giordano and Bert Gordijn in their research paper (Possibilities, limits, and implications of brain-computer interfacing technologies. Cambridge University Press: 07 May 2010

2. Ministerial Review Commission on the Intelligence Republic of South Africa, in its final report-10 September 2008.

3. Al Jazeera (02 Jul 2023

4. Christiaan Menkveld. Understanding the complexity of intelligence problems-08 Feb 2021

5. Associate researcher at CNRS and post-doctoral researcher at CERI Sciences in Paris, Felix Treguer in his paper (Major oversight gaps in the French intelligence legal framework. 25. March 2022.

6. Ibid

7. The report of Intelligence in a constitutional Democracy, Ministerial review commission on the intelligence in the Republic of South Africa (10 September 2008.

8. Professor Félix Tréguer- Overview of France's Intelligence Legal Framework. December 2021

9. Rise of the Reactionaries: Comparing the Ideologies of Salafi Jihadism and White Supremacist Extremism. (Alexander Meleagrou-Hitchens, Blyth Crawford, Valentin Wutke, the Program on Extremism, George Washington University, December 2021.

10. Laurence Bindner, Hugo Micheron, Aaron Y. Zelin (Policy Analysis, Policy Watch 3400. Terrorism in France: New and Old Trends in Jihadism. The Washington Institute for Near East Policy, 13 November 2020.

11. The EU's response to terrorism: Fighting terrorism is a top priority for the EU. Member states work closely together to prevent terrorist attacks and ensure the security of citizens. Council of the European Union.

12. Le Monde, June 16, 2023

13. FRA research report: Surveillance by intelligence services: Fundamental rights safeguards and remedies in the EU-2023.

14. The 2017 FRA report

15. The Euronews on 09 July 2023 reported France's intelligence authorities of violent actions by the ultra-right organizations. Director General of France Domestic Intelligence, Nicholas Lerner in his interview with Le Monde newspaper.

16. Mazzola, Stephanie in her research paper (War Studies Department. PhD Thesis: Intelligence services in Post Conflict State Building: a comprehensive study of Iraq and Afghanistan. July 2021, Kings College London. UK.

17. EURACTIV.de-19 July 2023

18. Al Jazeera November 17, 2015

19. Ibid

20. 23 December 2022, BBC

21. 05 July 2016, Associated Press

22. 05 July 2016, New York Times reporter Aurelien Breeden

23. Jacques Follorou in his commentary on the French intelligence reforms (France's tepid intelligence reform, 07 June 2021, About Intel.

24. Griff Witte and Loveday Morris (Failure to stop Paris attacks reveals fatal flaws at heart of European security-Washington Post, 28 November 2015.

25. Anne Lise Michelot (Reform of the French Intelligence Oversight System-30 November 2028

Chapter 9: The Tablighi Jamaat and its Intelligence Units Constitute Precarious Security Threat to France, and the European Union.

1, A unit of Aadhyaasi Media and Content Services Private Limited, OpIndia in its news commentary (Tablighi Jamaat and its links to terrorist organizations: History of association to Al Qaeda, Taliban and Kashmiri terrorists: Secret US documents released by WikiLeaks in 2011 revealed that some Al Qaeda operatives used the Jamaat to get visas and fund their travel to Pakistan. They also lived in and around Delhi, the documents said-31 March, 2020

2. Fred Burton and Scott Stewart in their report (Tablighi Jamaat: An Indirect Line to Terrorism-The Stratfor January 23, 2008

3. Arsalan Khan (Contested Sovereignty: Islamic Piety, Blasphemy politics and the paradox of Islamization in Pakistan-08 Jun 2022

4. South Asia Democratic Forum in its research paper (Policy Brief 10–Tablighi Jamaat and its role in the Global Jihad. South Asia Democratic Forum 11 December 2020

5. Ibid

6. Ibid

7. Vaibhav Singh's Tweet (04 April 2020

8. Hindustan Times (Pakistan stood in support of Tablighi Jamaat, is Imran Khan going against Saudi Arabia? 24 December 2021

9. EU today news report. Europe & US terror fears over Tablighi Jamaat Islamic group, 26 August 2020

Chapter 10: The Threat of Nuclear Weapons and the Jihadists use of Dirty Bomb, Chemical, Biological Weapons in France and the EU.

1. Jacques Follorou (Le Monde April 27, 2023).

2. Dick Toornstra (Parliamentary oversight of the security sector. OPPD Publisher: An OPPD publication on topical parliamentary affairs. European Parliament–OPPD, 2013.

3. Aidan Wills (Democratic and effective oversight of national security services. Issue paper published by the Council of Europe Commissioner for Human Rights. Council of Europe,. February 2019.

4. Franklin De Vrieze (Independent oversight institutions and regulatory agencies, and their relationship to parliament Outline of assessment framework. Westminster Foundation for Democracy, February-2019.

5. Muhammad Wajeeh, a Research Associate at Department of Development Studies, COMSATS Institute of Information Technology, Abbottabad Pakistan in his research paper (Nuclear Terrorism: A Potential Threat to World's Peace and Security-JSSA Vol II, No. 2.

6. Charles D. Ferguson in his paper (Assessing Radiological Weapons: Attack Methods and Estimated Effects. Defence against Terrorism Review Vol. 2, No. 2, fall 2009.

Chapter 11: Transformation of State Security and Intelligence Services in Poland: A Job Still Unfinished. Agnieszka Gogolewska.

1. Hans Born and Gabriel Geisler Mesevage, "Introducing Intelligence Oversight," Tool 1 in Overseeing Intelligence Services. A Toolkit, ed. Hans Born and Aidan Wills (Geneva: DCAF, 2012), https://www.dcaf.ch/sites/default/files/publications/documents/Born_Wills_Intelligence_oversight_TK_EN_0.pdf(link is external).

2. See the interview with the former functionary of the Internal Security Service ABW and former Head of Foreign Intelligence Service AW, Col. Grzegorz Małecki at http://www.defence24.pl/plk-grzegorz-malecki-panstwo-musi-byc-swiadome-roli-i-istoty-swoich-sluzb-wywiadowczych-wywiad(link is external). He voiced similar concerns about the lack of clarity in the functions of the Polish intelligence services in conversations with the author.

3. Among the academics, the most notable right-wing analyst of security and intelligence sector reform is professor Andrzej Zybertowicz from Toruń

University. He published numerous articles and books on the transformation, mostly critical of the conceptual approach to the reforms. See, i.e. "Chory rdzeń państwa" ("The Sick Core of the State"), interview with prof. Andrzej Zybertowicz, Rzeczpospolita daily, April 26, 2004.

4. Beyond the intelligence sector, the power to use covert surveillance techniques has been vested in several other security services in Poland: Police, including Central Investigative Bureau, Border Guards, Customs Services, Military Police and Treasury Intelligence, each in its respective field. The last of these is subordinated to the Ministry of Finance and criticized by some for its very extensive covert competencies. Despite this fact and the very name implying the function of intelligence gathering, the service is not considered as part of the intelligence sector.

5. Ustawa z 31 lipca 1985 r. o służbie funkcjonariuszy Służby Bezpieczeństwa i Milicji Obywatelskiej Polskiej Rzeczypospolitej Ludowej.

6. Jan Bodakowski, "Służby specjalne (wywiad, kontrwywiad, bezpieka) PRL," Salon 24, October 5, 2010, https://www.salon24.pl/u/jan-bodakowski/235906,sluzby-specjalne-wywiad-kontrwywiad-bezpieka-prl(link is external).

7. Ustawa z dnia 6 kwietnia 1990 r. o Urzędzie Ochrony Państwa.

8. Resolution No. 69 of the Council of Ministers of 21 May 1990 on the procedures and conditions for the admission of former Security Service officers to serve in the Office of State Protection and other organizational units subordinate to the Minister of Interior and to employ them in the Ministry of the Interior.

9. Rafal Leskiewicz, "Formalno-prawne aspekty powstania Urzędu Ochrony Państwa," in Urząd Ochrony Państwa 1990-2002 (Warszawa: Agencja Bezpieczeństwa Wewnętrznego, 2015), 53-79.

10. Antoni Dudek, Reglamentowana Rewolucja. Rozkład Dyktatury Komunistycznej w Polsce 1988-1990 (Warszawa, 2009).

11. See Andrzej Zybertowicz, W Uścisku Tajnych Służb. Upadek Komunizmu i Układ Postnomenklaturowy (Warszawa, 1993).

12. Zarządzenie nr. 39 prezesa Rady Ministrów z dnia 4 lipca 1990 roku w sprawie szczegółowego określenia zadań oraz struktury organizacyjnej Urzędu Ochrony Państwa, in Historyczno-prawna Analiza Struktur Organów Bezpieczeństwa Państwa w Polsce Ludowej (1944-1990). Zbiór studiów, ed. A. Jusupović and R. Leśkiewicz (Warszawa, 2013), 305-307.

13. See Andrzej Misiuk, "Cywilne Służby Specjalne w Polsce po 1989 r. Próba Refleksji," in Urząd Ochrony Państwa, 41-50.

14. In some private interviews, former UOP officers remembered the cases when the government politicians demanded that the cases of theft of expensive

alcohol from their studies be investigated, insisting that it falls within the purview of special services.

15. Ustawa z dnia 8 sierpnia 1996 r. o zmianie ustawy o Urzędzie Ochrony Państwa z 6 kwietnia 1990 r., Dz.U. 1996, No. 106, poz. 496.

16. The exact translation of the name of the institution from Polish would be "College for Special Services." That corroborates all the terminology-related problems in defining the meaning of "security sector" in Poland. The services commonly called 'intelligence' in most democratic countries, in Poland acquired the name 'special,' initially by habit, only to be incorporated later in the language used in legislative acts.

17. Misiuk, "Cywilne służby specjalne w Polsce," 46-47.

18. The series of internal structural transformations were introduced by the resolutions of the Prime Minister of December 6, 1996, August 19, 1998, May 12, 1999, and April 9, 2001. In 2002 the service was disbanded.

19. "Wszystkie służby III RP. Od UOP przez WSI do ABW i SKW," wiadomosci. dziennik.pl/polityka/artykuly/559825,sluzby-iii-rp-historia-powstanie-uop-abw-wsi.html(link is external).

20. Ustawa z dnia 24 maja 2002 r. o Agencji Bezpieczeństwa Wewnętrznego oraz Agencji Wywiadu, Dz.U. 2002 nr 74 poz. 676.

21. "Porządki po Nowku," interview with Andrzej Barcikowski, Trybuna, July 2, 2002.

22. Ustawa z dnia 9 czerwca 2006 r. o Centralnym Biurze Antykorupcyjnym Dz. U. z dnia 23 czerwca 2006 r.

23. See Marek Henzler, "Etaty i budżety służb specjalnych," https://www.polityka. pl/tygodnikpolityka/kraj/1500287,1,etaty-i-budzety-sluzb-specjalnych. read(link is external).

24. See https://mswia.gov.pl/pl/aktualnosci/11902,Rzad-przyjal-projekty-ustaw-o-ABW-i-AW.html(link is external).

25. Ustawy o powszechnym obowiązku obrony Rzeczypospolitej Polskiej z 21 listopada 1967 (Dz.U. z 1992 nr 4 poz. 16 i Dz. U. z 1994 nr 43 poz. 165).

26. Ustawa z dnia 9 lipca 2003 r. o Wojskowych Służbach Informacyjnych, Dz.U. 2003 nr 139 poz. 1326

27. Grzegorz Małecki, "UOP na tle innych służb europejskich," in Urząd Ochrony Państwa, 104.

28. Personal interviews of the author with former officers of the Military Intelligence.

29. Ustawa z dnia 9 czerwca 2006 r. o Służbie Kontrwywiadu Wojskowego oraz Służbie Wywiadu Wojskowego, Dz.U. 2006 nr 104 poz. 709.

30. Łukasz Rogojsz, "Łukasz Rogojsz," Newsweek, Polish edition, November 9, 2015, http://www.newsweek.pl/polska/antoni-macierewicz-raport-wsi-lista-macierewicza-specsluzby,artykuly,371988,1.html(link is external).

31. Załącznik do uchwały Sejmu RP z dnia 30 lipca 1992 r. – Regulamin Sejmu RP (tekst jednolity M.P. 2012 poz. 32 z późn. zm.)

32. http://orka.sejm.gov.pl/SQL.nsf/pracekom6?OpenAgent&SKBB(link is exte rnal).

33. Rozporządzenie Rady Ministrów z dnia 2 lipca 2002 r., Dz.U.02.103.929.

34. See Marta Kolendowska-Matejczuk, "Ile ograniczeń, a ile wolności w społeczeństwie obywatelskim w kontekście zapewnienia bezpieczeństwa państwa i obywateli," in Ochrona informacji niejawnych, biznesowych i danych osobowych, ed. Małgorzata Gajos (Katowice, 2012), 53-69.

35. Panoptykon Foundation, https://en.panoptykon.org/(link is external).

36. Helsinki Foundation for Human Rights, http://www.hfhr.pl/en/foundation/ (link is external).

37. Draft Bill on covert surveillance activities of February 7, 2008, parliamentary printout no. 353.

38. In Polish "działania operacyjno – rozpoznawcze" or to translate exactly "operational and surveillance activities," which collectively signify the operations with the use of covert human intelligence, intrusive investigations, direct surveillance, eavesdropping, interception of communication data, gathering of bulk data and the likes.

39. Dariusz Laskowski, "Prawne aspekty funkcjonowania służb specjalnych z perspektywy potrzeb obronnych państwa," Obronność. Zeszyty Naukowe 2, no. 10 (2014), 71.

40. Directive 2006/24/EC of the European Parliament and of the Council of 15 March 2006 on the retention of data generated or processed in connection with the provision of publicly available electronic communications services or of public communications networks and amending Directive 2002/58/EC, abolished 2014.

41. "Rok z ustawą inwigilacyjną. Co się zmieniło," Fundacja Panoptykon, January 18, 2017, https://panoptykon.org/biblio/rok-z-ustawa-inwigilacyjna(link is external).

42. Arkadiusz Król, „Działalność Operacyjna Służb Specjalnych w Systemie Bezpieczeństwa Państwa," Przegląd Bezpieczeństwa Wewnętrznego 9, no. 5 (2013), 287-289.

43. Król, „Działalność Operacyjna Służb Specjalnych w Systemie Bezpieczeństwa Państwa," 283-285.

44. Ustawa z 15 stycznia 2016 r. o zmianie ustawy o Policji oraz niektórych innych ustaw (Dz. U. 2016, poz. 147), dalej: tzw. ustawa inwigilacyjna, ustawa.

45. "Rok z ustawą inwigilacyjną. Co się zmieniło," 2-12.

46. Directive (EU) 2016/681 of the European Parliament and of the Council of 27 April 2016 on the use of passenger name record (PNR) data for the prevention, detection, investigation and prosecution of terrorist offences and serious crime.

47. Directive (EU) 2016/680 of the European Parliament and of the Council of 27 April 2016 on the protection of natural persons with regard to the processing of personal data by competent authorities for the purposes of the prevention, investigation, detection or prosecution of criminal offences or the execution of criminal penalties, and on the free movement of such data, and repealing Council Framework Decision 2008/977/JHA.

48. Letter from deputy Minister of Internal Affairs in response to watchdog enquiry, see https://www.rpo.gov.pl/sites/default/files/odpowied%C5%BA%20 MSWiA%20z%2015%20listopada%202017%20w%20sprawie%20 wdra%C5%BCania%20d.

Chapter 12: Soviet and Russian Diplomatic Expulsions: How Many and Why? Kevin P. Riehle

1 Jean d'Aspremont, "Persona Non Grata," in Max Planck Encyclopedias of International Law, edited by Anne Peters (Oxford: Oxford University Press).

2 Andrew Jordan, "You're Out! Explaining Non-Criminal Diplomatic Expulsion" (Ph.D. dissertation, University of Nevada, Las Vegas, 2018), p. 8.

3 See, for example, Carlos Cerda Duenas and Pablo Andrés Bonilla Hernandez, "Declaration of Persona Non Grata in Diplomacy: Experiences of Recent Practice in Guatemala," Derecho Global. Estudios sobre Serecho Justicia, Vol. 6, No. 17 (2021), pp. 167–194. https://doi.org/10.32870/dgedj.v6i17.351; Sean D. Murphy, "Expulsion of Cuban Diplomats for Spying," The American Journal of International Law, Vol. 97, No. 3 (2003), pp. 685–686.

4 U.S. Department of State, "Ensuring Reciprocity and Equivalence in the Functioning and Operations of Official Representatives of Soviet and Soviet Bloc Countries in the United States and Official Representatives of the United States in Soviet and Soviet Bloc Countries," 17 February 1984, CIA FOIA [Freedom of Information Act] Reading Room, https://www.cia.gov/readingroom/docs/CIA-RDP90B01370R000200330014-9.pdf, pp. 38–41.

5 Jordan, You're Out!, p. 9.

6 "Soviet Protests to Ghana over Expulsion of its Aides," New York Times, 4 April 1966, p. 25.

7 "Bolivia Is Ousting 119 Soviet Aides," New York Times, 30 March 1972, p. 1.

8   Steven R. David, "Soviet Involvement in Third World Coups," International Security, Vol. 11, No. 1 (1986), pp. 3–36.

9   Alvin Z. Rubinstein, "The Soviet Union and Iran under Khomeini," International Affairs (Royal Institute of International Affairs), Vol. 57, No. 4 (1981), pp. 599–617.

10 Jonathan Broder, "Egypt Expels Soviet Envoy and Six Aides," Chicago Tribune, 16 September 1981, p. 3.

11 U.S. Department of State, "Expulsions of Soviet Officials Worldwide, 1986," Foreign Affairs Note, January 1987.

12 U.S. Department of State, "Expulsions of Soviet Worldwide, 1983," Foreign Affairs Note, January 1984.

13 "Removed from Warsaw," Daily Telegraph (London), 10 June 1957, p. 9; Mirosław Golon, "Radzieckie służby dyplomatyczne i konsularne w Polsce w latach 1944–1961" ["Soviet Diplomatic and Consular Services in Poland in 1944-1961"], Czasy Nowożytne, Vol. 20 (2007), pp. 165–251.

14 CIA cable, 5 November 1971, CIA FOIA Reading Room, https://www.cia.gov/readingroom/docs/SCHULMEISTER%2C%20OTTO_0092.pdf; Alan Dean, "Russ, Romania In Nerve Battle," News-Pilot (San Pedro, CA), 16 May 1972, p. 4.

15 "Greece 'Orders Expulsion of Two Russian Diplomats,'" BBC, 11 July 2018, https://www.bbc.co.uk/news/world-europe-44792714

16 "Russian Diplomats Expelled by Obama over Hacking Leave US," BBC, 1 January 2017, https://www.bbc.co.uk/news/world-us-canada-38484735; Eric Tucker and Aamer Madhani, "US Expels Russian Diplomats, Imposes Sanctions for Hacking," Associated Press, 16 April 2021, https://apnews.com/article/us-expel-russia-diplomats-sanctions-6a8a54c7932ee8cbe51b0ce505121995

17 U.S. Congress, Senate, Congressional Record—Senate, 18 May 1960, p. 10549.

18 "Soviet Breaks Off Ties to Australia Over Petrov Case," New York Times, 24 April 1954, p. 1.

19 ohn Barron, KGB: The Secret Work of Soviet Agents (New York: Reader's Digest Press, 1974), pp. 379–415.

20 Christopher Andrew and Vasili Mitrokhin, The Sword and the Shield: The Mitrokhin Archive and the Secret History of the KGB (New York: Basic Books, 1999), p. 383.

21 Oleg Kalugin, Spymaster: My Thirty-Two Years in Intelligence and Espionage against the West (New York: Basic Books, 2009), p. 147. For a detailed treatment of Operation "Foot," see Christopher Andrew, Defend the Realm: The Authorized History of MI5 (New York: Vintage Books, 2009), 565–586.

22 Jeremiah O'Leary, "Defector Assails Russia," Evening Star, 16 March 1970, p. 9; Joseph B. Smith, Portrait of a Cold Warrior: Second Thoughts of a Top CIA Agent (New York: Ballantine Books, 1981), pp. 410–412.

23 U.S. Department of State, "Secretary of State William Rogers Is Informed of the Defection of a Mr. Tchebotarev, a Soviet Trade Mission Official Stationed in Brussels, Belgium," History-Lab,18 October 1971, http://history-lab.org/documents/2002110103192; "Soviet Official Defects to U.S. with List of Spies in Belgium," Washington Post, 19 October 1971, p. 14.

24 Mansoor Akbar, "USSR-Iran Relations (1979–86)," Pakistan Horizon, Vol. 41, No. 1 (1988), pp. 61–72.

25 U.S. Department of State, "Expulsions of Soviets Worldwide, 1983."

26 Gus Weiss, "The Farewell Dossier: Duping the Soviets," Studies in Intelligence, Vol. 39, No. 5 (1996), pp. 121–126.

27 James Coates, "Defector Pulls Plug on High-Tech Spies," Chicago Tribune, 10 April 1983, p. 5.

28 "Meeting Minutes of the Politburo of the CC CPSU, Regarding the Aftermath of the Reykjavik US-Soviet summit," 22 October 1986, History and Public Policy Program Digital Archive, TsKhSD, F. 89, Op. 42, D. 53, Ll. 1-14. https://digitalarchive.wilsoncenter.org/document/115984

29 "Kodenavn 'Steklov'" [Code Name "Steklov"], VG, 23 February 2003, https://www.vg.no/nyheter/innenriks/i/kaJoOj/kodenavn-steklov

30 Central Intelligence Agency, "Central Intelligence Bulletin," 29 September 1971, CIA FOIA Reading Room, https://www.cia.gov/readingroom/docs/CIA-RDP79T00975A020100070002-9.pdf

31 Charles Babcock, "Soviet Military Spy Caught in FBI Trap," Washington Post, 16 September 1983, https://www.washingtonpost.com/archive/politics/1983/09/16/soviet-military-spy-caught-in-fbi-trap/eab2d86f-405f-45bd-86dd-503e4e458f1b/

32 U.S. Department of State, "Expulsions of Soviet Officials Worldwide, 1986."

33 U.S. Senate, Subcommittee to Investigate the Internal Security Act and Other Internal Security Laws, Scope of Soviet Activity in the United States, Part 25, 84th Congress, Second Session, (Washington, DC: Government Printing Office, 1956), pp. 1366–1368.

34 John Van Camp, "U.N. Russian's Ouster Asked," Baltimore Sun, 26 October 1956, p. 7; Arthur North, "Boot UN Red Diplomat in Abduction of Tanya," New York Daily News, 1 December 1956, p. 144.

35 Vernon Loeb and Susan B. Glasser, "Bush Backs Expulsion of 50 Russians," Washington Post, 23 March 2001, https://www.washingtonpost.com/archive/politics/2001/03/23/bush-backs-expulsion-of-50-russians/c7a0770e-7139-4e6f-88bd-5d8a13f11810/

36 Siegfried Mortkowitz, "Czechs Expel More Russian Embassy Staff over Bombing Claims," Politico, 22 April 2021, https://www.politico.eu/article/ czech-republic-russia-embassy-staff-bombing-claims/; "Baltic States Expel Russian Diplomats in Solidarity with Prague," Euractiv, 23 April 2021, https://www.euractiv.com/section/politics/news/baltic-states-expel-russian- diplomats-in-solidarity-with-prague/

37 Kevin Riehle, "Assessing Foreign Intelligence Threats," American Intelligence Journal, Vol. 31, No. 1 (2014), pp. 96–101.

38 Weiss, "The Farewell Dossier," pp. 121–126.

39 Ibid., p. 126.

40 Roger Cohen, "Case of the Adaptable Spy: Agent for Soviets, and Russia, Too," New York Times, 12 May 1992, p. A11.

41 Kalugin, Spymaster, p. 198.

42 U.S. Department of State, "Ensuring Reciprocity and Equivalence in the Functioning and Operations of Official Representatives of Soviet and Soviet Bloc Countries in the United States and Official Representatives of the United States in Soviet and Soviet Bloc Countries," 17 February 1984, CIA FOIA Reading Room, https://www.cia.gov/readingroom/docs/CIA- RDP90B01370R000200330014-9.pdf, p. 36.

43 Norman Kempster and Eleanor Clift, "New Ousters Prompt U.S. Vow to 'Zap 'Em Again,'" Los Angeles Times, 12 October 1986, p. 1.

44 Bill Gertz, "55 Soviets Ousted, Experts See Limited Spy Activity Effects," Washington Times, 22 October 1986, p. 5-B.

45 Morten Heiberg, KGB's Kontakt- Og Agentnet i Danmark: Sagerne i PET's Arkiv Vedrørende Arne Herløv Petersen og Jørgen Dragsdahl [KGB's Contact and Agent Network in Denmark: PET Archival Cases Concerning Arne Herløv Petersen and Jørgen Dragsdahl] (Copenhagen: Ministry of Justice, 2009), p. 10.

46 Ninn-Hansen was quoted in the Danish newspaper Ekstra Bladet on 7 January 1992.

47 Natasha Bertrand and Jim Sciutto, "Russia's Ukraine War Effort Running 'Out of Steam' as Putin's Ability to Spy in Europe Cut in Half, MI6 Chief Says," CNN, 21 July 2022, https://edition.cnn.com/2022/07/21/politics/mi6-chief- russia-spying/index.html

48 Rod Mcguirk, "Australia Quietly Expels Major Russian Spy Ring, Report Says," Associated Press, 24 February 2023, https://apnews.com/article/australia-d69 e84c19cfdc83601d656cce3d82297

49 U.S. Congress, Senate, Congressional Record—Senate, 18 May 1960, p. 10548.

50 Fletcher Schoen and Christopher J. Lamb, Deception, Disinformation, and Strategic Communications: How One Interagency Group Made a Major Difference, Strategic Perspectives No. 11 (Washington, DC: National Defense University, Institute for National Security Studies, 2012), pp. 39–40.

51 Philip Agee and Louis Wolf, Dirty Work: The CIA in Western Europe (New York: Dorset Press, 1978); Ellen Ray, William Schaap, Karl Van Meter, and Louis Wolf (eds.), Dirty Work: The CIA in Africa (London, Zed Press, 1980).

52 Thomas Rid, Active Measures: The Secret History of Disinformation and Political Warfare (New York: Farrar, Strauss, and Giroux, 2020), pp. 222–227.

53 John Barron, KGB: The Secret Work of Soviet Agents (New York: Reader's Digest Press, 1974), pp. 379–415.

54 John Barron, KGB Today: The Hidden Hand (New York: Reader's Digest Press, 1983), pp. 437–442; see also U.S. Congress, Senate, Congressional Record—House, 18 June 1987, p. 16710.

55 CIA, "Appendix," undated but the latest entry in the list was dated April 1959, CIA FOIA Reading Room, https://www.cia.gov/readingroom/docs/CIA-RDP78-00915R000700260037-6.pdf

56 "Twice Removed," Daily Telegraph (London), 2 April 1979, p. 20.

57 Alistair Bunkall, "Russia 'Linked' to Election-Day Coup Plot in Montenegro," SkyNews, 21 February 2017, https://news.sky.com/story/russia-linked-to-election-day-coup-plot-in-montenegro-10775786; Dusica Tomovic and Natalia Zaba, "Montenegro Coup Suspect 'Was Russian Spy in Poland,'" Balkan Insight, 21 February 2017, https://balkaninsight.com/2017/02/21/montenegro-coup-suspect-was-russian-spy-in-poland-02-21-2017/

58 U.S. Department of State, "Expulsion of Russian Intelligence Officers," Press Statement, 22 March 2001, https://2001-2009.state.gov/r/pa/prs/ps/2001/1570.htm; "Expulsions Delayed by Hanssen Probe," UPI, 22 March 2001, https://www.upi.com/Archives/2001/03/22/Expulsions-delayed-by-Hanssen-probe/9858985237200/

Index

About the Author

Musa Khan Jalalzai is a journalist and research scholar. He has written extensively on Afghanistan, terrorism, nuclear and biological terrorism, human trafficking, drug trafficking, and intelligence research and analysis. He was an Executive Editor of the Daily Outlook Afghanistan from 2005-2011, and a permanent contributor in Pakistan's daily *The Post*, *Daily Times*, and *The Nation*, *Weekly the Nation*, (London). However, in 2004, US Library of Congress in its report for South Asia mentioned him as the biggest and prolific writer. He received Masters in English literature, Diploma in Geospatial Intelligence, University of Maryland, Washington DC, certificate in Surveillance Law from the University of Stanford, USA, and diploma in Counter terrorism from Pennsylvania State University, California, the United States.

Milton Keynes UK
Ingram Content Group UK Ltd.
UKHW010838100324
439069UK00002B/18